T5-BAV-679

THE SEMANTICS OF ASPECT AND MODALITY

STUDIES IN LANGUAGE COMPANION SERIES (SLCS)

The SLCS series has been established as a companion series to STUDIES IN LANGUAGE, International Journal, sponsored by the Foundation "Foundations of language".

Volume 34

Galia Hatav

The Semantics of Aspect and Modality
Evidence from English and Biblical Hebrew

THE SEMANTICS OF ASPECT AND MODALITY

EVIDENCE FROM ENGLISH AND BIBLICAL HEBREW

GALIA HATAV
University of Florida, Gainesville

JOHN BENJAMINS PUBLISHING COMPANY
AMSTERDAM/PHILADELPHIA

The paper used in this publication meets the minimum requirements of American National Standard for Information Sciences — Permanence of Paper for Printed Library Materials, ANSI Z39.48-1984.

Library of Congress Cataloging-in-Publication Data

Hatav, Galia.

The semantics of aspect and modality : evidence from English and biblical Hebrew / Galia Hatav.

p. cm. -- (Studies in language companion series, ISSN 0165-7763 ; v. 34)

Includes bibliographical references and indexes.

1. Hebrew language--Tense. 2. Hebrew language--Modality. 3. Bible. O.T.--Language, style. 4. English language--Tense. 5. English language--Modality. I. Title. II. Series.

PJ4569.H337 1997

401'.43--dc21 96-6117

ISBN 90 272 3037 4 (Eur.) / 1-55619-845-0 (US) (alk. paper) CIP

r97

John Benjamins Publishing Co. • P.O.Box 75577 • 1070 AN Amsterdam • The Netherlands

John Benjamins North America • P.O.Box 27519 • Philadelphia PA 19118-0519 • USA

Table of Contents

Preface

This study is a revision of my dissertation, written at Tel-Aviv University.

First I want to thank my teacher, Tanya Reinhart, for many stimulating discussions, for her insightful criticism, and her continuous encouragement in writing the dissertation and revising it as a book. I have learnt a great deal from her, not only on the subject of tense, aspect and modality, but also on thinking and writing in much broader sense.

I would also like to express my deep appreciation to Shlomo Izre'el, whose knowledge in Semitic languages has enabled me to lean on his criticism of the philological part of my thesis. Although he was not my official supervisor when writing my thesis, he agreed to read through it, and advise me on problems which arose during the writing. He, furthermore, continued to support me in revising my thesis for publication.

Thanks to Ruth Berman who read an early version of my thesis, for her detailed criticism, and for employing me on an important project on temporality.

Special thanks I gladly owe to Bernard Comrie, who read my dissertation and offered detailed improvements. The reader will find his "fingerprints" throughout this study. Remko Scha has read part of my dissertation, and given me very important, detailed comments.

My study has benefited from discussions with Meir Sternberg, Shalom Lappin, Edit Doron, Hagit Borer, Anita Mittwoch, Paul Wexler, and the late Eli'ezer Rubinstein.

I am indebted to Gabi Cohen in Tel-Aviv University and to the anonymous donor for a scholarship which allowed me to work on my thesis for a whole year without worrying about earning my living. My sincere thanks also to the Spharadic Federation for a scholarship which provided me the final push in writing the dissertation. I am also thankful to The University of

Florida for the substantial award which allowed me to spend a whole summer in revising my dissertation for publication.

Thanks also to Barbara Josman and Mickey Schafer for the language editing and their comments.

For helping me with the computer I am indebted to David Sitman in the support center in Tel-Aviv University, to The Porter Institute, to Pat Savinsky in the Faculty Support Center in The University of Florida, and the young students who work with her.

And last, but not least, I have the pleasure of thanking my beloved friends who have supported me during these long hard years. The list is very long, but I want to mention in particular my friend Dvora Zilberstein, who has been more than supportive to me, more than a friend.

Chapter 1

Introduction — Temporality in Language

The Tense-Aspect-Modal verb system of language (henceforth: TAM) has been given a great deal of attention in the literature. Traditional analyses of TAM usually regard the tense as having a temporal nature, while aspect and modality are described as dealing with attitude, perspective and the like. Recent semantic studies within the truth conditional approach tend to characterize all three features in terms of temporality. The analysis given in this study lies within truth conditional semantics, and hence proposes a temporal theory for TAM. The three parameters are, therefore, defined in terms of truth conditions, but pragmatic considerations are not irrelevant, and when necessary the analysis will take them, too, into account. For example, **Come here!** and **Would you please come here?** differ in their mood (the first being a command and the second a request), but both are modal propositions, and hence are discussed under the same category. This study aims to provide a general (semantic) theory for temporality (i.e., of TAM), but it also systematically examines the verb system in Biblical-Hebrew (henceforth: BH), which lacks tenses, as will be demonstrated, and thus enables us to see the nature of aspect and modality more clearly. The thesis is organized accordingly: the first part of each chapter deals with general notions and problems of the temporal parameter in question, while the second part is devoted to the verb system in BH.

1.1 Tense and Aspect

The major problem in the study of tense and aspect is to distinguish between these two notions, especially since in many languages (e.g., English) they intertwine, or (e.g., in French) they even coalesce into one form.

The term **tense** is used in the linguistic literature for morphological markers of the verb which function to characterize the temporal relations between the situation and the utterance time (e.g., Lyons 1977, Hartmann & Stork 1972, Kamp & Reyle 1993, and others).

The term **aspect** was first used to refer to the basic morphological distinction between **Perfective** and **Imperfective** in Russian and other Slavonic languages (see Hartmann & Stork 1972 and Binnick 1993), but has since been applied to other languages whose verb system has, presumably, the same distinction, semantically speaking. However, the problem was to define the *meaning* distinguished by the difference in morphology. Studies in the pragmatic approach view the difference as lying in the **attitude** of the speaker. For example, Comrie states (1976:3): "aspects are different ways of *viewing* the internal temporal constituency of a situation" (emphasis is mine). This approach faces difficulties in defining formally the notion of speaker perspective, especially when determining the different aspects themselves. But a more persuasive argument for rejecting this approach is the fact that, as will be shown in the coming chapters, it cannot account for many cases where the speaker's perspective is irrelevant, and where what determines a specific choice of aspect is temporal considerations, e.g., of the situations in the real world. (But, as said above, this is not to say that pragmatic features are completely irrelevant for characterizing aspects). Biblical-Hebrew is a language with no tense, but with aspect, and thereby enabling us to isolate issues of tense and aspect and to see their distinctive temporal features. The BH verb system is a mystery and, as I will show, despite the extensive analysis a completely satisfactory solution is not possible without a good theory of tense and aspect (see a survey in section 1.2 below).

Note that there is another notion — **Aktionsarten** — which is sometimes confused with aspect. In recent semantic studies it has been defined formally to distinguish between, e.g. events and states, but it has no morphological representation in language. However, Aktionsarten do have some impact on the temporal interpretation of sentences, as will be discussed in section 2.1 of chapter (2). But what, then, are the theoretical tools needed for analysing tense and aspect?

1.1.1 *Reference-Time*

The traditional systems of tense-logic — Prior (1967), Clifford (1969), Bull (1963) and others — analyze the temporal relations only in terms of E(vent) and S(peech) time. The truth conditions of a sentence are stipulated only according to the temporal relations between the E and the S time. For example, a sentence such as "John went to Jerusalem" is true iff the event of John's going to Jerusalem took place before the time in which the sentence is/ was/will-be uttered. Reichenbach (1947) shows that a system of traditional tense-logic cannot account for many differences holding between a large number of (English) sentences, such as the difference between (1a) and (1b):

(1) a. John ate.
b. John has eaten.

Both (1a) and (1b) denote events preceding the time of speech. Nonetheless they are not identical. Therefore, Reichenbach claims, languages express temporal relations not only between E-time and S-time in a two place structure, but also with reference to a third point of time which he labels R(eference)-time. Thus, (1a) differs from (1b) in the relation of R-time to the other two points of time, as represented in the following diagrams:

(1') a. ——R,E——S→
b. ——E——R,S→

The R-times of (1a) and (1b) are associated with E and S respectively. But the R-times can also be separated from the other points of time, as in the case of the past perfect in English:

(2) a. I had seen John (when you called me)
b. ————-E————R———-S→

The R-time (when you called me) not only follows the event (of me seeing John), as in (1b), but also precedes the S-time. Reichenbach illustrates every configuration of the temporal relations manifested in English grammar, in diagrams as in (1') and (2b), but he does not define the notion of R-time. Therefore, linguists who have adopted Reichenbach's three place relation interpret it in different ways.

Partee (1973), though she does not yet use the R-time notion, introduces the notion of "temporal anaphor" which seems to implicitly assume R-time. Hinrichs (1986 [1982]) expands Partee's analysis and incorporates into it the notion of R-time. In a later work, Partee (1984) herself, adopting Hinrichs's modification, explicitly relates the temporal anaphor to the notion of R-time. She claims that, just like pronouns, the R-time refers deictically or anaphorically to some interval (Cf. Fillmore 1971), e.g., in (3) below the (past) tense morpheme in the second sentence refers anaphorically to the adverb "last Friday" indicated in the first sentence:

(3) Sheila had a party last Friday and Sam got drunk.

However, as noted by Partee, the analogy to pronouns is not always as smooth as in (3). Consider, e.g., (4) below:

(4) John bought a watch. Two days later he lost it.

The interval referred to in the second clause is not the same interval indicated in the first clause, but rather some interval *following* it. In other words, the temporal "antecedent" is not identical to the temporal pronoun but precedes it. Partee notes in cases like (4) that "to say that the R-time of the first clause is the antecedent of the R-time of the second, is like saying that the antecedent is the 'father' of the pronoun" (p. 256). For similar reasons, McCawley (1981) introduces the notion of **indirect** R-time. He calls the first R-time the indirect R-time of the event reported in the second clause. Kamp & Reyle (1993) suggest a similar distinction. They claim that in a narrative there are two different kinds of R-time (discussed in their sections 5.2 and 5.4). One kind, labelled R_{pt}, functions as an anaphoric element which links the described situation to some element of the antecedent discourse, and hence is responsible for the time movement in the narrative. The other kind, labelled TP_{pt}, is "the temporal perspective point" which determines the different temporal meanings of the sentence in question: past, past in the past, etc. A different approach is suggested by Moens (1987). Discussing the anaphoric analysis suggested by Partee, Moens argues persuasively that tenses are not like pronouns but rather like definite descriptions. Like definite descriptions "tenses refer to a previous introduced entity and then create a new temporal entity that can be used for subsequent reference" (p.17). In other words, according to Moens there is only one kind of R-time, and that R-time behaves like definite descriptions. It seems to me that Moens captures the right behavior of R-time in discourse. But what is R-time? What is the temporal entity created by the R-time?

Moens himself admits that the notion of R-time is hard to define and suggests only an intuitive description: "It corresponds to the notion of the time that is being talked about" (p.17). Dowty (1986) defines R-time as "the time at which the event or the state mentioned by the sentence occurs (or obtains, respectively)" (p.45). However, if this is the definition of R-time, then what is E-time? Hinrichs (1986 [1982]) and Partee (1984) define the R-time as the time unit containing the event or being contained in the state. This definition has been partially adopted in this study. The R-time is, indeed, a time-unit, but it not only may contain or be contained in the E-time, but also be ordered with it. Secondly, the relation of the R-time to the situation (I use the term "situation" for referring either to events or states — see chapter 2 below for details) is determined, I claim, by the aspect rather than by the Aktionsarten (i.e., the event-state distinction). For example, in (6b) below the situation includes its R-time and therefore is in progressive, while in (6c) the situation is included in its respective R-time and hence the simple past is used. (But see below for a discussion of each aspect). To summarize, I define the notion of reference-time in the same spirit of Reichenbach, as the time-unit responsible for the temporal interpretation of the clause; a clause cannot have temporal interpretation without determining its R-time and the relationship of that R-time to the reported situation. (But contrary to Reichenbach I adopt the definition of Hinrichs and Partee who see the R-time as an interval rather than a point of time). For the nature of the R-time in narrative discourse I accept Moens' stipulation that the R-time functions like definite descriptions in creating a new temporal entity and referring to a previous R-time.

The notion of S-time also needs some discussion. Reichenbach (1947) defines it as "the time point of the act of speech, i.e., of the token uttered" (p. 288). Similarly, Hinrichs (1986 [1982]) defines it as the speech time, but he represents it as e_S, where 'e' stands for 'event' (referring to events as well as states). The fact that Reichenbach talks about an **act** of speech and Hinrichs uses the symbol of events to represent the speech time suggests that the utterance can be viewed as a special kind of event, and the S-time as a special kind of E-time. According to such an analysis we must assume a special R-time for the S-time. This is done, indeed, in Partee (1984), who claims that when interpreting a narrative discourse "we assume...a present reference time R_S..." (p. 255). This analysis is in accord with Prior (1967), Mittwoch (1988), Smith (1991), and others who stipulate that the S-time is the first unmarked R-time. The following examples will illustrate the R_S:

(5) a. David is/was/will-be in New-York this year/last year/next year.
b. Robert bought a dog yesterday.
c. Amos lives/lived in Tel-Aviv.

The R_S in (5a-b) is determined by different time units — "this year" and "today" respectively. In (5c) the R_S is not specified. (The present time, and hence R_S, is analyzed in Partee, p. 254, as an indexical). The R_S is crucial for determining the tense. Reinhart (1984b) suggests that the relation of the S-time to R-time determines the tense. In line with Reinhart: if the situation overlaps R_S, as in (6a) and (6b) below, the sentence denoting the situation will have the present tense. If the situation does not overlap R_S, the sentence denoting it will have the past tense if its R-time is prior to R_S (examples 6c-e below), and the future tense if it follows R_S (examples 6f-g):

(6) a. John has eaten.
b. John is eating.

c. John ate.
d. John had eaten (before Mary's arrival).
e. John was eating (when Mary came).

f. John will eat.
g. John will be eating/ will have eaten.

In BH R_S does not have a special "status"; It is treated just like any other R-time, and hence tense is not marked, as said above. (This will be the situation with any tenseless language). The aspect, on the other hand, plays a major role in the verbal system in BH. Thus the crucial temporal relations in BH are those holding between the situations and their R-times. The aspects will define: a) sequentiality; b) inclusion (=progressive); and c) perfect.

a) *Sequentiality*

According to the analysis suggested by Kamp (1979, & Reyle 1993) this aspect should have been labelled differently, as the aspect which moves the R-time forward. Kamp shows that this movement results in creating a sequence in a narrative discourse, and hence I label the aspect of verbs in clauses moving the R-time forward, the "sequence" aspect. I will show that a clause moves the R-time forward iff its situation has its own R-time in which it is included. If the situation is "parasitic" on another R-time it cannot move the R-time forward, and hence cannot appear on a sequence. This is the case with the progressive and the perfect aspects, as will be mentioned below. It is important to emphasize that if the sequential clause does not appear in a narrative discourse its potentiality to move the R-time forward may sometimes not be realized. For instance, if to the question "What did you do last night?" John answers in listing his deeds in clauses as (7) below, those clauses do not necessarily form a sequence, although they may appear in sequential forms.

(7) I managed to do a lot: I finished the article, played with the kids, did all the house work, and even read a novel.

In a narrative discourse, therefore, the verbs on the time-line are expected to always be in the aspect of sequence. This will be discussed in detail in the first part of chapter (2). The second part of chapter (2) will deal with the sequence aspect in BH, which is very rigid; the form *wayyiqtol* (see section 1.2.1 for the titles given to the BH forms) is the only form appearing in the time-line clauses, and it cannot appear in clauses off the time-line. BH, furthermore, has a special form — *wqatal* — marking the sequence in the modal material (i.e., sequences of orders, habitual events, future plannings, and the like — see section 2.2 for elaboration).

b) *Inclusion = Progressive*

Analyses dealing with the English verb system offer different explanations for the difference between sentences like (6c) and (6e). Tense cannot account for the difference since both sentences are in the past, so it is agreed that they differ rather in aspect. However, stipulating that the progressive differs from the simple past in aspect does not solve the problem of characterizing its meaning.

Traditional studies of the (English) progressive characterize it in terms of perspective only, i.e., they do not see a truth conditional difference between a sentence in progressive and a sentence in simple past. However, this is quite inadequate, and the choice between the two aspects depends rather on the temporal interpretation of the reported situation. Truth-conditional semantics studies such as Bennett & Partee (1978 [1972]), Mittwoch (1988) and others have shown that a situation denoted by a progressive clause necessarily includes its R-time. I will show that the reverse situation is also true, i.e., when an inclusive situation is reported it has to be in progressive (in a language which can mark the progressive). For example, in (6b) the situation of eating includes the R_S, and therefore the verb must be in progressive ("John eats" in this environment is ungrammatical in English). Vice versa, a progressive sentence cannot be interpreted without containing an R-time. As König (1980) and Mittwoch (1988) show, if R is not R_S such an R-time must come from the context, e.g., (6e) will be ill-formed if we remove the sentence in parantheses which provides the R-time. In other words, the progressive does not introduce an R-time, which means that it cannot move the R-time forward and therefore cannot comprise a sequence. In narrative discourse the progressive sentences are usually interpreted as including the neighboring event(s) since they usually draw their R-times from the events reported in the preceding or following clause(s). In the first part of chapter (3) I will define more formally the notion of inclusiveness, which characterizes the progressive aspect, and discuss issues hinging on its inclusive nature, e.g., its behavior in the narrative discourse. The second part of chapter (3) is devoted to the progressive form *qotel* in BH.

c) *Perfect = Anteriority, Simultaneity and Backgrounding*

In chapter (5) I will show that the **perfect** is also a parasitic aspect; that is, clauses in the perfect report situations which are dependent on some other situation's R-time (or on explicit time expressions such as adverbs) for their temporal interpretation. For example, in (6a) the situation depends on R_S, and in (6d) on Mary's arrival. The perfect may be used for different temporal relations holding between situations and R-time. The most common one is what I call *anteriority*. Anteriority is usually where the situations are reported in reverse order as in **When Mary arrived John had already left**. But as noted by Comrie (1986) and Reinhart (1984), the opposite order, paralleling chronological order, is also possible for the (English) perfect: **John had already left when Mary arrived**. This suggests that what defines anteriority is not the order of the situations, but the order of the R-time and the situation. The anterior situation precedes its R-time, regardless of the order in which they are introduced. Thus, in both examples the situation of John's leaving precedes its R-time which happens to be the time of Mary's arrival. (Note that defining the aspect of perfect in terms of relations between R-time and E-time aligns the perfect with the other two aspects. I.e., it provides us with a unified analysis of the different aspects.) It is usually the case, however, that when the R-time is provided by another clause (as in our both examples), the situations are reported in reverse order. The question of why we may have marked cases where those situations are reported in their chronological order is answered in Comrie and in Reinhart. Comrie and Reinhart independently claim that in such cases the narrator is merely interested in excluding those clauses from the time-line, backgrounding them. This suggests that the distinction of

foreground-background is relevant for characterizing the functions of the perfect aspect, although it does not affect its truth conditions. The BH *qatal* behaves like the English perfect in denoting anteriority and being used for backgrounding. However, there is at least one "parasitic" use of the *qatal* which does not coincide with the English perfect, namely the relation of simultaneity. Simultaneity could be of two kinds: inclusion or just overlapping, both parasitic relations. Inclusion was discussed under (b) above. Mere overlapping is when a situation is included in the same R-time with the situation reported by the previous clause, as in "John played the piano and sang (at the same time)". For the inclusion relation, as mentioned above, there are special forms in English (the progressive) and in BH (the *qotel*). For reporting overlapping situations, BH uses the *qatal*, but English uses the simple tenses rather than the perfect (as illustrated by our example). BH, then, is more consistent in using only parasitic forms in reporting parasitic situations. To conclude, the English and the BH perfects are not identical, but they both share the "parasitic" nature and many of the temporal and pragmatic functions. The analysis of the perfect aspect as "parasitic" concerning its R-time explains why it cannot form a sequence. Since a sequential clause must introduce a new R-time, clauses in perfect may not be a link on a chain of sequence, even when they precede the clause they depend on, which is demonstrated in English, BH and other languages. (Here we have further evidence that aspects, including sequentiality, must be determined by the relation of the R-time and the E-time rather than by relation of the E-time and the S-time.) In section (5.1) of Chapter (5) I will elaborate on the "parasitic" nature of the perfect, and discuss its different uses. The second part of the chapter — section (5.2) — will be devoted to the perfect aspect in BH.

1.1.2 *Modality*

Within pragmatic theory, modality, like aspect, is usually treated as an issue of the speaker's attitude, intention, desire, etc. However, these features cannot explain many phenomena concerning the modal system in language. It cannot account, e.g., for the seemingly peculiar phenomenon in BH in which the same verbal forms — *yiqtol* and *wqatal* — may be used to denote both future propositions as well as past habituals. This seems to be nicely solved by a truth conditional semantics theory, the general framework of this study. Within the approach of truth conditional semantics, modality, unlike tense and aspect, does not follow from R-time relations. Instead it involves the notion of **possible worlds** (or **branching options**). In the first part of chapter (4) I will discuss the different modal propositions and show that they all involve quantification over possible worlds. I will also show that many propositions such as conditionals and habituals (in the present as well as in the past) are modals, although traditionally they have not been treated as such (for not expressing, e.g., intention of the speaker). In the second part of the chapter I will present the BH data, which clearly show that all and only those propositions have the *yiqtol* or *wqatal* forms.

1.2 The Verbal System in Biblical-Hebrew

1.2.1 *The Problem*

One of the most puzzling problems in the study of Biblical-Hebrew is its verbal system, which is very rich in forms. These forms have been labelled in different ways, according to various scholars' analyses, the most neutral labelling being based solely on morphology. Hebrew, being a Semitic language, has a discontinuous morphology, where the root and the paradigm coalesce. The root, which is (generally) three consonantal, is usually denoted by the convention of *q.ṭ.l.*, where 'q' marks the first radical, 'ṭ' the second, and 'l' the third. The paradigm accords with one of the seven patterns, called *binyanim*. The convention for marking the binyan takes the conjugation of the third person masculine. Thus, the form *qa:ṭal*, for example, stands not only for the particular verb 'he killed' but also for verbs such as *ša:mar* 'he watched', *la:qaḥ* 'he took' on the one hand, and for verbs conjugated in other persons, e.g., *ša:marnu:* 'we watched', *la:qaḥti:* 'I took' etc., on the other. *Qa:ṭal*, furthermore, stands also for verbs from other patterns (*binyanim*), e.g., for verbs such as *hilbi:ša:* 'she clothed (someone)' (*hip̄ʕi:l*), *dibbe;r* 'he spoke' (*piʕe;l*) etc. I have adopted this labelling system, with some changes to match the Modern Hebrew pronunciation.[1]

Firstly I follow the accepted notation, e.g., McFall (1982) in using the letter 't' without the dot for the second radical of the root. Secondly, I do not always reflect the differences in some of the vowels; e.g., I use the same sign 'a' (without the two dots) for *qamaṣ* (also called *qameṣ*) as well for *pataḥ* as they are pronounced identically in Modern Israeli Hebrew (see discussion in next section). Therefore, instead of *qa:ṭal*, e.g., the form is represented as *qatal*. Thus we have the following forms: *qatal*, *wayyiqtol*[2], *yiqtol*, *wyiqtol*, *wqatal*, *qotel*, *qtol* (the imperative), *w*+imperative,"short"-*yiqtol* (the jussive), *w*+jussive, "long"-*yiqtol* (the cohortative), and *w*+cohortative. There is also a derived form *yiqtol*+*nun*-paragogicum (*yiqtlu:n*), which seems to play only a stylistic role (see, for instance, Joüon 1947, sections 44e-f), and therefore is represented here merely as *yiqtol*. The imperative may be "lengthened" by adding to it a final vowel 'a:' (like the cohortative — see section 4.2.1 for elaboration), e.g., *tna:* 'give' (as opposed to regular imperative *te;n*). However, the "long" imperative does not seem to differ from the "regular" imperative, semantically speaking, and hence they are represented the same way. (Fassberg 1994 explains the difference between the regular and the long imperative in terms of attitude towards the speaker.) I do not include here the infinitivals for reasons that will be explained in section 1.2.2 below.

All the attempts to account for the rich verbal system of Biblical Hebrew have failed as shown in Ben-Ḥayyim (1977), and in more detail in McFall (1982). McFall examines ten individual theories which represent six major approaches, from the tenth century till 1954. McFall, furthermore, analyzes each theory and points out the difficulties. In what follows I will sketch the main approaches summarized in McFall, relying in part on his summaries. I will add a short account of recent attempts in the analyses of Givón (1977, 1982), Longacre (1981), Andersen (1974), Niccacci (1990), Eskhult (1990) and Washburn (1994).

The main approaches dealing with the verbal system in the Bible are the tense-oriented and the aspect-oriented theories. Both approaches have faced problems primarily in analyzing the forms *wayyiqtol*, *qatal*, *yiqtol* and *wqatal*. They analyze them as being only two forms — *yiqtol* and *qatal*, which can be prefixed by the consonant 'w' called *waw* in Hebrew, yielding *wayyiqtol* and *wqatal* respectively.

The most famous tense-oriented theory is the *waw*-conversive theory of the Jewish scholars in the Middle Ages. This theory claims that *qatal* and *yiqtol* denote past and future time situations respectively, but when they are *waw* prefixed they denote the "opposite" tenses — *wayyiqtol* denotes past time events and *wqatal* futurates. The *waw*, according to this theory, converts the tense, and hence it is labelled *waw* conversive (*waw hahippux*, in Hebrew). This peculiar power of the *waw* is difficult to explain, especially since such a phenomenon is not known in any other language, as pointed out by

McFall. But this is not the only problem of the *waw*-conversive theory. The theory, furthermore, fails to account for a large number of counterexamples. As shown by Ben-Ḥayyim (1977) and McFall (1982), there are many verbs in *qatal* which are understood as denoting future situations and many *yiqtol* verbs which denote situations in the past. Similarly, the *waw* prefixed verbs do not always indicate "opposite" tenses. McFall reports another attempt to explain the forms as encoding tenses, namely the *waw* inductive theory introduced by Gell (1818). Gell accepts the claim that *qatal* is the past tense and *yiqtol* the future, but he denies the conversive power of the *waw* in the *waw* prefixed forms. However, he agrees that these forms denote the "opposite" tenses of their respective "free" forms, due to the *waw* which **conducts** the tense of the preceding verb into the verb in question. To replace the converting power of the *waw* into an inducive power does not solve the problems of the *waw* conversive theory, and in addition it cannot account for *wayyiqtol* verbs in openings of narratives, where there is no preceding verb from which those verbs can "pull" their tense. Another attempt to account for the difficulties raised by the *waw* conversive theory was the **Relative-Tense-Theory** (Schroeder 1766, Lee 1827, Weir 1849 and others). As summarized in McFall, this approach treats the verbal forms as denoting either absolute or relative tenses, according to the writers' standpoint. The writers may write either from the time *in* which they are living (the absolute standpoint), or from the time *of* which they are writing (the relative standpoint). For example, Lee (1827) claims that *yiqtol* (and hence *wayyiqtol*) denotes present, while *qatal* (and *wqatal*) denotes past. He explains the interpretation of *(way)yiqtol* as past events claiming that in these cases the writer took the relative standpoint putting himself in the time of the action. This contrasts with cases when the writer took the absolute standpoint of his speech-time and used, e.g., a *yiqtol* verb to denote an absolute present. This line of analysis provides a circular explanation, since it allows the writer to change his point-of-view at will, even from one verse to another. As a result, whenever a *qatal* verb is interpreted as denoting present or future time event, we may explain it as being from the relative point of view, and the same, *mutatis mutandis*, with *yiqtol* verbs interpreted as past events.

The failure of the tense-oriented theories to provide a satisfactory explanation for the different forms urged scholars to abandon this approach and search for other features to explain the choice of verb form. Against this background the aspect-oriented theories were developed, with the most well-known proponents being Ewald (1827, 1870) and Driver (1874).[3] Ewald was the first to replace the terms praeteritum (=past) and futuritum (=future) used at that time for the Hebrew forms, by the respective terms **perfect** and **imperfect**, not as in Latin and Greek, but in their etymological meaning, as signifying **complete** and **incomplete**. Ewald argues that the speaker uses the form *qatal* when the situation is **completed** and *yiqtol* when it is not. Hence the use of *qatal* for past time situations which are understood as being completed, and the use of *yiqtol* for future situations which are still to be completed. To account for cases where a *qatal* verb appears in a futurate clause and for cases where the *yiqtol* appears in sentences denoting past time situations he falls back on the relative-absolute distinction. According to Ewald, the speaker may regard a situation as being completed even if it is still to be done and then use a *qatal* verb, and vice versa, the speaker may regard the situation as in progress, incomplete, even if it has already occurred, and then use a *yiqtol* verb to denote it. This line of explanation is in the same spirit as the relative-tense theories and suffers, like them, from circularity. Ewald assumes, furthermore, that the *waw* prefixed forms can never stand by themselves, but must always relate either to the previous reported action (in the case of *wayyiqtol*) or to the speaker (in the case of *wqatal*). Hence, *wayyiqtol* denotes an incomplete action relative to the previous one and *wqatal* denotes a complete action relative to the speaker's point of view. Ewald fails to explain not only why the *waw* prefixed forms cannot be "independent" but also why there is such a difference between *wayyiqtol* and *wqatal*. Driver (1874) took the aspect approach to its extreme. Like Ewald he distinguishes between the perfect form *qatal* and the imperfect *yiqtol*. However, he does not accept Ewald's claim that the forms denote tenses, in addition to aspects, although he does agree that we usually regard past situations as perfect and future ones as imperfect. Driver differs from Ewald also in his interpretation of the notion of **imperfect**. While, like Ewald, he interprets **perfect** as "complete", the **imperfect** is not limited to incomplete situations, but has a number of interpretations, among which are nascency and progressive. When the speaker wishes to report the situation as nascent, progressive and the like s/he will use the form of *yiqtol*. The form *wayyiqtol* is interpreted accordingly (for being a *yiqtol* itself). Verbs in *wayyiqtol*, according to Driver, denote nascent situations in respect to the previous action, and the speakers (and readers) see the situations as unfolding before their eyes. The *waw* prefixed to them also has a role — it connects the events represented with a point already reached in the narrative, resulting in a consecutive narrative (hence the term *waw* consecutive). In time the whole form became the form which now denotes successive events in the narrative. The *waw* in *wqatal* is also explained as connecting events, but the form *wqatal* itself is not explained in the same way in which *wayyiqtol* is explained. This forces Driver to claim, like Ewald, that it behaves differently. As mentioned above, Driver claims that *qatal* denotes completed situations, but *wqatal* cannot (usually?) be interpreted in this way. This form, claims Driver, has lost its individuality and hence no longer indicates complete (perfect) situations, but acquires the meaning of the preceding verb which is usually *yiqtol* (which denotes imperfect actions). Driver does not explain why or how *wqatal* loses its individuality while *wayyiqtol* maintains its (Cf. Ewald). But this is not the main weakness in Driver's theory. Since he demands that *qatal* always denotes perfect situations and *yiqtol* imperfect ones, he is forced in many cases to give ad-hoc interpretations for the particular occurrences of *qatal* or *yiqtol* verbs to account for their perfectivity or their imperfectivity respectively (see Ben-Ḥayyim 1977 for examples). Moreover, his explanations are circular since he allows the speaker to change points of views as s/he wishes. In other words, if the reader has a different form from what s/he expected, s/he may always explain it as reflecting the writer's rather than the absolute point of view.

One of the opponents of Driver's theory was Bauer (1910), one of the most influential scholars who developed the historical-comparative approach. (McFall reports Knudtzon 1889 was the first to introduce a theory based on this approach. He also summarizes the theories of G.R. Driver 1936 and Thacker 1954). The historical-comparative approach goes back to the tense-oriented explanations of the Biblical verbal forms, i.e., that the forms indicate tenses rather than aspects. But although accepting this basic claim, Bauer does not accept most of the explanations given to the forms by the tense-oriented theories of the *waw* conversive, the *waw* inductive and the relative-tense theories. He does not accept the claim that *qatal* and *yiqtol* always indicate the same tenses — past and future respectively. Rather, he argues, each form has two functions and each function has two different forms. He explains the duality of the forms and functions as a result of historical developments. In Proto-Semitic, according to Bauer, the *qatal* indicated present-future and the *yiqtol* past time, but when the East-Semitic (Akkadian) split from the West-Semitic languages (which include the Hebrew language) the *yiqtol* started to report present-future and the *qatal* past time situations. The original past meaning of the *yiqtol* has been retained mainly in bound forms, which are less likely to change. This is how *wayyiqtol*, which is bound by a *waw*, is the praeterit form. Thus the *waw* does not **convert** the meaning of the form as claimed in the Middle Ages, but in the contrary, it **conserves** it, and hence the label '*waw*-conserving' given to this theory. A later development created a new form by analogy — *wqatal*, yielding the parallelism *yiqtol-wqatal* to indicate present-future on the one hand, and *wayyiqtol-qatal* for past tense on the other. The choice of the form in each group, he argues, depends on syntactical considerations: the *waw* prefixed forms are always clause initial, while the "free" forms can never appear in initial position. However, although very stimulating, Bauer's theory faces crucial difficulties. McFall criticizes Bauer's particular arguments in detail. But excluding the particular difficulties, McFall also points out more general problems, one of which is the fact that if we accept Bauer's view, it will never be clear to us when the verb in question belongs to the earlier and when to the later layer of the language (i.e., we, again, are faced with a circular theory). Ben-Ḥayyim (1977), too, rejects Bauer's theory, claiming that even if it is adequate to assume an amalgamation of two stages in the language, the system must have been crystallized by the time of the amalgamation and each form should have gained a special function.

Most of the new theories analyze the verbal forms in BH within a discourse analysis approach. Niccacci (1990) analyses the verbal forms in BH within the "text linguistics" approach of Weinrich (1978). As summarized in Niccacci (p. 19, 111), Weinrich sees texts from three different view points: linguistic attitude, foregrounding and linguistic perspective. Linguistic attitude distinguishes between narrative and commentary material. Foregrounding has to do with emphasis, where foreground clauses are emphasized or highlighted and background ones are not. (This is not how the distinction of foreground vs. background is used in studies such as Comrie 1986 and Longacre 1981 — see below for discussion.) Linguistic perspective distinguishes between three kinds of text: retrieved information (such as flashbacks), degree zero (which is the level of the story), and anticipated information (which reveals the end of the story). Niccacci suggests tables of the BH forms according to these distinctions (p.20). Thus, in the first table he lists the forms used in narrative vs. those used in the commentary material; in the second table he lists the forms which are used in the narrative foreground vs. the forms used in the narrative background, vs. the forms used for the direct-speech ('discourse' in his terms) foreground, etc. This pragmatic approach has many insightful local points (as well as local shortcomings), but it does not discern definite features for the forms and hence does not allow prediction for their uses. For example, the form *qatal* is found in the narrative as well as in the direct-speech material (see table 1), in the foreground of the direct-speech (table 2), in the recovered information of the narrative and the direct-speech (table 3), in degree zero of direct speech (table 3), and in the present volitive moods (also table 3). Niccacci himself admits that "Each case has to be judged on its own merits from literary criteria and the meaning of the text" (p. 59). Washburn (1994), correctly, notes that "such an approach takes us into the realm of semantic forces of *individual* verb and ultimately can tell us nothing about... WP (=*wayyiqtol*) in a more generalized sense" (p. 31; emphasis is mine).

A different approach is taken by Longacre (1981), Givón (1977,1982), Andersen (1974) and Eskhult (1990) who analyze the verbal system in Biblical Hebrew within a discourse analysis theory, which divides the narrative text into two main parts — the sequential situations on one hand and the rest of the material on the other. This approach seems to be fruitful in explaining the biblical Hebrew verb forms, and hence the studies of these scholars seem to be adequate in this respect. However, except for this argument, the other parts of their theories face theoretical difficulties and are not empirically valid. Let us briefly examine each of the theories.

Andersen (1974) argues that the text is divided between sequential material on the one hand, and clauses which function to elicit the poetic structure of chiasmus or to express some meaning of what he calls "circumstantial" clauses on the other hand. Chiasmus is the reversing order of the words in two parallel lines which is used for poetic effects. Circumstantial clauses, according to Andersen, may be used in order to introduce a new character, summarize events, mark a beginning or an end of an episode, etc. The verb forms, claims Andersen, are chosen according to those functions. Thus he observes that *wayyiqtol* and *wqatal* appear in sequential clauses in the narrative and in "predictive discourse" respectively, while the other forms appear in different kinds of circumstantial clauses. Andersen does not deny that the verb forms may have different temporal interpretations, but as by-product of the discourse functions of the clauses in which they appear. However, this point of departure seems to be inadequate. It seems to me that the choice of the verb is determined by the temporal relations expressed in the clause, rather than the poetic effects the writer wants to elicit. This does not mean that poetic and pragmatic effects are irrelevant, but they have to submit to the semantic (temporal) meaning of the verb form. To appreciate the difference between the two approaches consider the following examples:[4]

(8)

wayyiqra:	*ˀelo;hi:m*	*la:ˀo:r*	*yo:m*
WAYY:call:3SG:MASC	God	to-the-light	day
wlaḥo;šek̲	*qa:ra:*		*la:yla:*
and-to-the-darkness	QAT:call:3SG:MASC		night

'God called the light day, and the darkness he called night' (Gen. 1:5)

(9)

u:b̲ne:	*yiśra:e;l*	*ˀa:k̲lu:*	*ˀet̲*	*hamma:n...*
and-sons:of	Israel	QAT:eat:3PL	ACC	the-manna
ˀet̲	*hamma:n*	*ˀa:k̲lu:*		
ACC	the-manna	QAT:eat:3PL		

'And the Israelites ate the manna... the manna they ate...' (Ex. 16:35)

(8) is a famous example of chiasmus. As Andersen (p. 129) correctly shows, the clauses are in parallel constructions. The order in the first clause is as follows: verb - NP subject - PP - NP object. The second clause has a reverse order: PP - verb - NP object (the NP subject is missing since it is identical to that of the first clause). Now since a verb initial clause may come only in a *waw*-prefixed form, and a clause which does not open with a verb may have only a "simple" form, the verb in the first clause is in the *waw*-prefixed form *wayyiqtol*, and the form in the second clause is in the "simple" form *qatal*. For this reason, Silverman (1973:174) notes on such cases that "...the simple tenses do not signify anything inherently different than the consecutive ones..." Although I do not deny that there is a chiasmus structure in (8), I argue that the narrator could not have used it if the temporal relations did not allow it. I.e., since the second clause does not report a sequential event, it cannot be reported by a *wayyiqtol* clause but only by a *qatal* verb, enabling a chiasmus structure. In example (9) both clauses report the event of eating the manna and both are in *qatal*. Andersen explains the second *qatal* clause as functioning to end an episode (p.81). (He does not account in this example for the first *qatal* use.) Again, this might be a correct explanation for why the narrator reported the same situation twice. However, the fact that the second clause reports the same situation reported in the first assigns it the non-sequentiality property, and this is what enables the author to use the *qatal* form. Another problem with Andersen's analysis is the lack of a full account of all the forms. Since he is interested in describing the sentence and the discourse structure rather than explaining the forms themselves, Andersen does not try to give the forms a full account. For example, he treats *wqatal* and

yiqtol as denoting future situations, but realizing that they appear also in clauses interpreted as denoting situations in the past time sphere he discards the problem by noting that it is difficult to distinguish between narrative and predictive discourse (p. 71).

Eskhult (1990) also applies to the Biblical text the distinction of sequential vs. non-sequential material in the narrative, using the characterization of **foreground** vs. **background** respectively (as defined in Reinhart 1984 and other studies; not as in Niccacci 1990). Thus he claims that *wayyiqtol* is used in the foreground while the other forms appear in different kinds of clauses in the background. However, Eskhul lists a number of different background functions to each form instead of discerning one specific use. He explains this as a result of historical developments. For instance, he accepts the approach that *qatal* was originally a stative form, and therefore it functions in describing states. But when West-Semitic split from Akkadian the form had developed an active meaning, where it is used parallel to *wayyiqtol* in chiasmus structures. Similarly, *yiqtol*, according to Eskhult, usually denotes ongoing, cursive, actions, but when its clause is interpreted as reporting "a contingent present-future situation the cursive force is neutralized" (p. 34). (Eskhult does not explain how *yiqtol* lost its cursive meaning.) Although the historical explanations may be accurate, the forms must be assigned unique synchronic features (cf. Ben-Ḥayyim's criticisms of Bauer 1910). There are a few other shortcomings in Eskhult's theory. A major one is his inconsistency in categoraization, mainly his claim that the Foreground-Background distinction parallels the State-Motion one. According to Eskhult, *wayyiqtol* is a foreground-motion form, while *qatal* denotes states in the background, a stipulation consistent with his general claim. However, he also assigns the property of motion to the form of *yiqtol*, claiming that it denotes ongoing (=cursive) actions; yet he categorizes *yiqtol* under the category of background. To sum up, although the historical explanations may be accurate and his distinction of Foreground-Background seems to capture an important characterization of the verb forms in BH, Eskhult's analysis cannot account for the synchronic temporal features of the BH forms.

Givón (1977,1982) claims that the verbal system in BH is an aspectual one, identical to the aspect system in Creoles (as analyzed in Bickerton 1976). As in Universal Creole Aspectual System, he argues, the verbs in biblical Hebrew function first and foremost to distinguish between unmarked sequential events in the narrative, denoted by *wayyiqtol*, and counter-sequential events, denoted by other forms. But Givón accepts the usual analyses of dissecting *wayyiqtol* into *waw* and *yiqtol*, i.e., he accepts that *yiqtol* is the form in the narrative sequence, and hence characterizes it also as realis and punctual. In contrast to *yiqtol*, he claims, *qatal*, *qotel* and the other forms are counter-sequential, distinguished from one another by punctuality and irrealis (*qatal*, according to him, is punctual while *qotel* is non-punctual, and the other forms carry different functions of irrealis). However, although his distinction between sequential-nonsequential material is adequate, Givón's treatment is problematic as a whole. His main problem, it seems to me, is the characterizing of *yiqtol* as the realis sequential form. First, as he himself shows, *yiqtol* is used in irrealis clauses too. He faces a similar difficulty with the form *qatal*, which appears not only in realis, as expected by Givón's analysis, but also in irrealis material (a fact which bothers him, too). Secondly, it is clear that *yiqtol* by itself can never indicate a sequential event, unless it is *waw* prefixed. (But could it be the case that Givón meant to say that *yiqtol* indicates successive events if it is *waw* prefixed?). Another problem is the punctual parameter suggested by Givón. Givón does not define this parameter formally or even informally and uses it in an intuitive way, claiming that *yiqtol* (and hence *wayyiqtol*) and *qatal* denote punctual situations, while *qotel* reports non-punctual ones. Reinhart (1984a) gives some relative-intuitive definition of punctuality. She claims that some situations with comparatively shorter duration than others may be regarded as punctual, and hence are more likely to appear on the time-line. However, even when used in this intuitive-relative sense, punctuality does not seem to be a relevant criterion for identifying the time-line in BH, since we find *wayyiqtol* or *qatal* clauses reporting "long" situations alongside much "shorter" ones, sometimes even "longer" than (neighboring) *qotel* clauses. (Givón himself admits that *qotel* clauses may have non-punctual use — 1982:131.) Givón has at least two more inaccuracies. Firstly, he claims that a *qatal* verb may indicate only anterior event, which is data invalid, as will be shown in chapter (5). Givón himself realizes that there are *qatal* clauses which do not report anterior events. These cases he explains as a device for changing the subject/topic (1977:215). Givón claims that when speakers want to shift the topic they use the *qatal* form instead of *(way)yiqtol* (1977:195,200,215; 1982:129). Givón does not specify if he relates to the sentence or the discourse topic, but his discussion implies that he is relating to sentence topic, since he claims that the topic is usually the subject, but emphasizes that sometimes it might be some other element "what one is talking about rather than the strict grammatical subject" (1977:FN. 16). (Cf. Reinhart 1981). However, Givón seems to be wrong on this issue too. On the one hand there are many cases when the subject/topic changes and yet the verb form in those clauses is *wayyiqtol*. For example, in conversation each turn of the speech act is reported by a verb of saying in *wayyiqtol*, although in each turn there is a different speaker. (But would Givón consider these cases as having the same topic?) Another set of examples are *wayyiqtol* clauses at the opening of a narrative discourse (Gen. 34:1, Gen. 30:1, Lev. 1:1, among others) where it is evident that the topic is a new one. Similarly, we also find many cases where the subject/topic does not change and still the verb is in *qatal*. Consider the following example:

(10) 9. ...*wayyo;mer* *lo:* *baḥ^{a}lo:mi:* *whinne:* *gep̄en*
WAYY:say:3SG:MASC to-him in-dream-my and-behold vine
10. *lp̄a:na:y* *u:ḇaggep̄en* *šlo;ša:* *śa:ri:ḡim* *whi:*
to-front:of-me and-in-the-vine three:MASC branches and-she
kp̄o;raḥaṯ *ˁa:lṯa:* *niṣṣa:h*
as-QOT:budded:SG:FEM QAT:rise:3SG:FEM blossom-her
hiḇši:lu: *ˀaškloṯe:ha:* *ˁana:ḇi:m*
QAT:ripen:3PL clusters-her grapes
'9. ... and he said to him. In my dream there was a vine. 10. On the vine there were three branches, and it budded and blossomed and its clusters ripened into grapes.' (Gen. 40:9-10)

All the clauses in (10) describe the vine, yet two of them have *qatal* verbs. (See Zewi 1992 for more discussion on the inaccuracy of the topic shift analysis of Givón.)

Longacre (1981), too, applies to the Biblical text the distinction of sequential vs. non-sequential material in the narrative, drawing attention to studies which characterize it as **foreground** vs. **background** material respectively. He adds other parameters to this distinction to account for the different forms. The parameter of "spectrum", which is a scale measuring the "dynamism" of the verb form is the most important. According to him, *wayyiqtol* is the most dynamic form and nominal clauses are the most static (or the least dynamic) in the narrative discourse. He claims that such a hierarchy exists also in prophetic texts, in which the form *wqatal* is the most dynamic. Longacre has two important points in his analysis: the application of the foreground-background distinction to the Biblical text and the observation that there are non-narrative texts, such as prophetic discourse, which behave similarly to narratives in having sequential vs. non-sequential material. Furthermore, he is not faced with most of the difficulties raised by Givón's analysis, for he does not dissect the *waw* prefixed forms, and treats them as a whole, where *wayyiqtol* is labelled "praeterit". However, his *dynamism* scale which was meant primarily to account for the different forms in the non-sequential material is problematic, although it does seem to me to capture the intuitive observation that the *wayyiqtol* and the *wqatal* clauses move the time forward (see chapter 2 for analysis). The main difficulty with this notion (pointed out to me by Ruth Berman, personal communication) is that it is not defined by objective metalinguistic means, which results in a circular claim (*wayyiqtol* is a dynamic form because the situation it denotes is dynamic, and the situation is dynamic because it is denoted by a dynamic form). Even the criteria for determining the level of dynamism are not given full formal treatment. Therefore, it is not possible to evaluate this analysis or to judge the classification determined by it. For instance, Longacre states that the degree of informativity or relevance is responsible for the degree of dynamism and hence the choice of the form. How, however, are we to measure the degree of informativity or relevance? This vagueness allows Longacre to provide, at times, ad-hoc explanations to account for an occurrence of a specific form, explaining it as relevant (or irrelevant), informative or not highly informative, etc.

Washburn (1994) rejects the discourse analysis approach altogether. He claims that the prefix in *wayyiqtol* is not a conjunction, although it uses the same consonant *waw* as the conjunction, and therefore the meaning of the form does not depend on the previous clause. The prefix in the *wayyiqtol* form, claims Washburn, is rather "a specified grammatical formative; it is inflectional, part of the verb to which it is prefixed" (p. 40). This analysis of the prefix is in accord with Joüon (1947) who argues that there are two kinds of *waw*, one functions to coordinate phrases, and one which he labels "energetic *waw*" functions to mark succession, parallel to Arabic *wa* and *fa* respectively. However, although he does not consider the *waw* in *wayyiqtol* to be a pure coordinator, Joüon still analyses *wayyiqtol* clauses with respect to the previous clauses. This, claims Washburn, is inadequate, since there are many *wayyiqtol* clauses which open new discourse. (Cf. Bauer 1910's objection to Driver's analysis.) It is, indeed, problematic to define sequence according to the definition implicitly used by Joüon, Driver and others, namely that sequential clauses are only those which report situations following the previous reported situations. However, analyses such as Givón (1977, 1982) and Longacre (1981) analyze sequential material as forming the time-line, *all* of whose "beads", including the first one, should have sequential verb forms. Their shortcoming in this respect is that they assume an existing text, but do not explain how a narrator forms such a time-line. Kamp's (1979) definition of sequentiality, adopted in this study, seems to overcome this difficulty, and accounts for Washburn's objection. Recall that Kamp defines sequential clauses as moving the R-time forward (regardless of what they have in their neighboring clauses). This definition not only does not contradict Washburn's analysis of the form *wayyiqtol*, but it is even in accord with it. Washburn claims that each *wayyiqtol* clause "makes its individual statement, nothing more" (p. 45). I argue that this feature of *wayyiqtol* entails its power to move the R-time forward. The fact that clauses in *wayyiqtol* have their own "thought" (in Washburn's terms) manifests their character of introducing their own R-time, and hence their *potentiality* of forming a sequence. This potentiality may not be realized when such clauses appear in isolation or in non-narratives. But when building narratives their characteristic feature of forming new R-times causes them to use their potentiality of moving the R-time forward, resulting in forming sequences. (The same is to be said about *wqatal*, but Washburn discusses only *wayyiqtol*.)

This study treats the *waw* prefixed forms in a way similar to Longacre in that it does not dissect them into components. The main problem of dissecting these forms is, that to date, there is no adequate description for the component following the *waw*. There is much controversy among scholars on whether the form *wqatal* includes the form *qatal* and also, though less controversial, whether *wayyiqtol* is composed of *yiqtol*, jussive or another "free" form following the *waw*. Since I have done no morphological research on the subject I do not intend to take a stand on this controversy, but if an analysis in the future showing regularity in the differences between the free forms and the forms attached to the *waw* in the *waw* prefixed forms is proposed, I will be able to enrich my analysis on the subject. Thus the following overview aims only to show that we cannot yet dissect the *waw* prefixed forms. For many years, from the Middle Ages till the beginning of the 20th century, the common belief was that *wayyiqtol* is composed of *waw* and *yiqtol* (hence the *waw* conversive theory claiming that the *yiqtol* which denotes future changes its function to denote past when it is *waw* prefixed, the *waw* conserving theory which sees *wayyiqtol* as conserving the old function of *yiqtol* to denote past time events, etc.). Now most Hebraists believe that this is not the case, and the form in *wayyiqtol* does not contain *yiqtol*, an approach which started to be developed already in the nineteenth century. Ewald (1827) argues that it is the form of the jussive that is attached to the *waw* in *wayyiqtol*, but Gesenius (1909), Bergsträsser (1972)[5] and Driver (1874) disagree. Driver rejects Ewald's claim on the basis that the forms differ in their tone position and in many cases in the ultimate vowel also, as in the following pair: *yo:lé;k̲* (jussive) vs. *wayyó:lek̲* (*wayyiqtol*). However, it may be the case that the difference in the ultimate vowels in the two forms is due to the tone shift in the *wayyiqtol* verb. Washburn (1994) suggests that the shortening of the vowel (and the tone shift) was to restore the balance which had been undermined when a close syllable *way* was added. Moreover, as shown by Blau (1972) the tone position of *wayyiqtol* is not always on the penultimate vowel, but it is context dependent: it is on the penultimate syllable when it is open and on the ultimate when that syllable is closed. Thus we have pairs such as *wayyišá:mer-wayyišmó;r*. The question whether we have a jussive form attached to *wayyiqtol* or some other form is still open. However, note that if we accept the claim that it is jussive, we have to account for the occurrence of *w*-jussive, which clearly has the same meaning as the "free" jussive, and explain how *wayyiqtol* has lost its jussive meaning. We have a similar debate with the form of *wqatal*. Through the period from the Middle Ages until the nineteenth century the common belief was that *wqatal* has *qatal* as a basic form. But McFall (1982) reports Hebraists who argue that the form following the *waw* in *wqatal* is different from the "free" *qatal*. They find support for their claim in the difference of the tone positions in the first and second person singular masculine. In *qatal* the tone is on the penultimate vowel, e.g., *ša:márta:*, while in *wqatal* it is on the ultimate, e.g., *wša:martá:*. However, McFall shows that this rule is not valid as there are many *wqatal* verbs which are accentuated on the penultimate vowel even in the persons mentioned above. McFall claims that the tone position is not phonematic (semantic) but has syntactic significance. According to McFall, the tone position is determined by the relationship of the verb to the other members of the sentence. (Note, furthermore, that in first person plural the tone is on the penultimate rather than the ultimate vowel, which also suggests that the tone position is context-dependent). In sum, in the absence of an adequate non-controversial (generally accepted) account of the morphology of the *waw* prefixed forms there is no way of specifying them in any well motivated fashion. Note, however, that in the case of the *w*-imperative, the *w*-jussive (*w* with a shwa and without geminating the prefix *y*) and the *w*-cohortative we have no such confusion, and can easily identify them when they are attached to a *waw*. Therefore, the approach adopted in this study considers these forms as independent.

1.2.2 *The Corpus*

As Ben-Ḥayyim (1977) notes, one of the problems of the theories dealing to date with the Biblical verbal system lies in treating the Bible as a single entity. Rather, one should differentiate between different genres of texts and different periods of the language, and maybe also between different dialects.

Gesenius (1909), Ben-Ḥayyim (1977), Qimron (1981) and others claim that the language in the poetry texts differs in many respects from the prose discourse (which is true about many languages, and might even have universal validity). This is clear in the case of the aspect system. The verb forms function differently in prose as opposed to poetry. I have chosen in this study to examine narrative texts since, as pointed out to me by Bernard Comrie (pc), poetry often violates otherwise valid linguistic norms for poetic effect, often harking back to archaic styles, etc. In addition, only narratives can clearly manifest R-time movement. Therefore the poetry texts have been excluded from the corpus. Gesenius (1909), Bergsträsser (1972) and others show that prophetic texts in the Bible behave like poetry, and hence they, too, are excluded from the corpus of this study. The law part of the Bible, however, was not omitted for two reasons. First, it was pointed out to me by Meir Sternberg (pc) that the law text is part of direct speech, which is part of narrative discourse. Secondly, such texts manifest what Longacre (1981) calls "foreground in the background", i.e., they, too, are divided into sequential and non-sequential material, for it is possible to give, e.g., orders which are supposed to be carried out one after the other.

Bergsträsser (1972), Rabin (1971) and others point to some evidence for the existence of different dialects in the Biblical text. However, as they themselves show, the examples are very few in number. Moreover, there is no evidence for dialectical differences in the aspect-modal system, and hence dialect considerations were not taken into account in this study.

In contrast, diachronic considerations are very significant for the aspect-modal system. It is well known that the Bible includes material from different periods of time. This is reflected in the vocabulary as well as in the grammar. In the most important division the Biblical language is seen as split into two periods — the First Temple and the Second Temple periods. Hurvitz (1972) and Eskhult (1990) show that this division is manifested very clearly in the case of the aspect system. In the period of the First Temple the aspect system is very rich, but after the Babylonian exile and during the Second Temple it collapses. This study, then, takes into account only the texts from the period of the First Temple, namely Genesis through Kings. Note that this period lasted for about 400-500 years, but my study clearly shows that the aspect system was consistent throughout this long period (or maybe it manifests the fact that it was edited at a certain point of time). More serious is the fact that for a long time the Bible was not written but was transmitted orally from father to son. The editing of the text came even later. Moreover, the spelling changed in time, from a spelling which did not mark vowels at all to one which marked many of them. This resulted in different versions of spellings in the canonized Bible. But even after the Bible was written, the reading still depended on oral tradition, for most of the vowels were not marked, until the pointing (*niqud*) systems were developed. At least three systems of pointings were developed to mark the vowels, one of which is the Tiberian. The Tiberian system was developed during the 8th-9th centuries and is the one which has been accepted in "our" Bible. The late development of the vowel markers may have caused some "mispointings", which is reflected in the Massoretic corrections of the *Tiqune Sofrim*, and the different versions of some of the word pointings (see Biblia Hebraica). This is probably why Ben-Ḥayyim (1977) suggests depending mainly on the consonants when dealing with the verbal system in the Bible. However, this is not always possible since there are forms which can be distinguished only by their vowels, e.g., the forms *wayyiqtol-wyiqtol* have identical spelling; they differ only in the vowels of the *waw* (and the dagesh forte in the first form). Moreover, as reflected in the corrections of the Massora and grammarians such as Gesenius (1909) and Bergsträsser (1972) it seems that the pointing is consistent and the "mispointings" are rare. However, there is some debate among scholars about the correct pronunciation of the vowels, and to some extent of the consonants, too. For instance, Gesenius (1909) argues that the vowel called *qamaṣ* was pronounced (usually) as a long 'a:', but Joüon (1947) and Bergsträsser (1972), who believe that the vowels marked quality rather than quantity, claim that it was a back (low) '**ɔ**'. The assumption of the consonants' pronunciation is less debatable, but there are still some differences. However, this is not our concern since we are dealing here only with the different vowels as distinct from one another, regardless of how they were pronounced. This "policy" was adopted in my transcription which, therefore, does not intend to reflect the "right" pronunciation; it only gives a loyal graphemic "translation" of the Hebrew text, relying mainly on Gesenius' analysis since it seems to be the one most acceptable to Hebraists in Israel, and is the closest to the Modern Hebrew pronunciation. (For the pronunciation of the consonants and the vowels in present Israeli Hebrew see Muraoka 1993 p. 33 and 41 respectively.) Note that even when there is wide agreement on the assumed pronunciation, Hebraists prefer a transcription which reflects the spelling. For example, it is widely accepted that the phoneme /p/ has two allophones — [p] & [f] — (which has some reflection in Modern Israeli Hebrew, too), which are distinguished by the existence and non-existence of the dagesh in the letter *pe*. In this study I follow this convention, and these two allophones, e.g., are both marked by the letter 'p', distinguished here by a superline in the case of the [f]. The following tables list the transcription used in this study.

Table 1.1. The consonant transcription

ʔ –	א		l –	ל	
b –	בּ	(with a dagesh)	m –	ם, מ	
ḇ –	ב	(without a dagesh)	n –	ן, נ	
g –	גּ	(with a dagesh)	s –	ס	
ḡ –	ג	(without a dagesh)	ʕ –	ע	
d –	דּ	(with a dagesh)	p –	פּ	(with a dagesh)
ḏ –	ד	(without a dagesh)	p̄ –	ף, פ	(without a dagesh)
h –	ה		ṣ –	ץ, צ	
w –	ו		q –	ק	
z –	ז		r –	ר	
ḥ –	ח		š –	שׁ	
ṭ –	ט		ś –	שׂ	
y –	י		t –	תּ	(with a dagesh)
k –	ךּ, כּ	(with a dagesh)	ṯ –	ת	(without a dagesh)
ḵ –	ך, כ	(without a dagesh)			

As said above, the pronunciations of the vowels is controversial, and I am not taking a stand. My marking some vowels, e.g., *qamaṣ* by a long vowel 'a:' does not manifest any assumption, but it is merely a technical device to distinguish them from the other vowels.

Table 1.2. The vowel transcription ('X' stands for a consonant)

a:	—	qamaṣ	X̸ָ
a	—	pataḥ	Xַ
ᵃ (superscript a)	—	ḥaṭap̄ pataḥ	Xֲ
e:	—	ṣere male ("full" ṣere)	Xֵי
e;	—	ṣere ḥaser (regular ṣere)	Xֵ
e	—	segol	Xֶ
ᵉ (superscript e)	—	ḥaṭap̄ segol	Xֱ
o:	—	ḥolam male ("full" ḥolam)	Xוֹ
o;	—	ḥolam ḥaser (regular ḥolam)	Xֹ
ᵒ (superscript o)	—	ḥaṭap̄ qamaṣ	Xֳ
o	—	qamaṣ qaṭan	Xָ
u:	—	Šuruq	Xוּ
u	—	qibbuṣ	Xֻ
i:	—	ḥiriq male	Xִי
i	—	ḥiriq ḥaser	Xִ

As seen in the table, the *qamaṣ qaṭan* is marked in the Bible by the same sign as regular *qamaṣ*, but nevertheless it is marked differently in this study since there are some Hebraists like Rabin (1965), who see it as different in length from the "regular" *qamaṣ*. This makes it also more convenient for the Israeli Hebrew reader, for there is a difference in pronunciation between the two vowels — 'a' for the regular *qamaṣ* and 'o' for the *qamaṣ qaṭan*.

The shwa is not indicated; e.g., *d<u>b</u>a:ri:m* 'things', because as shown by Garbel (1959) it is not phonematic.

A furtive patah (*pataḥ gnu:<u>b</u>a:*) is marked by a subscript $_a$, e.g., *ru:$_a$h* 'wind'. A dagesh forte (*dageš ḥazaq*) is indicated by geminating the consonant, e.g., *sippe;r* 'he told'.

Vowel letters (called *ˀimo<u>t</u> qriˀa:* in Hebrew) are not indicated, e.g., לֵאָה is transcribed as *le;ˀa:* (without an 'h' at the end). But when the letter *he* is in word-final position (and therefore has a dot in it called a *mappiq*), it is consonantal and transcribed by an 'h', e.g., שְׁמָהּ is transcribed as *šma:h*.

When a (root) letter is silent it is not indicated; compare: *ʔa:mar* to *yo;mar* — the first letter *ʔ* of the root *ʔmr* is pronounced in the first verb which is in form *qatal* and hence it is indicated, but it is not pronounced in the second verb which is in *yiqtol* form, and therefore it is not indicated there.

Apart from the vowels, another marking system was also developed, namely the accents, called *ṭʕᵃme: hammiqra:* in Hebrew. These markers were developed mainly to indicate the musical way of reading the Bible in the synagogue, i.e., as musical notes. But the majority of these markers also indicate the position of the word stress and the punctuation. These two functions are, sometimes, significant for determining the verb form. I refer mainly to two cases. Firstly, when the root has a *waw* or a *yud* in its second position, as in *qwm*, *bwʔ*, *šyr*, etc, it has the same conjugation in *qatal* and *qotel* in third person singular feminine, as in *qa:ma:*, *ba:ʔa:*, *ša:ra:*, etc. The distinction between the *qatal* and the *qotel* forms in such verbs lies only in the tone position — in *qatal* it is on the penultimate vowel and in *qotel* on the ultimate. Thus we have pairs such as *qá:ma:-qa:má:*. In contrast, the *ṭaʕam* may sometimes neutralize a distinction. Verbs in pattern *nip̄ʕal* in third person singular, such as *nilḥam* (*qatal*) — *nilḥa:m* (*qotel*) 'fight' have a *pataḥ* in the ultimate syllable when they are in *qatal*, but a qamaṣ in *qotel*. However, in its pausal form (in *hefseq*), the ultimate vowel is a *qamaṣ* in both forms. The accents are not indicated in this study, but I will mention them in the discussion when it is relevant for a particular argument.

1.2.3 *The Biblical Hebrew Verb System and the Temporal Parameters*

My study clearly shows that the BH system organizes the text into sequential and non-sequential material, as observed by Givón, Longacre and others. That is, the aspect of sequence, as said in section 1.1.1 above, allows the valid prediction of the choice of the verb form. But this is not sufficient, since there are several verb forms denoting sequentiality and even more forms appearing in non-sequential clauses, e.g., both the *wayyiqtol* and the *wqatal* forms appear in sequential chains only. I will show that the choice of the specific form depends on the other temporal parameters mentioned in sections 1.1.1-1.1.2. Table (1.3) summarizes the BH verb forms that I will develop in the following chapters according to those parameters, where **SEQ** stands for "sequentiality", **MOD** for "modality", **INC** for "inclusion" (i.e. "progressive") and **PER** for "perfect":

Table 1.3. The Forms and Temporality

FORM PARAMETER	*wayyiqtol*	*wqatal*	*yiqtol*	*qatal*	*qotel*
SEQ	+	+	–	–	–
MOD	–	+	+	–	–
INC	–	–	–	–	+
PER	–	–	–	+	–

There are two forms indicating sequential clauses (i.e., clauses moving the R-time forward) — *wayyiqtol* and *wqatal*. They differ on the MOD parameter. This shows that BH has a special form, *wayyiqtol*, for the clauses on the time-line, and a special form — *wqatal* — for sequential modal clauses. The form *qotel* functions as the progressive (i.e., inclusive) aspect, and *qatal* as the perfect, both non-sequential forms. *Yiqtol* is also a non-sequential form, but it is modal. There are a few extra points I want to make.

First, the column for the perfect aspect is redundant. The fact that *qatal* has negative values on the first three parameters reflects its "parasitic" character which is characteristic of the perfect form (see section 5.2 in chapter 5 for a detailed discussion). However, in order to represent all four parameters explicitly I included the perfect.

Second, the picture emerging from table (1.3) may be misleading, concerning the forms *qotel* and *qatal*. Contrary to what might be predicted from the table, these forms may and do appear in modal clauses. The way this works will be explained in chapters 3-5.

Third, in the case of modals the table specifies only two — *yiqtol* and *wqatal* — these two represent all the other forms. In fact there are many more forms the modals can take, but here *wqatal* stands for all the sequential *waw* prefixed forms, and the *yiqtol* for all the non-sequential "simple" forms. Thus: *wqatal* represents (in addition to *wqatal* itself): *wyiqtol*, *w*+jussive, *w*+cohortative and *w*+imperative. In section 4.2.1 I will show that the forms are semantically identical, i.e., they have the same truth conditions. All these forms refer to sequences of modal situations which might take place in some possible world. This means that had they been represented in the table they would all have had positive values on the [SEQ] and [MOD] parameter (and negative values on [INC] and [PER]), and could have been reduced to one form. Similarly, the forms represented by *yiqtol*: the imperative, the jussive, and the cohortative (and *yiqtol* itself, naturally) all function to denote modal situations like the *waw* prefixed forms, except that they are not sequential. The forms differ from one another in the kind of modality they indicate — see section 4.2.1 in chapter 4 for discussion. The forms *yiqtol* and *wqatal* were chosen to represent all the other modal forms since they are the most neutral, and are sometimes used instead of the more specific forms. (The reader is referred again to section 4.2.1 for elaboration).

The infinitive forms were also omitted from the table, but for a different reason. They were omitted altogether not only from the table, but also from the discussion of the verbal system. In Hebrew there are two kinds of infinitives, labelled as "absolute" and "construct" by Hebraists. The construct is in part similar to the English infinitive, e.g., *lišmo;r* 'to watch' is constructed of *l* 'to' and the stem *šmo;r* 'watch', which (usually?) behaves like the parallel English form. Within the Chomskian approach, infinitivals are usually treated as subordinate sentences, but unlike subordinate clauses with finite verbs, infinitivals do not have their own temporal features. It is not clear, however, where they get to be assigned those features, e.g., it is not clear how in sentences such as "John wanted to eat" the infinitival "to eat" is assigned a modal feature although the matrix is non-modal. In Hebrew the infinitive can also be used as a verbal noun, but then it is preceded by different prepositions, e.g., *k* or *b*, usually meaning 'when'. In such cases the verbal noun functions as a **when**-clause, but its temporal features seem to be determined syntactically, e.g., *kišmo;aʕ yaʕᵃqo;b̲* may be interpreted as a non-modal 'when Jacob heard' or as a modal 'when Jacob will hear'. Prefixing the words *wayhi:* or *wha:ya:* to them will disambiguate the clause to mean the non-modal and the modal 'when' respectively. (See discussion on these words in chapter 2.) To complicate the picture, the so called **absolute infinitive** seems to behave quite differently from the other infinitive. It is found in matrix sentences such as in *ša:mo:r ʔet̲ yo:m haššabba:t̲ lqaddšo:* 'keep the Shabat day...', where the infinitive 'keep' is used for a commandment (instead of the imperative), but it is also found in other constructions. Goldenberg (1971) calls the most common construction a 'tautological infinitive', when it is added to a finite verb of the same root and pattern, adding no semantic content but used as syntactic "filler" (see example 30 in chapter 5). However, all the description given above is based on unsystematic observations. It seems to me that there is a need for extensive research on the infinitive in Hebrew before we can determine its temporal character, and therefore infinitivals were not included in this study.

1.2.4 *Method*

The full corpus, as defined in section (1.2.2) above, was examined repeatedly during the research, each time for a different purpose; e.g., to find out if *wayyiqtol* is indeed the only form to identify the sequential non-modal clauses, to check the behavior of the inclusive (*qotel*) aspect, etc. While reading through the data I examined all the counter- (or seemingly counter-) examples, trying to find an explanation. Most of the time there were explanations for these apparent counterexamples, but there still remained a few verses without an explanation. To find out if the number of unexplained cases is significant a statistical count was also done, but on a sample only. To obtain a non-biased random sample of all the books in the corpus, the first three and the last three chapters of each book were included. Where the book consisted of thirty or more chapters, its three middle chapters were also included. This seems to be a better method than taking every fifth or third chapter in each book, because it yields larger stretches of narratives and, usually, a complete topic. When one (or more) chapter (or part of it) of the sample was poetic material, the chapter was omitted, e.g., SamuelII's last three chapters are 22-24, but since chapter 22 consists of David's words of song, the chapters included in the sample were only 23 and 24. While omitting poetry, prophecy, etc., from the sample, the law part of the Bible, appearing mainly in Leviticus, was not omitted, for reasons explained above. However, since my main concern is the narrative, I decided to include in the sample only three chapters of the book of Leviticus — the first, the middle and the last one. The sample, then, consists of 62 chapters as follows:
Genesis: 1-3, 25-27 and 48-50; Exodus: 1-3; Leviticus: 1, 14 and 27; Numbers: 20-22; Deuteronomy: 1-3 and 32-34; Joshua: 1-3 and 22-24; Judges: 1-3 and 19-21; SamuelI: 1-3, 14-16 and 29-31; SamuelII: 1-3 and 23-24; KingsI: 1-3 and 20-22; KingsII: 1-3 and 23-25.

The forms' distribution in this sample is summarized in table (1.4) below:

Table 1.4. The Distribution of the Forms

TOTAL	wayyiqtol	yiqtol	wqatal	qatal	qotel	n-qotel	?	other
6293	2445 ~39%	1121 ~18%	573 ~9%	1190 19%	425 ~7%	253 ~4%	144 ~2%	142 ~2%

The label '*n-qotel*' in the table stands for 'nominal *qotel*', referring to clauses with predicates which do not consist of a verbal form. These predicates behave like the *qotel* in terms of temporality and hence the label given to them. (For this reason they will be discussed together with the *qotel* in chapter 3). The *2445* verbs in *wayyiqtol* do not include the 104 occurrences of *wayhi:* for reasons to be explained in chapter (2). For the same reasons the 38 occurrences of *wha:ya:* are not included in the statistics of *wqatal*. In table (1.4) they are represented together under the column labelled 'Other'. The column '?' represents 144 verbs ambiguous with respect to morphology. These verbs are mainly *ʕayin-waw* and *ʕayin-yud* forms. I.e., verbs whose roots have *w* or *y* as their second radical, as in *q.w.m* and *m.w.t* or *š.y.r* and *ś.y.m*. Verbs with such roots have the same form in *qatal* and *qotel* for the third singular person masculine e.g., *qa:m*, *ša:r*, etc. (in third person singular feminine they also have the same form, but are distinguished by the location of the stress — which is on the penultimate vowel in *qatal* but on the ultimate in *qotel*). Another group of ambiguous verb forms is the paradigms *qatel* and *qatol*. Verbs in these paradigms can be interpreted either as *qotel* or as *qatal*, in third person singular masculine, e.g., *ya:še;n* and *ya:k̲o;l*. Excluding the ambiguous clauses (less than 2%), each clause was given a value on each of the four parameters — SEQ, MOD, PER and INC. The method can be illustrated by the verse under (11) below:

(11) *wayye;lek̲* *rˀu:b̲e;n* *bi:me:* *qṣi:r* *ḥiṭṭi:m*
WAYY:go:3SG:MASC Reuben in-days:of harvest:of wheat
wayyimṣa: *d̲u:d̲a:ˀi:m* *baśśa:d̲e*
WAYY:find:3SG:MASC mandrakes in-the-field
wayya:b̲e; *ˀo;t̲a:m* *ˀel* *le;ˀa:* *ˀimmo:*
WAYY:bring:3SG:MASC them to Leah mother-his
watto;mer *ra:ḥe;l* *ˀel* *le;ˀa:* *tni:* *na:*
WAYY:say:3SG:FEM Rachel to Leah IMP:give:2SG:FEM please
li: *middu:d̲a:ˀe:* *bne;k̲*
to-me from-mandrakes:of son-your
'In the time of wheat-harvest Reuben went out and found some mandrakes in the field and brought them to his mother Leah. Rachel said to Leah, Give me, please, some of your son's mandrakes.' (Gen. 30:14)

The first predicate (*wayye;lek̲*) was given a positive value on the SEQ parameter, since it initiates the sequence, but a negative value on MOD, INC and PER parameters. The second predicate (*wayyimṣa:*) was also assigned a positive value on SEQ and negative on the other three parameters, since it denotes a non-modal event occurring after the event reported in the preceding clause and before the next reported one. The following clause (*wayya:b̲e;...*) was assigned the same values for the same reasons, as was the next clause (*watto;mer...*). Now the next predicate is direct speech which consists of Rachel's request *tni: na:....* The request, naturally, has not yet been fulfilled and therefore is a modal, and does not include or overlap or follow the event reported in the preceding clause. It therefore is assigned negative values on SEQ, PER and INC criteria, but a positive value on MOD. But while in this example the context enables us to evaluate all the clauses, there are cases in which it is not possible. There are cases where the context cannot independently determine if the situation reported is sequential or inclusive, modal or non-modal. This can be illustrated by (12) below:

(12) *whaːˀa:d̲a:m* *ya:d̲aˁ* *ˀet̲* *ḥawwa:* *ˀišto:*
and-the-man QAT:know:3SG:MASC ACC Eve wife-his
wattahar *watte;led̲* *ˀet̲* *qayin...*
WAYY:conceive:3SG:FEM WAYY:bear:3SG:FEM ACC Cain
'The man lay (had laid?) with his wife Eve, and she conceived and gave birth to Cain.' (Gen. 4:1)

The three clauses in this verse are obviously temporally ordered. This we know from our world knowledge — the event reported in the second clause is a result of the one represented in the first clause, and the event reported in the third clause is a result of the one represented in the second. We can, therefore, determine the SEQ value of the second and the third clause, i.e., they are both assigned a positive value on this parameter (and negative values on MOD, PER and INC). However, it is not possible to determine the temporal relation of the first clause with the clause preceding it, the last clause in verse 3:24:

(12') *wayḡa:reš* *ˀet̲* *ha:ˀa:d̲a:m* *wayyaške;n*
WAYY:expel:3SG:MASC ACC the-man WAYY:place:3SG:MASC
miqqed̲em *lḡan* *ˁe;d̲en* *ˀet̲* *hakkrub̲i:m* *wˀe;t̲*
from-east to-garden:of Eden ACC the-Cherubim and-ACC
lahaṭ *haḥereb̲* *hammit̲happek̲et̲* *lišmo;r*
flame:of the-sword the:QOT-turning-over:SG:FEM to-INF:guard
ʔet̲ *derek̲* *ʕe;ṣ* *haḥayyi:m*
ACC way:of tree:of the-life
'He cast the man out, and to the east of the garden of Eden he stationed the cherubim and the flame of the whirling sword to guard the way to the tree of life.' (Gen. 3:24)

Neither our world knowledge nor the text provide clues for the temporal relations between the events reported in (12) and those reported in (12'): Adam could know Eve before or after they were exiled from the Garden-of-Eden and the cherubim were placed at its east. This point may be further demonstrated by the following example:

(13) 28. ...*wayyitten* *lo:* *?e<u>t</u>* *ra:ḥe;l* *bitto:* *lo:*
WAYY:give:3SG:MASC to-him ACC Rachel daughter-his to-him
29. *l?iša:* ***wayyitte;n*** ***la:ḇa:n*** ***lra:ḥe;l*** ***bitto:*** ***?e<u>t</u>***
for-wife WAYY:give:3SG:MASC Laban to-Rachel daughter-his ACC
bilha: šip̄ḥa:<u>t</u>o: la:h lšip̄ḥa:
Bilhah slave-his to-her for-servant
'28. Laban gave him his daughter Rachel as wife; 29. **and he gave Rachel his slave-girl Bilhah to serve her.**' (Gen. 29:28-29)

The temporal relations of the event reported in the boldfaced clause with the situations of the neighboring clauses cannot be independently determined from the context. For (my) lack of knowledge of marriage habits in those days, I cannot determine if the gift given to Rachel preceded or followed her marriage. Cases like (12) and (13) remained unanalyzed concerning the SEQ criterion.[6] The same was done, mutatis-mutandis, with the other two parameters, e.g., out of 2445 verbs in *wayyiqtol* 494 (i.e., 20%) appear in clauses where it was impossible to determine the temporal relation with the previous clause, and therefore, only 80% of the *wayyiqtol* verbs in the sample (1951 verbs) were counted — 1834 of them (94%) were correctly sequential, while 117 (6%) were counter-examples (most of them have an explanation). On the other hand, only 7 *wayyiqtol* verbs (i.e., less than 1 percent — 0.28%) were vague concerning the MOD parameter, and hence the counts here of 2438 verbs, and for the INC parameter only 18 (0.73%) were vague and hence excluded from the statistics.

The statistical results will be presented in the respective chapters, but I would like to emphasize again that each parameter and each issue were examined on the *whole* corpus, and therefore examples and counter-examples from the whole corpus will be explained and/or discussed, as has been done in this and the previous sections.

NOTES

1. I do not do this for the transcription of particular verbs, since there the phonemic contrast is significant.

2. a. The consonant *y* in the form of *wayyiqtol* is the third person marker; the second person has, instead, *t*, the first person singular and plural have the consonants *?* and *n* respectively.
b. Some of the verbs represented by *wayyiqtol* have different vowels. Most of the verbs do, indeed, have a pataḥ after the *waw* followed by a dagesh forte geminating the next consonant (hence the vowel 'a' and the double 'y' in the form's name). However, when the consonant following the first vowel is '?' (in first person singular) it is not geminated and the vowel preceding it is a qamaṣ, which is represented here as a long 'a:' (see next section for the transcription). When the consonant is a 'y' with a shwa it is not geminated either, but the vowel of the first syllable is still a pataḥ. The following examples illustrate each of the cases. *wayyo;mer* 'he said', *wanno;mar* 'we said', but *wa:?o;mar* 'I said' and *waydabbe;r* 'he spoke'.

3. Ben-Ḥayyim (1977) believes that the seeds of this approach had been planted long before in Dalmash (1523), but admits that only in the 19th century was the aspect-oriented approach explicitly developed.

4. a) The forms are represented in the glossary by their first three or four letters, e.g., *wayyiqtol* is represented as WAYY in front of the verb, which in turn is followed by its features concerning person, number and gender (as in WAYY:call:3SG:MASC in example 8), 'imperative' is represented as IMP, etc.
b) The translation is generally my own, relying in part on *The New English Bible* and sometimes on the King James' Version.
c) For the consonants and the vowel transcriptions see tables 1.1 and 1.2 below respectively.

5. I refer to the Hebrew translation of Bergsträsser (1918).

6. Such cases can be reduced by poetic methods and/or historical investigation. For the poetic methods the reader is referred to the works of Sternberg, mainly Sternberg (1985). Historical considerations, e.g., marriage contracts in the Ancient East, will also contribute to disambiguate cases such as (13).

Chapter 2

Sequence

In the previous chapter I claimed that the sequence aspect is to be defined in the spirit of the analysis first introduced by Kamp (1979), namely as the aspect moving the time forward. The *result* of this movement is what we identify as a sequence. In the first part of this chapter I will define the concept of time movement, i.e., the sequence aspect, in a more formal way, demonstrating it mainly from French, Russian and English, since most of the literature on sequence discusses these languages. The second part of the chapter will be devoted to the sequence aspect in BH.

2.1 Definition of Sequence

Formal studies dealing with sequence have defined the narrative sequence only. Since the clauses on the narrative time-line are understood as preceding the speech time, or rather the R_S (in tensed languages, therefore, those clauses will usually have the past tense), the sequence is usually defined not only by the notions of Reference and Event time, but also with respect to the Speech-time. However, as mentioned in chapter (1) above, informal analyses such as Polanyi & Hopper (ms.) illustrate other kinds of sequences, e.g., future plannings, habitual activities, military orders, recipe directions and the like. In our terms, modal clauses in the present or the future (as well as in the past) may also constitute a sequence, which suggests that the R_S, i.e., the tense, is irrelevant for defining sequentiality. The question is whether the R-time is irrelevant too, i.e., whether we can define the sequence by the E-time only. The answer is negative. Consider example (1):

(1) Rachel took a shower, got dressed and went to school.

If we describe (1) only in terms of E-time, we would not be able to account for the fact that there might be (and probably are) other events occurring between the first and the second event and between the second and the third event. The narrator refers to them as uninterrupted intervals, and such a sequence of intervals can hold only between R-times. But more persuasive is the fact that if the events are included in the same R-time, they will not constitute a linguistic sequence, as in the following examples:

(2) a) The party has died out because John has left and Bob has got drunk.
b) Israel was established in 1948. In that year John left Europe.

The temporal relations between the events reported in the last two clauses of (2a) or the two sentences of (2b) are ambiguous: the first reported event may have happened before the second, after it or exactly at the same time. That is, one possible interpretation that the event of the second clause follows the event reported in the first one, but nevertheless they cannot compose a sequence. We explain this by noting that the two events share the same R-time — the R_S and '1948' respectively. For the same reason, a sentence in perfect cannot be a link on a chain of sequence (see chapter 5 for discussion). We generalize, then, that clauses bear the sequence relation iff their R-times follow each other, which is the result of the R-time movement. That is, to define a sequence one needs to lean on an analysis which takes the R-time as a basic notion.

Kamp (1979, & Reyle 1993) developed the Discourse-Representation-Structures (henceforth: DRS or just DR) in analyzing the narrative discourse. The central idea of Kamp's analysis is that each sentence in the discourse is temporally processed not only by itself but also in relation to the preceding clauses. The syntactic structure of the sentence signals to the recipient how to incorporate the information it brings into the representation which s/he has already formed of the preceding section(s) of the text of which the sentence is part. The representations which the recipient constructs in the course of the text processing have the form of DRS. The internal temporal structure which the representation possesses was developed in the theory to explain how such structures might semantically relate to the real time structure of the actual world. To illustrate how this works reconsider example (1). In the chain of sequential clauses such as (1) the truth conditions of the first sentence are determined according to its past tense, which requires that the event took place in some interval preceding the S-time. With the other syntactic components it determines the first DR. When the second sentence is processed its syntactic structure functions to incorporate the information from the first DR_1, now forming the second DR_2 which contains the first DR. The third sentence, in turn, yields an expanded DR_3 which contains the second DR_2 (and since DR_2 contains DR_1 it follows that DR_3 contains also DR_1), and so forth. In other words, to determine the truth conditions of the second, the third... the nth sentences in a discourse such as (1) it is not sufficient to determine that they precede the R_S, but also that their R-times follow the R-times of the event(s) reported in the preceding clause(s). (The same is to be said, *mutatis mutandis*, about other temporal relations; see the following chapters for detailed discussions). In Kamp & Rohrer (1983), Hinrichs (1986 [1982]), Partee (1984), Kamp & Reyle (1993) and others this is described in terms of R-time movements, i.e., each of the sentences moves the R-time forward, and as a result the R-times are temporally ordered. Kamp has supported his analysis with an examination of the French verbal system, which marks the clauses on the time-line. In written French narrative, the simple past (passé simple) carries the story line (see also Kamp & Rohrer 1983, Guenthner, Hoepelman & Rohrer 1978, Hoepelman & Rohrer 1980, Hopper 1979 and others). Kamp's analysis can be applied to other languages such as Russian and BH, which mark the sequential clauses aspectually. In Russian, every verb has perfective or imperfective form. The verb in the sequential clauses are in perfective, while the verbs in the rest of the text are usually in imperfective, as Chvany (1980), Forsyth (1970), Hopper (1979) and others have shown. As to BH, this works even better, since the sequential form *wayyiqtol* would not appear in clauses off the time line under any circumstances. This will be illustrated and discussed further in the next section of this chapter. However, languages such as English (and Modern Hebrew) do not have a special aspect for this purpose, and the simple past may be used either for sequential material as in example (1) above, or off the time-line as in the following example:

(3) John lay on the bed and listened to the radio.[1]

Hinrichs (1986 [1982]) tries to apply Kamp's theory to English, by developing a theory leaning on the concept of Ak(tionsarten), first suggested informally by Dry (1981). Dry was the first to show that "perception of forward time movement in narrative correlates with textual phenomenon suggesting definite change of state" (p. 233). In general, Dry suggests that when a sentence is understood as an event it is interpreted as involving a change of state, and hence moving the time forward, while a stative sentence is not. However, as shown in the study of Miller & Johnson-Laird (1976), while events are perceived *only* when a change occurs, not all changes are perceived as events. A sequence of two or more changes in the physical objective world can be perceived either as two (or more) events, or as one single event, or even as a state. A flickering light, e.g., is perceived as a state, although it consists of many successive changes. Moreover, identification of events might even depend on social conventions: trips, meetings, games and other social activities may be regarded as single events "simply because that is how we talk about it" (p. 90). This means that as far as language is concerned one must not only consider the perceptual events, but also the conceptual ones. In other words, the event-state distinction must be characterized as a language rather than a real world distinction, as implied by Dry (1981) and argued explicitly by Bach (1981), Moens (1987), Moens & Steedman (1988), Tenny (1992), Depraetere (1995), Kearns (1991) and others. Recent semantic studies have characterized the distinction in terms of the inherent temporal properties of the predicate type. These studies, sometimes referred to in the literature as Ak(tionsarten),[2] try to capture the temporal properties according to the lexical verb and its arguments. The typology of predicates according to Ak' dates back as far as Aristotle (see, e.g., Hinrichs 1985, Mourelatos 1978 and Binnick 1991). The Aristotelian classification forms the basis for much of the research on Ak' carried out by philosophers of language (Ryle 1949, being the first, as noted by Hinrichs 1985) and later by linguists, with the most influential being that of Vendler (1967). His classification is accepted, basically, by most linguists, although with slight modifications.[3]

Vendler identified four different categories of verbs: st(ates), act(ivities), acc(omplishments) and ach(ievements):

(4) a. Mary lives in London. (st.)
b. Jasmin ran (for an hour). (act.)
c. Lucie made a chair. (acc.)
d. Carol found her bird. (ach.)

Vendler groups the first two and the last two together, according to a semantic characterization which he calls homogeneity. While st' and act' are homogeneous, acc' and ach' are heterogeneous.[4] In recent semantic studies resting on the notion of interval semantics the property of homogeneity has been called 'the distributive property' and analyzed in a more formal way (Bennett & Partee 1978 [1972], Dowty 1979, 1986, Taylor 1977, Bach 1981, Hinrichs 1985). Interval semantics is the idea of evaluating the truth of a sentence with respect to time intervals (rather than to moments or points of time as has been done in tense logic). The distributive property defined within this framework is concerned with the relationship of the situation and any of its subparts. It has been stipulated that states and activities are true in every subinterval. For example, if John lived in Tel-Aviv (for ten years), then he lived in Tel-Aviv during any subinterval of these ten years. The same is true for activities: if John laughed (for six minutes), then he laughed for every subinterval of these six minutes. (But see below a discussion accounting for intervals of activities and states which contain gaps.) However, acc' and ach' are both heterogeneous (i.e.,nondistributive). If John drew a circle (say it took him ten minutes), it is not the case that he drew a circle in every subinterval of those ten minutes. (Rather he was drawing a circle, or was busy drawing a circle in the subintervals of the event "he drew a circle".) It has been noted that the distinction correlates with Aristotle's **energeia-kinesis**, **telic-atelic** (e.g., Gary 1957, Depraetere 1995, Krifka 1992), **bound-unbound** (Allen 1966, Verkuyl 1993), **delimited-non-delimited** (Tenny 1992), **terminative-durative** (also Verkuyl 1993) and other similar distinctions. This binary distinction tries to capture an intuitive property which also has been given different terminology: "(natural) end-points" of the situation (Smith 1978, 1983 and elsewhere, Dry 1981, Tenny 1992), "culmination points" (Parsons 1990, Moens 1987, Moens & Steedman 1988, Kamp & Reyle 1993), "(set) terminal points" (Krifka 1992), "conclusion" (Kamp & Reyle 1993).[5]

One of the most challenging tasks for linguists has been to determine how activities such as "eat" acquire endpoints. The most acceptable one is the stipulation that a direct object with a countable head noun as in "eat the apple" serves to delimit the event, as opposed to objects with a bare plural noun phrase as in "eat apples" or a mass noun as in "eat cheese". Another kind of modifiers which affects the Ak' is a directional PP. For example, the PP "to the store" changes the unbound "John walked" into a bound situation "John walked to the store" (Dowty 1979, 1986; Verkuyl 1972, 1993; Tenny 1992; Depraetere 1995, among others). However, most of these analyses do not provide an explanation for the phenomenon, and hence cannot account for predicates such as "push a cart" which are unbounded although they have a countable NP as an object. Moens (1987) implicitly argues that there could not be an explanation for the phenomenon, claiming that it is only a pragmatic inference. For example, direct objects such as "an apple" are an indication that "the process [=activity] had a particular culmination point associated with it and provide extra context to help determine that point" (p.110), while a bare plural NP or a mass term "do not help the hearer in determining the culmination point". Verkuyl (1993) does not rely solely on the intuitive interpretation of the context, and claims that on the basis of semantic information associated with specific syntactic elements the Ak' ("aspect" in his terms) can be predicted (p. 3 and elsewhere). Verkuyl develops a compositional analysis within the localism framework introduced by Gruber (1976) and developed as a set-theory approach by Jackendoff (1976 and elsewhere). Interpreting thematic roles semantically, the localist theory argues that there are verbs which express movement of the Theme from Source to Goal, and verbs which do not. Verkuyl claims that this movement constructs a PATH which consists of a set of positions, cumulated on the way from the Source to the Goal. Hence he determines a parameter [ADD TO] as the property of such movement. Thus stative verbs have the property [-ADD TO], while verbs expressing activities, acc' and ach' have the property [+ADD TO]. Now the [+ADD TO] verbs may form two different categories of predicates: "terminative" (=bounded) vs. "durative" (=unbounded), depending on their arguments. For the categorization of the arguments Verkuyl defines an atemporal parameter [SQA], meaning "Specified Quantity of A", where "A" is the head noun of the NP argument. If that NP reports a specified quantity such as "three sandwiches" its predicate is terminative (=bounded), but if the NP does not express specified quantity as in the case of bare plurals or mass nouns, it is durative (=unbounded). Let us illustrate his analysis by examples (5a-c) below (his: 65 p. 218, 72 p.224 and 50 p. 236 respectively):

(5) a. John walked home.
b. John walked.
c. John walked to the store.

All the sentences under (5) have [+ADD TO] verbs, each expressing a set of spatio-temporal positions at which John (the Theme) was on his way from the Source (say, his office) to the Goal (which is home in a, the store in c, but not determined in b). The first point in all the cases is the set <t_0,office>, i.e., John was at his office at t_0. The second is <t_1, book shop>, i.e., at time t_1 John was in the book shop (on his way home or to the store), the third point is <t_2, office> (in case John returned to his office), etc. The last point of (5a) is <t_n, home>, determined by the NP object "home", and for (5c) it is <t_n, the store>, determined by the directional PP "to the store" which has a specified NP "the store". For a lack of a phrase bearing [+SQA] property, the last point in (5b) is not determined. Thus we say that (5a) and (5c) are bound, but (5b) is unbound. In a metaphorical way Verkuyl (p. 239) characterizes sentences such as "Judith ate three sandwiches" as bound, where the Theme Judith "goes" through a Path of eating from the Source of the first sandwich to the Goal of the third sandwich (and the second sandwich is a position located between the Source and the Goal). As the analysis is not merely syntactic but relies also on semantic considerations, Verkuyl is able to account for predicates such as "push the cart". The verb "push", claims Verkuyl, does not require a 'source-goal movement' and hence it is not terminative (see his ch. 14 for the analysis of such verbs).[6] Verkuyl claims that his analysis manifests the way we perceive time: discrete, measured by cardinality, rather than dense. Therefore he rejects the approach of interval semantics as being inadequate for analysing Ak'. However, Verkuyl believes that when using tenses and the progressive we map the discrete time movements into an interval of real time, which means that according to Verkuyl, too, interval semantics is the adequate framework for analysing tense and aspect. Incorporating Verkuyl's analysis of Ak' into interval semantics of tense and aspect might solve one of the most disturbing problems noted in the interval semantic approach. It has been realized (e.g., by Dowty 1986) that many activities do not realize the same activity in all of their subintervals. For example, a sentence such as

(6) John worked for seven hours.

may be true even though John probably took a break or two during those seven hours. Therefore Dowty stipulates that activities are true only in their "most subintervals" (criterion 13b on p.42). However, note that although it is probably the case that John did not actually work every minute of those seven hours, we still perceive the seven hours as a whole, one uninterrupted interval. Thinking of the seven hour interval of John's working as underlying the total sum of the positions on the Path through which John "moved", where the coffee break is one of the positions, say $<t_{20}$, coffee-break$>$, will explain why we do not conceive the gaps within the seven hours as interrupting the working interval. In other words, we consider John to be working also at the time of the coffee break t_{20}, because coffee breaks are considered to be part of the working path. (This is in accord with what has been emphasized by many linguists, that distributivity is not a property of the real world but of the way speakers refer to it.) This line of analysis can be modified to account also for states with gaps. A state like "John lived in London (for ten years)" will be true even if John used to take vacations during those ten years and live abroad. Verkuyl, as mentioned above, characterizes states as bearing the property [-ADD TO], which means that they do not go through a Path. However, tense and aspect, according to Verkuyl, apply to states the same way as to events and activities, i.e., to their underlined interval. Thus we may see the gaps of the states as part of that interval. To summarize, I adopt Verkuyl's analysis of Ak', but at the same time maintain the distributive property, in the way just described. Bach (1981), followed by Partee (1984), labels the non-distributive group EVENT. I, too, will use the term **event** for referring to accomplishments or achievements. For the group of activities and states I will use the term **distributive (situation)**, and for the general term referring to all the groups I will use Comrie's (1976) generic term **situation**. Figure 2.1 below summarizes the classification adopted here:

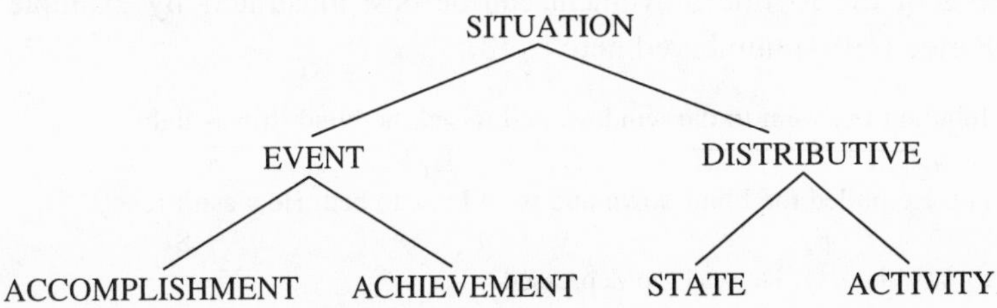

Figure 2.1. Aktionsarten Classification

Since the identification of the events is so crucial, Vendler and others have pointed out a series of related semantic properties that distinguish between different Ak'. The most complete account of these properties is that of Dowty (1979). The most useful test, used by many linguists, is the "in" phrase. Events expressions can occur with this phrase as in sentences (7c-d) below, while distributives cannot, as shown by the ungrammaticality of (7a-b)

(7)	a.	*Dan slept in two hours.	(st.)
	b.	*Dan cried in two hours.	(act.)
	c.	Dan wrote his thesis in one month.	(acc.)
	d.	Dan died in a few minutes.	(ach.)

Another useful criterion (although not as reliable as the first one) is the occurrence of the modifier "for" as in the phrase "for two hours" which gives a mirror picture, i.e., it rules out sentences denoting events but provides well-formed sentences with states and activities.

Hinrichs (1986 [1982]) followed by Partee (1984) stipulates different relations of R-time with the situations. He argues that events are contained in their R-time, while states and activities always contain theirs. He further argues that sequentiality is determined by the relations of the R-time with the situation, namely that only when the situation is included in its R-time can it be a candidate for sequentiality. Now, since they argue that events are contained in their R-time but distributives contain theirs, their conclusion is that only event clauses in the discourse move the R-time forward. They assume that, in addition to R_S, a past R-time R_0 at the beginning of the discourse contains the first introduced event, where the rest of the R-times are introduced by the events, always containing the **following** event. Distributive clauses do not introduce a new R-time, and always include the current one. Their analysis of the R-time movement can be best illustrated by example (14) from Partee (1984) numbered here as (8):

(8) John got up, went to the window, and raised the blind. It was light
E_1 E_2 E_3 S_1
out. He pulled the blind down and went back to bed. He wasn't ready
E_4 E_5 S_2
to face the day. He was too depressed.
S_3

The first clause denotes an event E_1, which is contained in an R-time R_0, already existing in the discourse, and introduces a new R-time R_1, in which E_2 reported in the second clause is contained. The second event E_2, in turn, introduces R_2 in which the *next* event E_3 is contained. Now this third event also introduces a new R-time — R_3, but since the situation in the fourth clause is not an event but a state, it *includes* R_3 rather than being included in it. In this particular narrative, which is the default case, we understand it also to include the previous R-times (i.e., R_0, R_1 and R_2), and hence their events too. Since it is a state the fourth situation does not introduce a new R-time and the next event (of the fifth clause) is included in the R-time R_3 (and hence follows R_2 and E_3), and so on till the whole discourse has been processed. Hinrichs' motivation for requiring the event to introduce the *next* R-time rather than its own was the observation that states and activities may, sometimes, be understood as following the last mentioned event, rather than including it. He illustrates this possibility by the following discourse:

(9) Jameson entered the room, shut the door carefully and switched off the light. It was pitch dark around him because the venetian blinds were closed.

Hinrichs explains the last sentences as denoting two states — the state of the room's being dark and the state of the venetian blinds' being closed. The first follows an accomplishment (switched off the light), but since it is the result of that accomplishment it is necessarily understood as following it. This analysis accounts for a distributive situation following the previous event, but it cannot account for distributives on the sequence, i.e., distributives which are not only preceded but also followed by other situations. Suppose that discourse (9) comprises two more events:

(9') ...Jameson took off his clothes and went to bed.

Since, according to Hinrichs, states do not introduce new R-times, the first event in (9') will be included in R_3 (introduced by the event "switched off the light") which is included in the state of the room's being dark. That is, the event of John's taking off his clothes will necessarily be included in that state. It follows that the state is not temporally ordered with the event following it, as required by the definition of sequence. In other words, in the case of (9) the theory suggested by Hinrichs happened to give a distributive situation on the time-line, but this happened just because the stative clause was not followed by another event. However, it cannot account for cases where distributives are clearly on the time-line (or other sequence), which will be demonstrated shortly.

Scha (1983), realizing that states can also appear in sequence, suggests a different mechanism for the R-time introduction. However, he still maintains that only event clauses move the R-time forward. He formulates the following rule:

(10) *Rule for R-time introduction (Scha 1983)*:
Given the current R, (R_n):
a) if the new situation is a state do nothing;
b) if the new situation is an event, introduce R_{n+1} to contain the event and then introduce the next R_{n+2}.

Scha, too, assumes R_0 as the current R-time available in the discourse before the first situation is implemented. Let us illustrate his rule of R-introduction:

(11) a) Max entered the room. It was dark in the room and the radio was playing some strange music. Max switched on the light...
E_1 (entered), S_1 (was dark), S_2 (was playing), E_3 (switched on)

b) $R_0\ [_{R1}E_1][_{R2}S_1,S_2][_{R3}E_3]R_4$

The first event E_1 introduces R_1 which is R_{0+1} to be contained in it, and then introduces the next R_2. The new situation S_1 does not introduce its own R-time, and therefore it is contained in R_2. Since it does not introduce a new R-time either, the next situation S_2 is also contained in R_2. When the third situation E_3 is implemented into the discourse a new R-time is introduced — R_3 — which contains E_3 introduced by it. E_3 introduces the next R_4, but since there is no new situation implemented in the discourse the new R-time remains "empty". The mechanism suggested by Scha predicts that two successive states reported in two successive clauses as S_1 and S_2 in (11) overlap each other. It also accounts for states appearing in a sequence, provided that they are preceded and followed by event clauses, as in (12) below:

(12) a. John reached the summit, stayed there for a while, and went down.
E_1 (reached), S_1 (stayed), E_3 (went down)

b. $R_0[_{R1}E_1][_{R2}S_1][_{R3}E_3]R_4$

However, there are a number of difficulties in Scha's analysis. First notice the redundancy of R-times it produces. R_0 in (11) and (12) has no role in the respective DRSs, since E_1 comes with its own R_1 in which it is contained. R_4 is also redundant. In (11) and (12) there are only two redundant R-times — the first and the last one. However, whenever we have a sequence of two or more events (i.e., in most of the narrative discourses) there will be many more. Secondly, although it is statistically rare, we can find sequences with stative clauses, provided that they are modified by a delimiter such as "for three hours":

(13) a) [It was a lovely performance]. The entertainer told jokes for fifteen minutes, sang for half an hour and danced for another half an hour.

b) We were in Mexico for couple of weeks, travelled in Guatemala for three weeks, visited Chile for two months [and came back home].

In order to develop an alternative analysis, let me reexamine the analysis suggested by Hinrichs and Partee. The wrong prediction of Hinrichs and Partee concerning the behavior of distributives on the time-line (and sequence in general) is a result of the relationship they assume between distributives and their R-times. Recall that they argue that only events are contained in their R-time, while distributives always contain theirs. I want to challenge this argument which seems to be only partially true. While events are, indeed, contained in their R-time, distributives do not always contain theirs. This can be illustrated by the following examples, where the R-time is specified as the day-unit preceding the time-of-speech denoted by the adverb "yesterday":

(14) a) **I was sick yesterday**, but my friend came and gave me a pill, and by midday I was feeling well.
b) **I was sick yesterday**, all day long, but after a good night's sleep I got up in the morning feeling better than ever.
c) A: Why didn't you come to my party yesterday?
B: **I was sick yesterday**; You know I have been sick for the last three weeks, and, unfortunately, I have not recovered yet.

While in (14c) the state, indeed, contains the R-time, in (14a) the state is rather included in its R-time and in (14b) it overlaps it. Reinhart (1986), accepting the claim that states may bear three different relations to their R-time, suggests a more general definition for the relation of R-time with the situation, as follows:

(15) R-time must contain *at least one* interval at which the eventuality (=situation) expressed by a given clause obtains.

From (15) it follows, that since an event can be true only at one such interval it has to be properly contained in its R-time. But in the case of states and activities we do not have such a constraint, and they may also obtain at intervals which are not contained in the R-time. The difference between events and distributives as to their relation with R-time explains the different entailments noted by Reinhart (1986) and Dowty (1986):

(16) a. I ate the apple yesterday. → I am not eating it now.
b. I will eat the apple tomorrow. → I am not eating it today.
c. I was at home yesterday. ~ → I am not at home now.
d. I walked in the park yesterday. ~ → I am not walking in the park.
e. I will be at home tomorrow. ~ → I am not at home today.

The antecedents of the implications (16a) and (16b) denote events, and thus they imply that the events cannot obtain after or before their respective R-time.[7] However, (16c-e) denote states, and thus do not entail that the R-time restricts the existence of the states — they can exist after and/or before their respective R-time. However, the logical entailments show that distributives do not necessarily continue beyond their R-time, as in the examples (14a-b) above. When they are included in their R-time, i.e., when they do not continue beyond it, distributives may appear in a sequence. This may happen in two cases: when they are interpreted as inchoatives or as holistic situations. In what follows I will first discuss inchoativity and then define the notion of "holistic" situations and account for the phenomenon.

It is widely acknowledged that stative clauses may be interpreted as inchoative (Dry 1981, Comrie 1985b, Dowty 1986, Partee 1984, Smith 1978, 1983 and elsewhere). Dry and Smith argue that only events may appear in a sequence due to their endpoints. However, they show that sometimes distributive sentences may be understood as events, due to linguistic clues or pragmatic inferences, and hence have natural endpoints and then be candidates for the time-line. Dry illustrates the phenomenon by a few sentences from *A Wrinkle of Time*:

(17) This was more than silence. Here there was nothing to feel. *Suddenly she was aware of her heart beating.*

(18) [Mrs. Murry said,] "Meg, come let me look at that bruise". *Meg knelt at her mother's feet.*

In her analysis, the underlined sentence in (17) has a stative predicate 'was aware', but the adverb "suddenly" which modifies it, suggests an inchoative meaning, which turns the whole sentence into an achievement. In (18) the underlined sentence is an activity by itself, but since it is the result of the event of the previous clause, the accomplishment reading 'assumed a kneeling position' is forced. Dowty (1986) agrees with Dry's and Smith's analyses, but suggests a pragmatic theory to account for superficial distributives on the time-line in model theoretic terms. Dowty, like Nerbonne (1986), claims that all the situations in the narrative, including distributives, have their own R-time (i.e., distributives too introduce new R-times), but by pragmatic implicatures distributives are usually understood to continue beyond their R-time, and hence to overlap each other and their neighboring event(s). But, since although the distributive character of states and activities *allows* them to begin earlier than their asserted R-time, it does not *require* them to do so (see the logical entailments he notes, given under 16), there may be cases when the default pragmatic inference is cancelled, as in examples (17) and (18) above. Dowty, agreeing with Dry (1981), points to the adverb "suddenly" and the causality inference respectively (in similar sentences) as being responsible for the event readings. He argues that the adverb and the causality inference cancel the pragmatic inference that the state obtained earlier, and give inceptive (=inchoative) interpretations to the stative sentences. As argued in Hatav (1989), it seems to me that pragmatic inferences for turning a superficial distributive into an event are rare since there are many linguistic devices for this purpose. In addition to adverbs such as "suddenly", we find other lexical means as well as morphological and aspectual devices. For example, in English, apart from adverbials, we find different lexical phrases for the inchoative-stative distinction, such as *fall in love* vs. *be in love*, *fall asleep* vs. *be asleep*, *sit* vs. *sit up* or *realize* vs. *know*. In Modern Hebrew, the distinction is usually encoded in the verb patterns (called "*binyanim*" or "conjugations"). MH 'love' is *ʔahav* while 'fall in love' is *hitʔahev*, and compare, too, pairs like *ʕamad* 'stand' vs. *neʕemad* 'stand up', *yašav* 'sit' vs. *hityašev* 'sit down' and even *šaḥor* 'be black' vs. *hišḥir* 'become black'. Languages which mark sequential clauses aspectually do not need lexical or other means for the contrast. They use their aspectual system to distinguish between inchoative and stative situations. Comrie (1985b) illustrates this by the Russian imperfective verb *sidet* 'be in a position of sitting', vs, the perfective *set'* 'to adopt a sitting position', 'sit down'. A similar account is found in Hoepelman & Rohrer (1980) for the French passé-simple. They claim that stative verbs such as *être* 'be' denote inchoatives if they have the passé-simple form, as in the following example:

(19)	*Quand*	*on*	*fut*	*exténué*	*on*	*fit*	*la*	*paix*
	when	one	be:PS	tired	one	make:PS	the	peace

'When they got tired they made peace'

(R. Carrier, *La Guerre, Yes Sir*, p. 16)

Examples (37), (40) and (62b) in section (2.2.1) illustrate incohatives in BH. To conclude, I accept the claim that when a situation has an inchoative meaning it should be analyzed as an event, and move the R-time forward. However, what has gone unnoticed is that "real" distributives may also appear in sequence. Recall that a situation has to be included in its R-time in order to be a candidate for a sequence. This requirement means that candidates for a sequence may not continue beyond their respective R-times. In other words, the duration of such situation must be restricted. Now Recall that the intervals of a distributive situation are not limited (as opposed to events which are always restricted, by definition, to one single interval). Therefore, in order for a distributive situation to be able to appear on the time-line or in another kind of sequence it has to be restricted explicitly by, e.g., a durational adverb such as "for three days". Since they function to *delimit* a distributive situation it is reasonable, therefore, to label such adverbs *delimiters* as suggested to me by Reinhart (pc). When it is restricted such a situation is conceived as contained in its R-time, although *logically* the situation may hold beyond the time, e.g., the three days. It should also be emphasized that the property of intervals' restriction is strictly semantic, and not a property of the real world, as can be shown in the difference between (20a) and (20b):

(20) a. John lived in Boston (when he studied for his Ph.D.).
b. John lived in Boston for three years.

In (20a) as well as in (20b) the situation of John's living in Boston must be bound to a certain duration in the real world (assuming that John cannot live in Boston forever), but only in (20b) is the duration restricted linguistically (where its initial point of the first interval is the first day of the three years, and the last day is the final point of the last interval). Therefore, we say that in (20a) the state is open, unrestricted or unbound, while in (20b) it is restricted, bound, and hence seen as a closed holistic situation (the term "holistic" is taken from Partee 1984) and is understood as contained in its R-time. If the number of the intervals of a situation is not restricted (semantically) the situation must contain its R-time and therefore cannot appear in a sequence. Conversely, when a situation contains its R-time it cannot be semantically restricted and hence cannot be a candidate for a sequence, as in the case of the progressive in English (see ch. 3 for discussion). The claim that only when it is modified by a delimiter can a distributive situation be a candidate for a sequence seems to be adequate for states, and in less extent for activities. Therefore I will first demonstrate it through states, and then account for activities. This claim explains the difference in the acceptability of sentences (a) and (b) in (21) below:

(21) a. { John slept for ten hours, } and (only then he) started to work.
b. { ?John slept, }

While (21a) is a well-formed acceptable sentence, (21b) is not very good. This is because in (21a) the clause denoting the state of sleeping also contains a durational adverb which bounds the state duration. The clause in (21b), on the other hand, seems to be "loose" as far as its duration is concerned. (It is more natural to interpret it as a containment situation, whose duration is not bound, so that the event denoted in the second clause seems to be denoting an event occurring during the time of sleeping, which is incompatible with our knowledge of the world, and hence the uncomfortable feeling). This analysis finds support in the choice of the sequential forms in BH, Russian and French. States will appear in *wayyiqtol* in BH, perfective in Russian and passé-simple in French only if they are modified by a delimiter. For BH see next section (ex. 39). Here consider two examples from Russian, taken from Forsyth (1970) (I thank Baruch Podolsky for the phonetic transcription):

(22) a. *On prožil v moskve tri goda i peryexal v leningrad*
he lived:P in Moskow three years and moved:P to Leningrad
'He lived in Moskow for three years and moved to Leningrad' (p.12)

b. *On proležal v gospitale polgoda, potom vernuls^{y}a*
he spent:P in hospital half-a-year then came-back:P
na fronti i provoyeval do konča
to front and fought:P to end
'He was in the hospital for half a year, then returned to the front and fought till the end of the war' (p. 63)

All the clauses in (22) represent chains in the sequences and their verbs are, therefore, in perfective. The stative verbs 'live' and 'spend' in (a) and (b) respectively are modified by the durationals "(for) three years" and "(for) half a year" and therefore they, too, are part of the sequences. If we remove the durationals, we will have to change the perfective verbs *prožil* and *proležal* into their imperfective counterparts (Lonya Volozky, personal communication). When changed into imperfectives, the verbs no longer can appear in sequential clauses, as argued by Forsyth (1970). In a different context, however, the verbs may remain in perfective, but then they are understood as inchoative events.

It must be emphasized that what is delimited by the delimiter adverbs is the state and not the R-time. The R-time which is always delimited (specifically or unspecifically) does not delimit the situation itself. Recall in this connection example (14c) in which the situation denoted by the sentence "I was sick yesterday" is not restricted to the interval of "yesterday", which is the R-time of the state "being sick", and see also "I slept for three hours yesterday" where the R-time is "yesterday" and the "three hours" interval is included in it. Therefore only adverbials delimiting the state itself can be included in the group of the delimiters. This is demonstrated further by the fact, that when the situation itself cannot be bound, it will yield an ill-formed sentence when combined with a delimiter, as claimed by Mittwoch (1988). Mittwoch shows that situations denoted by progressive sentences in English cannot be modified by durationals:

(23) *John was eating supper for three hours (when the phone suddenly rang).

(Note, however, that this analysis is controversial, not accepted by at least two linguists: Comrie [pc] and Kearns [1991]. Their view will be discussed in ch. 3.) Mittwoch, furthermore, shows that progressives must contain their R-time, which excludes them from being able to appear in sequence (see ch. 3 for more details). Apart from durationals there are other delimiters such as "ten times", which are labelled "cardinal count adverbs" (Mourelatos 1978) and "iteratives" by others (e.g., Reinhart, personal communication). Such adverbs refer to a number of occurrences of the same situation as a whole, as if it were a single situation where its initial point is the first occurrence and its final point is the last occurrence. Leech (1969) differentiates between cases where an event takes place on a number of separate occasions and between a number of events taking place on a single occasion. He claims that only the latter may appear in a narrative sequence, e.g.,:

(24) He leapt his horse, knocked three times on the door, and demanded immediate admittance.

It seems to me that "occasion" in Leech's terms corresponds with "R-time". In other words, delimiters such as "three times" force the situations to be contained in one R-time, and hence allows them to appear, as a holistic situation, in a sequence. In effect, such delimiters, too, interact only with sequential verb forms. For example, Hoepelman & Rohrer (1980) show that cardinal count adverbs can interact only with the passé-simple. Compare the sentences under (25) (theirs 49-50):

(25) a. **Jean dansait trois fois.*
b. *Jean dansa trois fois.*
'Jean danced three times'.

When the delimiter "three times" combines with the predicate verb in the imparfait in (25a) the sentence is ill-formed, while when combined with the same verb in passé-simple in (25b) it is well-formed. The progressive in English, too, would not be able to appear with such an adverb, as the ungrammaticality of (26) shows:

(26) *John was dancing three times.

Activities, as mentioned above, do not seem to follow the restrictions as rigidly as states, although they too are distributives. Like states they may be modified by a "for" phrase to delimit their intervals number, and hence be able to compose a sequence, as in the following example:

(27) John read for a while and went to bed.

However, unlike states, they may appear in sequence without a delimiter and be understood as a holistic situation whose length is not specified. Consider the following examples (ex. 28b is from Comrie pc):

(28) a) Mary ate and went to bed.
b) I came home, had my supper, read, then went out for a walk.

The clause "Mary ate" in (28a) and the clause "read" in (28b) are interpreted as holistic situations rather than inceptive events. It is worth checking whether Scha's (1983) analysis (discussed above) can be modified to account for this phenomenon. It can be the case that activities without a delimiter may appear in sequence only between two events. However, we have occurrences in BH where two activities follow each other, both without delimiters (see ex. 42 in next section). A different line of explanation should be adopted: States with a sequential form are interpreted as inchoatives, unless they are modified by a delimiter, while activities in this form may be modified by a delimiter and then denote a holistic situation, but they may also appear without a delimiter and then be understood either as an inchoative or a holistic situation.

Ignoring the problem of activities, I conclude that a distributive situation may be a candidate for a sequence only if it is semantically restricted. This generalization can fit into Dowty's (1986) analysis discussed above, with the modification that delimiters, like "suddenly" and other such adverbs, cancel the pragmatic inference that the state or the activity continue beyond their R-time. However, I cannot accept his requirement that any situation, including distributives, has its own R-time, for I find it counter-intuitive to assume different R-times for states such as the situations in the three middle sentences of the following example analyzed by Dowty (his:25):

(29) Mary entered the president's office. A copy of the budget was on the president's desk. The president's financial advisor stood beside it. The president sat regarding both admiringly. The advisor spoke.

Dowty claims that we do not perceive that time moves in these sentences because their R-times are very short, as short as it takes an observer to perceive the states. If the observer's perception is the relevant factor here, it seems to me that Mary in (29) observes the states at a glance, simultaneously. Hence while I adopt Hinrichs's claim, in this matter, and assume that distributives do not introduce their own R-time, I add the modification that when they are semantically restricted they behave like events in this respect and introduce an R-time. In addition, Partee (1984), Dowty (1986) and others acknowledge that events do not always move the R-time forward. Events can appear off the time-line as well as out of modal sequences when they are simultaneous with or anterior to the situation reported in the preceding clauses, as in examples (30a-b):

(30) a. John opened his mouth and closed his eyes (at the same time).
b. When Mary came John had already left.

In these (and other cases — see discussion in chapter 5) the R-time does not move forward.

In view of the fact that events or restricted distributives can also appear in non-sequential clauses we must conclude that the property of restricted situation is a necessary but not sufficient condition for forming a sequence. That is, the following rule is optional rather than obligatory.

(31) *A Rule of R-time Movement*
Given the current R-time, R_n,
introduce a new R-time R_{n+1} if the clause introduced into the narrative discourse denotes a situation whose set of intervals are restricted, i.e., an event (including inchoatives) or a distributive situation with a delimiter.
(The first situation in the sequence introduces the first R_1.)

The analysis I suggest differs from Hinrichs', as mentioned earlier, on two points. First, the R-time introduced by the situation contains that situation rather than the following one. Secondly, as illustrated by the brackets in (31), I do not require an R_0 to be assumed at the beginning of the discourse, since an R-time is introduced only via a restricted situation (or a frame adverb). The following stretch of narrative will illustrate the mechanism of rule (31):

(32) Mira entered the room and sat on the piano stool. She was
E1 E2 S1
very happy that day. She was ready to share her happiness with the
S2
world. She played the piano for a while and went to bed.
S3 E3

The first event introduces R_1 in which it is included. The second E_2, in turn, introduces R_2 in which this event is included. The next situation introduced into the discourse is a state S_1, and since it does not introduce an R-time it includes the last introduced R_2. The next clause also reports a state, S_2, and therefore S_2 also includes R_2. The situation reported next is an activity S_3 but with a delimiter "for a while", which makes it introduce a new R-time R_3 including that activity. E_3 introduces R_4 and is included in it. The theory accounts for the fact that S_1 and S_2 overlap, but it does not indicate whether the states overlap other R-times, in addition to the current one. For example, in (32) the state of Mary being happy overlaps not only R_2 (and naturally E_2 included in R_2) but also R_1, R_3 and R_4. (For seeming counterexamples of states which are understood as not including the current R-time, see discussion in chapter 3.)

Note that reference to the final point of a distributive situation does not allow it to introduce a new R-time, and hence it cannot appear on a sequence. For example, in a discourse such as *It was pitch dark. John turned on the light...* the event of John turning on the light, terminating the state of being dark is included in the state, and does not follow it. In other words, when a state is interpreted as terminative it behaves as a "regular" state and cannot be a chain in a sequence, while when it is interpreted as inchoative or holistic it can.

But while in languages such as English the best rule we can have for the movement of R-time is the optional Rule (31), the rule will be much simpler and non-optional for languages which mark the sequence aspect morphologically:

(33) *A Rule for Sequence Aspect*
Given the current R-time, R_n,
introduce a new R-time R_{n+1} to include E_{n+1}, if the verb in the new clause is in sequential aspect.
(The first clause with a verb in sequential aspect introduces R_1.)

Rule (31) is relevant for languages with sequence aspect when the interpretation of a distributive clause is concerned. If a clause in sequential aspect has a "bare" distributive verb, it is interpreted as an inchoative event; if it has a distributive verb modified by a delimiter, it is interpreted as a holistic situation.

2.2 The Sequence Aspect in Biblical-Hebrew

As mentioned in chapter 1, BH marks sequential clauses morphologically. It has two sequential forms: *wayyiqtol* for clauses on the time-line, and *wqatal* for marking sequentiality in modal clauses. These two forms will not appear in non-sequential clauses. Thus we can apply to BH Rule (33) formulated in the previous section as follows:

(34) *Rule of R-time Movement in BH*
Given the current R-time R_n,
introduce a new R-time R_{n+1} to include E_{n+1}, if the verb in the new clause is in *wayyiqtol* or *wqatal*.

As described in section (1.2) of the introduction, the sequential forms *wayyiqtol* and *wqatal* have usually been analyzed as composed of two parts: a prefixed *waw* and a "simple" form — *yiqtol* and *qatal* respectively. According to this approach the *waw* in these forms is analyzed as an operator for sequentiality.[8] This line of analysis goes along with the fact that the directives — the imperative, the jussive and the cohortative — are prefixed by *waw* when they denote sequentiality. However, as discussed in the introduction, the radicals of *wayyiqtol* and *wqatal* are not yet clear, and hence we cannot assert for sure that the *waw* prefixed to them is an operator for sequentiality. Hence, I abandon this idea, and only draw attention to the interesting phenomenon, namely that (usually) all and only the *waw* prefixed forms are used in sequential clauses. This generalization has also been supported by the results of statistical examination presented in table 2.1 below, where 'N' stands for the number of the verb form occurrences in the corpus (the corpus is described in section 1.2 of chapter 1), and '+SEQ' for the occurrences reporting situations which are sequential to the situations reported in the preceding and/or the following clauses. (A clause in the opening of the discourse was, naturally, examined only with respect to the following clause and a clause at the end of the discourse was checked with respect to the preceding clause only, while all the rest of the clauses were examined with respect to the preceding **and** the following clause.) As mentioned in chapter (1) above, there were a number of cases where the text itself could not determine with respect to (my) knowledge of the world whether there was sequentiality, but where the interpretation of sequentiality is possible. (See discussion on examples 12 and 13 in chapter 1.) The number of the questionable cases is given in the '?' column. The 'rest' column includes the clear cases, and the percentage of sequential clauses is calculated from the 'rest' cases. For example, there are 2445 occurrences of *wayyiqtol* in the corpus; 494 of them (i.e., 20% of all the occurrences) are questionable, and so the number of clear cases is 1951 (80%) — of which 1834 (94% of 1951) are clearly sequential. Another point in reading table 2.1: As in table (1.3) in section (1.2), all the modal sequential forms are represented by *wqatal*, and all the non-sequentional modal forms are represented by *yiqtol*. (The table does not include the 680 occurrences of nominal verbs, i.e., the infinitivals, for reasons explained in chapter 1.)

Table 2.1. Sequentiality and the Biblical Hebrew Verb Forms

FORM	*wayyiqtol*	*qatal*	*wqatal*	*yiqtol*	*qotel*
Total	N=2445	N=1190	N=573	N=1121	N=678
?	N=494	N=89	N=176	N=54	N=0
	20%	7.5%	30.7%	4.8%	0%
REST	N=1951	N=1101	N=397	N=1067	N=678
+SEQ	N=1834	N=11	N=471	N=7	N=0
	94%	1%	93.5%	0.65%	0%

Table 2.1 clearly shows that the argument that all and only the *waw* prefixed forms appear in sequential clauses is empirically valid. In the following sections I will discuss the findings of the table. In section 2.2.1 I will show that *waw*-prefixed verbs do indeed appear only in clauses denoting sequential situations. In section 2.2.2 I will account for the 6% of *wayyiqtol* and 6.5% of *wqatal* which do *not* denote sequential clauses (most of which have explanations), and in section 2.2.3 I will discuss the special particles *wayhi:* and *wha:ya:*. Section 2.2.4 will demonstrate that only *waw*-prefixed verbs appear in sequential clauses, and deal with the problematic cases where *qatal*, *qotel* and *yiqtol* seem to violate this claim.

2.2.1 *The Sequential Forms*

The vast majority of the *waw*-prefixed verbs in our corpus (94% for *wayyiqtol* and 93.5% for *wqatal*) appear in clauses comprising a sequence. Most of them, naturally, appear in "middle" chains, which follow the previous *wayyiqtol* or *wqatal* clause and precede the next one. Only at the beginning of the sequence do they precede sequential clauses, but do not follow them, and only at the end of the sequence are they not followed by such clauses. In order to determine if a certain clause is part of a sequence, then, it was crucial to determine when a narrative discourse starts and when it ends, and moreover when its time-line starts and when a modal sequence starts. The Biblical narrative has been segmented in different ways, but only the segmentation into open and closed sections (called *parašot ptuḥot* and *parašot stumot* in Hebrew) is relevant for identifying the different stories, because this is the only segmentation according to discourse topics. (For a discussion on Biblical text segmentation see Ring 1967, among others.) Therefore this segmentation was used to identify the narrative segments; only once or twice did I use my intuitions. The identification of the beginning of the modal sequences was easier, since modal clauses are always a transition from the flow of the text.

First consider example (35) below (discussed also in chapter 1 under 11) for the non-modal clauses (the verbs in *wayyiqtol* are boldfaced):

(35) 14. ***wayye;leḵ*** *rˀu:ḇe;n* *bi:me:* *qṣi:r* *ḥitti:m*
WAYY:go:3SG:MASC Reuben in-days:of harvest:of wheat
wayyimṣa: *du:ḏa:?i:m* *baśśa:ḏe* ***wayya:ḇe;***
WAYY:find:3SG:MASC mandrakes in-the-field WAYY:bring:3SG:MASC
?o;ṯa:m ?el le;?a: *?immo:* ***watto;mer*** *ra:ḥe;l* *?el* *le;?a:*
them to Leah mother-his WAYY:say:3SG:FEM Rachel to Leah
tni: *na:* *li:* *middu:ḏ?e:* *bne;ḵ*
IMP:give:2SG:FEM please to-me from-mandrakes:of son-your
15. ***watto;mer*** *la:h* *hamˁaṭ* *qaḥte;ḵ* *?eṯ* *?i:ši:*
WAYY:say:3SG:FEM to-her QUE-little INF:take:-you:SG:FEM ACC man-my
wla:qaḥaṯ *gam* *?eṯ* *du:ḏa:?e:* *bni:* ***watto;mer*** *ra:ḥe;l*
INF:take also ACC mandrakes:of son-my WAYY:say:3SG:FEM Rachel
la:ḵe;n *yiškaḇ* *ʕimma:ḵ* *hallayla:* *taḥaṯ*
therefore YIQ:sleep:3SG:MASC with-you:SG:FEM the-night instead:of
du:ḏa:?e: *ḇne;ḵ*
mandrakes:of son-your:SG:FEM
'14. In the time of wheat-harvest Reuben **went out** and **found** some mandrakes in the field and **brought** them to his mother Leah. Rachel **said** to Leah, Give me, please, some of your son's mandrakes 15. Leah **said**, Is it so small a thing to have taken away my husband, that you should take my son's mandrakes as well? Rachel **said**, Therefore he will sleep with you tonight in exchange for your son's mandrakes.' (Gen. 30:14-15)

As we can see, all the verbs in *wayyiqtol* form appear in non-modal clauses which are temporally ordered, comprising the narrative time-line. The sequential clauses in the modal material are marked by the form *wqatal*, while *yiqtol* is used for the non-sequential (modal) clauses. The difference between the modal forms *yiqtol* and *wqatal* is nicely illustrated in the following fragment of discourse:

(36) 2. *wayyar* *whinne:* *b̲ʔe;r* *baśśa:d̲e* *whinne:* *ša:m*
WAYY:see:3SG:MASC and-behold well in-the-field and-behold there
šlo;ša: *ʕed̲re:* *ṣo;n* *ro;b̲ṣi:m* *ʕa:leha:* *ki:* ***min***
three:MASC flocks:of sheep QOT:lie:PL:MASC on-her because from
habbˀe;r hahi: ***yašqu:*** ***ha:ʕad̲a:ri:m*** *wha:ʔeb̲en*
the-well the-she YIQ:water:3PL:MASC the-flocks and-the-stone
gd̲o;la: *ʕal* *pi:* *habbˀe;r* 3. ***wneʔesp̄u:*** ***ša:ma:*** ***k̲ol***
big:SG:FEM on mouth:of the-well WQAT:gather:3PL there:to all:of
ha:ʕad̲a:ri:m ***wḡa:llu:*** ***ʔet̲*** ***ha:ʔeb̲en*** ***me;ʕal*** ***pi:*** ***habbʔe;r***
the-flocks WQAT:roll:3PL ACC the-stone from-on mouth:of the-well
whišqu: ***ʔet̲*** ***haṣṣo;n*** ***whe;ši:b̲u:*** ***ʔet̲*** ***ha:ʔeb̲en*** ***ʕal***
WQAT:water:3PL ACC the-flock WQAT:return:3PL ACC the-stone on
pi: ***habbʔe;r*** ***limqo;ma:h***
mouth:of the-well to-place-her
'2. He saw a well in the field and three flocks of sheep lying beside it, **because they used to water the flocks from that well**. Over the well's mouth was a huge stone. 3. **All the herdsmen used to gather there, roll the stone off the mouth of the well, water the flocks, and put it back in its place over the well.**' (Gen. 29:2-3)

The clauses boldfaced in (36) describe habitual events. The first of these clauses has a *yiqtol* verb — *yašqu:* 'they watered'; while the rest of them consist of verbs in wqatal. As predicted, all the clauses with the *waw*-prefixed verbs describe sequential habitualities: they first used to gather, then roll away the stone, water the sheep, and put the stone back on the well. The first habitual clause with the *yiqtol* verb cannot be interpreted as being part of this sequence, but as summarizing it. (Note also that it is in a subordinate causal clause which demonstrates further that it is not part of the modal "narrative".)

Both sequential aspects interact with Ak' in the way described in the previous section. Distributives in *wayyiqtol* or *wqatal* are understood as inchoatives, but with a delimiter modifying their verb they are understood as "regular" states. Consider first an example for inchoatives. The same lexical *ʔhb̲* is used for denoting the inchoative 'fall in love' or the state 'be in love', using *wayyiqtol* or *qatal* respectively, as in (37) and (38) below:

(37) *wayye^{ʔe}hab̲ ya^{ʕa}qo;b̲ ^{ʔ}et̲ ra:ḥe;l*
WAYY:love:3SG:MASC Jacob ACC Rachel
'Jacob fell in love with Rachel.' (Gen. 29:18)

(38) *wyiśra:ʔe;l ʔa:hab̲ ʔet̲ yo:se;p̄ mikkol ba:na:w*
and-Israel QAT:love:3SG:MASC ACC Joseph from-all sons-his
'Now Israel loved Joseph more than any other of his sons...' (Gen. 37:3)

The following examples illustrate states modified by "for" phrases:

(39) a. *wayya:b̲o: mo;še bt̲o:k̲ heʕa:na:n wayyaʕal*
WAYY:come:3SG:MASC Moses inside the-cloud WAYY:go-up:3SG:MASC
ʔel ha:ha:r ***wayhi: mo;še ba:ha:r ʔarba:ʕi:m***
to the-mount WAYY:be:3SG:MASC Moses in-the-mount forty
yo:m wʔarba:ʕi:m la:yla:
day and-forty night
'Moses entered the cloud and went up the mountain; **There he stayed forty days and forty nights.**' (Ex. 24:18)

b. 10. *...watta:ʕoz ya:d̲o: ʕal ku:ša:n rišʕa:t̲a:yim*
WAYY:prevail:3SG:FEM hand-his on Chushan Rishathayim
11. ***wattišqo;ṭ ha:^{ʔ}a:reṣ ^{ʔ}arba:^{ʕ}i:m ša:na:***
WAYY:rest:3SG:FEM the-land forty year
wayyamot̲ ʕot̲ni:^{ʔ}e;l ben qnaz
WAYY:die:3SG:MASC Othniel son:of Kenaz
'10. ...Othniel prevailed on Chushan-Rishatayim 11. **The land was at peace for forty years** and Othniel son of Kenaz died.' (Jud. 3:10-12)

The durational "(for) forty days and forty nights" in (39a) refers to the state of Moses being on the mount as a holistic situation which is in sequence with the other situations. Similarly, the stative verb 'rest' in (39b) is modified by the delimiter "for forty years". The situation it denotes is interpreted as happening after the previous reported situation, and before the following one. This is why the stative verbs "be" and "rest" in (39a) and (39b) respectively are in the sequential form *wayyiqtol*. To demonstrate further the difference between statives interpreted as inchoatives and statives interpreted as holistic situations let us compare (39a) to the following paragraph:

(40) 2. *wayyo;mer ʔe;la:w yhwh mazze*
WAYY:say:3SG:MASC to-him God what-this:MASC
b̲ya:d̲ek̲a: 3. *wayyo;mer maṭṭe wayy;omer*
in-hand-yours:MASC WAYY:say:3SG:MASC rod WAYY:say:3SG:MASC
hašli:k̲e;hu: ʔarṣa: wayyašli:k̲e;hu: ʔarṣa:
IMP:cast:2SG:MASC-him ground-to WAYY:cast:3SG:MASC-him ground-to

wayhi: ***lna:ḥa:š...***
WAYY:be:3SG:MASC to-snake
'2. The Lord said to him, What do you have in your hand? He (Moses) said "A staff", 3. He (The Lord) said, "Throw it on the ground." He threw it on the ground **and it turned into a snake**...' (Ex. 4:2-3)

The verb *wayhi:* is interpreted as 'turned into' in (40), but as 'stayed' in (39) where it is modified by the delimiter "(for) forty days and forty nights'. Activities, too, may be modified by a delimiter and appear on sequence:

(41) a. *wayya:qu:mu:* *kol* *ʔi:š* *ḥayil* ***wayye;lk̲u:*** ***k̲ol***
WAYY:rise:3PL:MASC all:of man hero WAYY:go:3PL:MASC all:of
halla:yla: *wayyiqḥu:* *ʔet̲* *gwiyyat* *ša:ʔu:l* *wʔet̲*
the-night WAYY:take:3PL:MASC ACC body:of Saul and-ACC
gwiyyo;t̲ *ba:na:w...*
bodies:of sons-his...
'So the bravest of them **journeyed together all night long** and took the bodies of Saul and his sons...' (SamI. 31:12)

b. *wayya^{ʕa}b̲o;d̲* *ya^{ʕa}qo;b̲* *bra:ḥe;l* *šeb̲aʕ* *ša:ni:m...*
WAYY:work:3SG:MASC Jacob in-Rachel seven years
'So Jacob worked seven years for Rachel...' (Gen. 29:20)

In (41a) the activity verb 'go' (or 'walk' or 'journey') is modified by the delimiter 'all the night (long)', and the situation denoted by its clause is in sequence with the other clauses, which justifies the *wayyiqtol* form of this verb. Similarly, in (41b) there is an activity verb 'work' in *wayyiqtol* modified by a durational 'seven years'. However, as discussed in the previous section, activities may appear without a delimiter and still be a link in a sequence. Consider the following example:

(42) *wayyippo;l* *ab̲ra:ha:m* *ʕal* *pa:na:w* ***wayyiṣḥaq***
WAYY:fall:3SG:MASC Abraham on face-his WAYY:laugh:3SG:MASC
wayyo;mer blibbo:...
WAYY:say:3SG:MASC *in-heart-his*
'Abraham threw himself down on his face, **laughed** and said to himself...' (Gen. 17:17)

The situation depicted in the boldfaced clause — 'laughed' — is a distributive activity, but although it is not modified by a delimiter its verb is in *wayyiqtol*. Furthermore, as also mentioned in the previous section, two activities without a delimiter may follow each other, denoting sequential situations and have *wayyiqtol* verb forms, as the two boldfaced clauses in the following example:

(43) 54. *wayyizbaḥ* *ya^{ʕa}qo;b̲* *zeb̲aḥ* *wayyiqra:*
WAYY:slaughter:3SG:MASC Jacob feast WAYY:call:3SG:MASC
l?eḥa:w *le^{?e}k̲ol* *la:ḥem* ***wayyo:k̲lu:*** *leḥem*
to-brothers-his to-INF:eat bread WAYY:eat:3PL:MASC bread
55. ***wayya:li:nu:*** *ba:ha:r* *wayyaške;m* *la:b̲a:n*
WAYY:sleep:3PL:MASC in-the-mount WAYY:get-up:3SG:MASC Laban
babbo;qer...
in-the-morning
'54. 'Jacob slaughtered an animal and called his brothers to eat. They ate and spent the night on the mountain. 55. Laban rose early in the morning,...' (Gen. 31:54-55)

The following example illustrates a distributive situation modified by a cardinal number phrase:

(44) *wayye;red̲* *wayyiṭbo;l* *bayyarde;n* *šeb̲aʕ*
WAYY:descend:3SG:MASC WAYY:dip:3SG:MASC in-the-Jordan seven:FEM
pʕa:mi:m *kid̲b̲ar* *?i:š* *ha:[?]elo;hi:m* *wayya:šob̲*
times as-word:of man:of the-God WAYY:return:3SG:MASC
bśa:ro: *kib̲śar* *naʕar* *qa:ṭo;n* *wayyiṭh:ar*
flesh-his as-flesh:of lad little WAYY:pure:3SG:MASC
'He went down, and dipped himself in Jordan seven times, as the man of God told him, and his flesh was restored as a little child, and he was clean.' (KingsII, 5:14)

The dipping event occurred seven times (in a row), but since no other situation is reported between the occurrences of dipping, the verb denoting the dipping is in *wayyiqtol*.

2.2.2 *Formulas, Hyhdiyadums and paraphrases*

The frequency counts in table 2.1 above show that 6% of the *wayyiqtol* and 6.5% of the *wqatal* occurrences in our sample are not sequential. However, about half of these occurrences can be explained, which reduces the number of counter-examples to 3% only and increases the supportive examples to 97%. Table 2.2a and table 2.2b below summarize the *wayyiqtol* and the *wqatal* respectively according to the SEQ criterion:

Table 2.2a. ***wayyiqtol*** *and sequentiality*

Total	+SEQ	–SEQ		
		Explained		*Unexplained*
		Formula	*Paraphrase*	
N=1951 100%	N=1834 94%	N=50 2.6%	N=10 0.5%	N=57 2.9%

Table 2.2b. ***wqatal*** *and sequentiality*

Total	+SEQ	–SEQ		
		Explained		*Unexplained*
		Formula	*Paraphrase*	
N=397 100%	N=382 96%	N=3 0.76%	N=1 0.25%	N=11 2.75%

The largest group of the explained counter-examples, labelled "formula," contains, mostly, phrases with two successive verbs of saying, both in *wayyiqtol* or both in *wqatal*, such as the two verbs *waydabber-wayyo;mer* reporting only one event of saying (following the situation reported in the clause preceding the first verb). The second verb appears in *wayyiqtol* (or in *wqatal*) although it does not report a situation in sequence with the situation reported by the first verb of saying, which seemingly violates the sequential criterion of *wayyiqtol*. However, this verb is not used to report an event, but functions as a citation marker. In BH there are a number of ways to report an event of saying announcing direct speech. Firstly, the event can be reported simply by the general neutral *ʔmr*; when it appears in a sequential non-modal clause it is *wayyo;mer* 'said', as in the following example:

(45) *wayyo;mer* *ʔelo;hi:m* *yhi:* *ʔo:r...*
WAYY:say:3SG:MASC God JUS:be:3SG:MASC light
'God said, Let there be light.' (Gen. 1:3)

When the specific kind of speech-act is denoted as in *wayṣaw* 'ordered', *wayyaʕan* 'answered', *wayyitḥannan* 'begged', etc., the two verbs of saying are used — one denotes the specific speech-act and one is the neutral generic *wayyo;mer*. In these cases, the second verb does not indicate a sequential situation, but is used to announce the quotation (functions as quotation marks in modern languages), as in (46) below:

(46) *wattitpalle;l* *ḥanna:* *watto;mer* *ʕa:laṣ*
WAYY:pray:3SG:FEM Hanna WAYY:say:3SG:FEM QAT:rejoice:3SG:MASC
libbi:...
heart-my
'Hannah prayed and said, My heart rejoice...' (SamI 2:1)

When the text reports only the speech-act, without providing the speech itself, it uses only one verb — the verb denoting the speech act, e.g.,:

(47) a. *waysappe;r* *ha:ʕebed* *leyiṣḥa:q* *ʔe:t* *kol* *haddba:ri:m*
WAYY:tell:3SG:MASC the-servant to-Isaac ACC all:of the-things
ʔašer *ʕa:śa:*
that QAT:do:3SG:MASC
'And the servant told Isaac all things that he had done.' (Gen. 24:66)
b. *...wayya:bo;* *ʔel* *be:to:* *wayyiš ʔal*
WAYY:come:3SG:MASC to home-his WAYY:request:3SG:MASC
wayya:śi:mu: *lo:* *leḥem* *wayyo;kal*
WAYY:put:3PL:MASC to-him bread WAYY:eat:3SG:MASC
'He went home and asked for food. They gave him food and he ate.' (SamII. 12:20)

In (47a) the content of the servant's report to his master Isaac is summarized and presented as indirect speech, and in (47b) the content of King David's request is not mentioned at all (it is understood from the context as "food"). Hence the verb *wayyo;mer* is not added to *waysappe;r* and *wayyiš ʔal* respectively.[9] The same rules apply to modal reports too. Compare (48) and (49):

(48) 1. *waydabbe;r* *yhwh* *ʔel* *mo;še* *le;mo;r* 2. *dabbe;r*
WAYY:speak:3SG:MASC God to Moses to-INF:say IMP:speak:2SG:MASC
ʔel *bne:* *yiśra:ʔe;l* *wʔa:marta:* *ʔale:hem* *ʔani:* *yhwh*
to sons:of Israel WQAT:say:2SG:MASC to-them:MASC I God
ʔelo;he:kem
God-your:PL:MASC
'1. The Lord spoke to Moses and said, 2. Speak to the Israelites in these words: I am the Lord your God.' (Lev. 18:1-2)

(49) *wayyo;mer* *yhwh* *ʔel* *mo;še* *dabbe;r* *ʔel* *ʔahaｒo;n*
WAYY:say:3SG:MASC God to Moses IMP:speak:2SG:MASC to Aaron
ʔa:ḥi:ka: *wʔal* *ya:bo;* *bkol* *ʕe;t* *ʔel*
brother-your:SG:MASC and-NEG YIQ:come:3SG:MASC in-all:of time to

haqqo;deš	*mibbe:t̲*	*lappa:ro;k̲et̲*	*ʔel*	*pne:*	*hakkappo;ret̲*
the-sanctuary	from-house:of	to-the-veil	to	face-of	the-cover
ʔᵃšer ʕal ha:ʔa:ro;n	*wlo;*	*ya:mu:t̲*		*ki:*	*beʕa:na:n*
that on the-ark	and-NEG	YIQ:die:3SG:MASC		because	in-cloud
ʔe;ra:ʔe	*ʕal*	*hakkappo;ret̲*			
YIQ:seen:1SG	on	the-cover			

'God said to Moses: Tell your brother Aaron that he must not enter the sanctuary within the Veil, in front of the cover, over the Ark, except at the appointed time, on pain of death; for I appear in the cloud above the cover.' (Lev. 16:2)

In both examples God orders Moses to carry his order to the sons of Israel or to his brother. In (48) he wants him to repeat his exact words, and therefore, the order (in verse 2) includes two verbs of saying: the specific one is in the IMP form *dabbe;r* and the neutral one in *wqatal* — *wʔa:marta:*. (Note the English translation which I took in this case from *The New English Bible*.) In (49), on the other hand, the Lord wants Moses to warn his brother. He leaves Moses to decide how to do it, and what exactly to say; he only tells him the content of that warning, and hence the "quotation marker" *ʔmr* is missing. However, the Bible could, in the cases described above, have used a different form for the second neutral verb, the infinitival *le;mo;r* which would have avoided the violation of the rules concerning the forms *wayyiqtol* and *wqatal*, as in the first verse of example (48).

In addition to phrases with two verbs of saying, there are other phrases of two successive *wayyiqtol* (or *wqatal*) verbs which must be regarded as constructing a formula in a similar way. Consider the following examples:

(50) a. ... *wayyiśśa:* *ʕe;śa:w* *qo;lo:* *wayye;b̲k*
WAYY:lift:3SG:MASC Esau voice-his WAYY:cry:3SG:MASC
'...Esau lifted up his voice and wept.' (Gen. 27:38)

b. *wayyiśśa:* *yaʕᵃqo;b̲* *rag̅la:w* *wayye;lek̲* *ʔarṣa:*
WAYY:lift:3SG:MASC Jacob feet-his WAYY:go:3SG:MASC land-to
b̲ne: *qed̲em*
sons:of east
'Jacob took off and went to the land of the people of the east.' (Gen. 29:1)

In these and other examples the first verb *wayyiśśa:* 'lift' is followed by a noun phrase such as *qo;lo:* 'his voice' in (50a), *rag̅la:w* 'his feet' in (50b), *ʕe:na:w* 'his eyes' in other examples, etc. The phrases containing this verb may be regarded as indicating inchoativity, and then the combination of one of the phrases with the activity verb denotes inchoative situations, 'started to cry', 'started to walk' etc. But the two verbs may also be interpreted as a hyndiyadum, i.e., a special case of formula, like the two verbs in the following example:

(51) *...wayyimšk̲u:* *wayya*^{ʕa}*lu:* *ʔeṯ* *yo:se;p̄* *min* *habbo:r*
WAYY:pull:3PL:MASC WAYY:lift:3PL:MASC ACC Joseph from the-pit
'...and they drew Joseph up out of the pit...' (Gen. 37:28)

The verb 'pull' in (51) does not denote an event separate from 'lift up', but adds some information on how the lifting was done. The two verbs, then, form a hyndiyadum which denotes the event and the way it was done. The following examples are modal formulas of the kind described above.

(52) *wyhwh* *ʔa:mar* *ʔel* *ʔab̲ra:m* *...śa:* *na:*
and-God QAT:say:3SG:MASC to Abram IMP:lift:2SG:MASC please
ʕe:ne:k̲a: *urʔe;...*
eyes-your:SG:MASC and-IMP:see:2SG:MASC
'God said to Abram...Lift up your eyes and see...' (Gen. 13:14)

(53) *...wayyo;mer* ^{ʔa}*le:hem* *mišk̲u:*
WAYY:say:3SG:MASC to-them:MASC IMP:pull:2PL:MASC
uqḥu: *la:k̲em* *ṣo;n* *lmišpḥo;ṯe:k̲em*
and-IMP:take:2PL:MASC to-you:PL:MASC sheep to-families-yours:PL:MASC
wšaḥ^{a}*ṭu:* *happa:saḥ*
WQAT:slaughter:2PL:MASC the-Passover
'...and said to them, Go and get sheep for your families and slaughter the Passover.' (Ex. 12:21)

However, unlike the non-modal counterparts, such formulas in modal clauses may also be reported by non prefixed forms, as in the following examples:

(54) a. *wayyo;mer* *yhwh* *ʔel* *mo;še* *bmid̲ya:n* ***le;k̲***
WAYY:say:3SG:MASC God to Moses in-Midian IMP:go:2SG:MASC
šu:b̲ ***miṣ ra:yim***...
IMP:return:2SG:MASC Egypt
'The Lord said to Moses in Midian, **Go back into Egypt**...' (Ex. 4:19)

b. *wʕatta:* ***lk̲u:*** ***ʕib̲du:***...
and-now IMP:go:2PL:MASC IMP:work:2PL:MASC
'and now **go work**...' (Ex. 5:18)

The second group of explained counter-examples is the group labelled "paraphrases". It includes cases where the writer starts a sentence, stops, starts it again and then completes it (Sternberg, personal communication, likes to call the phenomenon by the illustrative term “stuttering”). Consider the example in (55) below:

(55) 8. *wattiḵto;ḇ* *sp̄a:ri:m* *bše;m* *ʔaḥˀa:ḇ* *wattaḥto;m*
WAYY:write:3SG:FEM letters in-name:of Ahab WAYY:seal:3SG:FEM
bḥo;ṯa:mo: *wattišlaḥ* *hasp̄a:ri:m* *ʔel* *haz̲z̲qe;ni:m* *wʔel*
in-seal-his WAYY:send:3SG:FEM the-letters to the-elders:MASC and-to
haḥo;ri:m *ʔašer* *bʕi:ro:* *hayyo;šḇi:m* *ʔeṯ* *na:ḇoṯ*
the-nobles:MASC that in-city-his that-QOT:sit:PL:MASC with Naboth
9. *wattiḵto;ḇ* *bassp̄a:ri:m* *le;mo;r* *qirˀu:*
WAYY:write:3SG:FEM in-the-letters to-INF:say IMP:declare:2PL:MASC
ṣo:m...
fast
‘8. She wrote letters in Ahab’s name, sealed them with his seal, and sent them to the elders and notables of Naboth’s city who were dwelling with Naboth 9. She wrote in the letters saying: Proclaim a fast...’ (KingsI 21:8-9)

In verse 8, we have a report of the deeds of Jezebel, Ahab’s wife, in the same order in which they were done. Verse 9 goes back to the first event of this report to add the content of her letters.

Let us discuss now the 3% of the unexplained counter-examples. It is interesting that some kinds of the counter-examples found in BH are also found in other languages. Kamp & Rohrer (1983) point out some violations of the passé-simple in the French narrative. Consider their example (9) given here in (56):

(56) *L’été de cette année-là vit plusieurs changements dans la vie de nos héros. Francios épousa Adèle, Jean-Louis partit pour le Brésil et Paul s’achèta une maison à la campagne.*
‘The summer of that year saw several changes in the life of our heroes. Froncios married Adele, Jean-louis went to Brasil and Paul bought himself a house in the country.’

The first clause in (56) does not indicate a situation separated from those reported in the following clauses, but rather “summarizes” them. However, its verb is in simple past. Moreover, the temporal relations of the events reported in the following clauses are unresolved: the clauses can be interpreted not only as denoting sequential situations, but also as denoting simultaneous events or even situations bearing the anteriority relation. However, as pointed out to me by Comrie (pc), in examples like (56), one is moving out of strict narrative. This might account for some of the counterexamples given by

Washburn (1994) to refute the sequence hypothesis of the BH form *wayyiqtol* (see discussion in section 1.2 above). Consider one of his examples (p. 32) given here under (57):

(57) 8. *wayyišpo;ṭ* *ʔaḥ^{a}ra:w* *ʔet̲* *yiśra:^{ʔ}e;l* *ʔib̲ṣa:n*
WAYY:judge:3SG:MASC after-him ACC Israel Ibzan
9. *mibbe:t̲-la:ḥem* *wayhi:* *lo:* *šlo;ši:m* *ba:ni:m* *ušlo;ši:m*
from-bethlehem WAYY:be:3SG:MASC to-him thirty sons and-thirty
ba:no:t̲ *šillaḥ* *haḥu:ṣa:* *ušlo;ši:m* *ba:no:t̲*
daughters QAT:send:3SG:MASC the-out-to and-thirty girls
he;b̲i: *lb̲a:na:w* *min* *haḥu:ṣ* *wayyišpo;ṭ* *ʔet̲*
QAT:bring:3SG:MASC to-sons-his from the-out WAYY:judge-3SG:MASC ACC
10. *yiśra:^{ʔ}e;l* *šeb̲aʕ* *ša:ni:m* *wayya:mot̲* *ʔib̲ṣa:n*
Israel seven:FEM years WAYY:die:3SG:MASC Ibzan
wayyiqa:b̲e;r *bb̲e:t̲-la:ḥem*
WAYY:be-buried:3SG:MASC in-Bethlehem
'8. After him Ibzan from Bethlehem judged Israel. 9. He had thirty sons and thirty daughters whom he gave away, and brought in thirty girls for his sons. He judged Israel for seven years. 10. He died and was burried in Bethlehem.' (Jud. 12:8-10)

As Washburn correctly notes, it cannot be the case that Ibzan judged for an indeterminate period of time, took time off to have 60 kids and marry them all off, then returned to judge for 7 more years. Now although I have included this kind of examples in the 3% of unexplained counterexamples, it seems to me that they should not be there. It seems to be the case that texts like (57) are not narratives, but rather chronicles, historical texts. However, in order to validate this hypothesis one needs to determine independently the features of chronicles and the difference between them and narrative texts.

But while examples such as (57) may be explained as forming a non-narrative text, examples like (58) and (59) cannot:

(58) 16. *wayyar* *yo:se;p̄* *ʔitta:m* *ʔet̲* *binya:mi:n*
WAYY:see:3SG:MASC Joseph with-them:MASC ACC Benjamin
wayyo;mer *la^{ʔa}šer* *ʕal* *be:t̲o:* *ha:b̲e;* *ʔet̲*
WAYY:say:3SG:MASC to-that on house-his IMP:bring:2SG:MASC ACC
ha:^{ʔa}na:ši:m *habbayt̲a:* *u:ṭb̲o;$_{a}$ḥ* *ṭeb̲aḥ*
the-people the-house-to and-IMP:slay:2SG:MASC slay
wha:k̲e;n *ki:* *ʔitti:* *yo;k̲lu:*
and-IMP:prepare:2SG:MASC because with-me YIQ:eat:3PL:MASC
ha:^{ʔa}na:ši:m *baṣṣoh^{o}ra:yim* 17. *wayyaʕaś* *ha:ʔi:š* *ka^{ʔa}šer*
the-people in-the-noon WAYY:do:3SG:MASC the-man as-that

ʔa:mar *yo:se;p̄* ***wayya:ḇe;*** ***ʔeṯ*** ***ha^{ʔa}naši:m***
QAT:say:3SG:MASC Joseph WAYY:bring:3SG:MASC ACC the-people
be:ṯa: ***yo:se;p***
house-to:of Joseph
'16. Joseph saw Benjamin with them, and said to his steward, Bring these men indoors, kill a beast and make dinner ready; for they will eat with me at noon. 17. The man did as Joseph told him **and brought the people to Joseph's house.**' (Gen. 43:16-17)

In verse 16, Joseph orders his servant to do a number of things, which the servant carried out as we are told by the first clause of verse 17. However, the next clause specifies one of the things he had done, but instead of using a *qatal* verb it uses the *wayyiqtol* form. Similarly:

(59) *wya^{ʕa}qo;ḇ* *na:ṯan* *lʕe;śa:w* *leḥem* *u:nz:iḏ* *^{ʕa}ḏa:ši:m*
and-Jacob QAT:give:3SG:MASC to-Esau bread and-pattage:of lentils
wayyo;ḵal *wayye;št* *wayya:qom*
WAYY:eat:3SG:MASC WAYY:drink:3SG:MASC WAYY:rise:3SG:MASC
wayye;laḵ *wayyiḇez* *ʕe;ś:aw* *ʔeṯ* *habbḵo:ra:*
WAYY:go:3SG:MASC WAYY:despise:3SG:MASC Esau ACC the-birthright
'Jacob gave Esau bread and the lentil broth, and he ate and drank, rose up and went away. Esau despised the birthright.' (Gen. 25:34)

The verbs denoting the eating and the drinking events are both in *wayyiqtol* forms. However, it is unlikely that they follow each other; it is more likely that Esau ate and drank in some simultaneous way. But the examples in (58) and (59) may be analyzed as special kinds of formulas. However the last clause in (59) cannot. See also the following case:

(60) 11. *wayya^{ʕa}śu:* *bne:* *yiśra:^{ʔ}e;l* *ʔeṯ* *ha:raʕ* *bʕe:ne:* *yhwh*
WAYY:do:3PL:MASC sons:of Israel ACC the-bad in-eyes:of God
wayyaʕaḇdu: *ʔeṯ* *habbʕa:li:m* 12. *wayyaʕazḇu:* *ʔeṯ*
WAYY:work:3PL:MASC ACC the-gods WAYY:leave:3PL:MASC ACC
yhwh *^{ʔ}elo;he:* *^{ʔa}ḇo:ṯa:m* *hammo:ṣi:*
God God:of fathers-their:MASC the-QOT:bring-out:SG:MASC
ʔo:ṯa:m *me;^{ʔ}ereṣ* *miṣrayim* *wayye;lḵu:*
them:MASC from-land:of Egypt WAYY:go:3PL:MASC
ʔaḥ^{a}re: *^{ʔe}lo;hi:m* *^{ʔa}ḥe;ri:m* *me;^{ʔe}lo;he:* *ha:^{ʕ}ammi:m*
after Gods other from-the-gods:of the-people
^{ʔa}šer *sḇi:ḇo:ṯe:hem* *wayyištaḥ^{a}wu:* *la:hem*
that around-them:MASC WAYY:bow:3PL:MASC to-them:MASC
wayyaḵ^{ʕ}i:su: *ʔeṯ* *yhwh* 13. *wayya^{ʕ}azḇu:*
WAYY:anger:3PL:MASC ACC God WAYY:leave:3PL:MASC
ʔeṯ *yhwh* *wayyaʕḇdu:* *labbaʕal* *wla:ʕašta:ro:ṯ* 14...
ACC God WAYY:work:3PL:MASC to-the-Baal and-to-the-Astarot

> '11. The Israelites did what was wrong in the eyes of the Lord, and worshipped the Baalim. 12. They forsook the Lord, their fathers' God who had brought them out of Egypt, and went after other gods, gods of the races among whom they lived; they bowed down before them and provoked the Lord anger; 13. they forsook the Lord and worshipped the Baal and the Ashtaroth. 14....' (Jud. 2:11-16)

As in the French example, the first clause in this paragraph functions as a discourse topic introducing all the evils of the sons of Israel, which are told in detail in the following clauses, an example similar to (59). However, in this paragraph the *wayyiqtol* clauses in the details' section do not denote sequential events either.[10]

We find examples of this kind in the modal material, too:

(61) 12. *ki: ʔim šo:b̲ ta:šu:b̲u: u:d̲b̲aqtem*
because if INF:return YIQ:return:2PL:MASC WQAT:stick:2PL:MASC
byet̲er haggo:yim ... whit̲ḥatantem ba:hem
in-rest:of the-people WQAT:marry:2PL:MASC in-them
13. *ub̲a:t̲em ba:hem... ya:d̲o*$_{a}$*ʕ te;d̲ʕu:...*
WQAT:mingle:2PL:MASC in-them INF:know YIQ:know:2PL:MASC
'12. If you turn away and attach yourselves to the peoples... and intermarry with them and associate with them... 13. then be sure...' (Jos. 23:12-13)

The clauses comprising the apodosis of the conditional do not comprise a sequence of situations, but report some possible habits which are somehow simultaneous with each other. Nevertheless they are reported by the sequential *wqatal* form.

2.2.3 *wayhi: and wha:ya:*

Tables 2.2a and 2.2b do not represent the verbs *wayhi:* and *wha:ya:*. That was deliberate, since they do not function only as verbs.

The word *wayhi:* and its modal parallel *wha:ya:* function in the Bible in two different ways: 1) As a *wayyiqtol* and *wqatal* verb respectively of 'be' in 3rd person masculine singular; 2) As a segmentational particle, marking mainly temporal segmentation. In section 2.2.3.1 I will discuss the predicate function of *wayhi:* and *wha:ya:*, and in 2.2.3.2 their segmentational function. It seems that, in addition to these two functions, we have signs of a later function of the verb 'be' as an auxiliary verb. This will also be discussed in section 2.2.3.1. Usually it is easy to interpret a *wayhi:* and a *wha:ya:*; from 104 occurrences of *wayhi:* in our sample only 7 (i.e., less than 7%) and from

38 occurrences of *wha:ya:* only 1 (less than 3%) were questionable (for the meaning of 'questionable' see the explanation in section 1.2). Table 2.3a summarizes the 97 unquestionable occurrences of *wayhi:* in our sample; table 2.3b represents the distribution of the unquestionable occurrences of *wha:ya:*.

Table 2.3a. ***wayhi:***

Total	Verbal	Temporal Segmentation	Other Segmentation
97	31	52	14
100%	31%	54.5%	14.5%

Table 2.3b. ***wha:ya:***

Total	Verbal	Temporal Marker
N=37	N=15	N=22
100%	40.5%	59.5%

2.2.3.1 *The Predicative Function of wayhi: and wha:ya:*

In their predicative meaning *wayhi:* and *wha:ya:* are a *wayyiqtol* and a *wqatal* forms respectively of the root *hyy* 'be'. Being a part of the verbal system, they function in opposition to other forms: *ha:ya:-qatal*, *yihye-yiqtol*, etc. Being a part of a paradigm, *wayhi:* and *wha:ya:* are one of the conjugations — 3rd person masculine singular, as opposed to other persons: *watthi:* (3rd. person feminine singular), *wannhi:* (1st person plural), *wha:yu:* (3rd. person plural), etc.

Being a stative verb *hyy* 'be' can be used to denote inchoative or holistic situations. Consider first some examples illustrating the inchoative meaning:

(62) a) *wayya:ḇo;* *mo;še* *w?ah^{a}ro;n* *?el* *par^{ʕ}o;*
WAYY:come:3SG:MASC Moses and-Aaron to Pharaoh
wayya^{ʕa}śu: *ke̱;n* *ka$^{?a}$šer* *ṣiwwa:* *yhwh*
WAYY:do:3PL:MASC so as-that QAT:order:3SG:MASC God
wayyašle;ḵ *?ah^{a}ro;n* *?eṯ* *maṭṭe;hu:* *lip̄ne:* *parʕo;*
WAYY:throw:3SG:MASC Aaron ACC staff-his before Pharaoh
wlip̄ne: *ʕaḇa:ḏa:w* ***wayhi:*** ***lṯanni:n***
and-before servants-his WAYY:be:3SG:MASC to-serpent
'Moses and Aaron came to Pharaoh, and did as the Lord had told. Aaron threw down his staff in front of Pharaoh and his courtiers, **and it became a serpent.**' (Ex. 7:10)

b) *wattabbe;ṭ* *?išto:* *me;?aḥ^{a}ra:w* ***watthi:***
WAYY:look:3SG:FEM wife-his from-behind-his WAYY:be:3SG:FEM
nṣi:b̲ ***melaḥ***
pillar:of salt
'Lot's wife looked back, **and turned into a pillar of salt.**' (Gen. 19:26)

c) *wayyo;mer* *ʔ^{e}lo;hi:m* *yhi:* *ʔo:r*
WAYY:say:3SG:MASC God JUS:be:3SG:MASC light
wayhi: ***ʔo:r***
WAYY:be:3SG:MASC light
'God said, Let there be light; **and there was light.**' (Gen. 1:3)

All the boldfaced clauses denote a change of state. In (a) and (b) this is demonstrated also by the English translation 'become'. In (c) the verb *wayhi:* is translated by 'was' only because English does not have a special verb denoting 'coming into existence'.

The claim that *hyy* 'be' may indicate inchoativity can be further demonstrated by the comparison of this verb with the verb *hp̄k̲* 'become' in (63):

(63) 19. *wayyo;mer* *yhwh* *ʔel* *mo;še* *ʔ^{e}mo;r* *ʔel* *ʔah^{a}ro;n*
WAYY:say:3SG:MASC God to Moses IMP:say:2SG:MASC to Aaron
qaḥ *maṭṭk̲a:* *u:nṭe:*
IMP:take:2SG:MASC staff-your:MASC and-IMP:stretch-out:2SG:MASC
ya:d̲k̲a: *ʕal* *me:me:* *miṣrayim...**wyihyu:*** ***d̲a:m***...
hand-your:SG:MASC on waters:of Egypt WYIQ:be:3PL:MASC blood
20. *wayyaʕ^{a}śu:* *k̲e:n* *mo;še* *wʔaharo;n* *kaʔ^{a}šer*
WAYY:do:3PL:MASC so Moses and-Aaron as-that
ṣiwwa: *yhwh* *wayya:rem* *bammaṭṭe*
QAT:order:3SG:MASC God WAYY:lift:3SG:MASC in-the-staff
wayyak̲ *ʔet̲* *hammayim* *ʔ^{a}šer* *bayʔo;r* *lʕe:ne:* *parʕo;*
WAYY:hit:3SG:MASC ACC the-water that in-the-Nile to-eyes:of Phraoh
u:lʕe:ne: *ʕ^{a}b̲a:d̲a:w* ***wayye;ha:p̄k̲u:*** ***kol*** ***hammayim***
and-to-eyes:of servants-his WAYY:become:3PL:MASC all:of the-water
ʔ^{a}šer ***bayʔo;r*** ***ld̲a:m***
that in-the-Nile to-blood
'19. The Lord told Moses to say to Aaron, Take your staff and stretch your hand out over the waters of Egypt...**To turn them into blood**... 20. Moses and Aaron did as the Lord had commanded them. He lifted up his staff and struck the water of the Nile in the sight of Pharaoh and his courtiers, **and all the water was changed into blood.**' (Ex. 7:19-20)

Here is an example to illustrate the inchoative meaning of the modal *wh:ya:*:

(64) *wayyo;mer* *yhwh* *ˀel* *mo;še* *ˀᵉmo;r* *ˀel* *ˀahᵃro;n*
WAYY:say:3SG:MASC God to Moses IMP:say:2SG:MASC to Aaron
nṭe; *ˀet̲* *maṭṭk̲a* *whak̲*
IMP:stretch-out:2SG:MASC ACC rod-yours:SG:MASC and-IMP:hit:2SG:MASC
ˀet̲ *ˤap̄ar* *ha:ˀa:reṣ* ***wha:ya:*** *lk̲innim* *bk̲ol*
ACC earth:of the-land WQAT:be:3SG:MASC to-lice in-all:of
ˀereṣ *miṣra:yim*
land:of Egypt
'The Lord told Moses to say to Aaron, stretch out your staff and strike the dust on the ground, and **it will turn into** maggots throughout the land of Egypt.' (Ex. 8:12)

Example (39a) above repeated here as (65) illustrates the function of *hyy* in reporting holistic states of being:

(65) *wayya:b̲o;* *mo;še* *bt̲o:k̲* *heˤa:na:n* *wayyaˤal*
WAYY:come:3SG:MASC Moses inside the-cloud WAYY:go-up:3SG:MASC
ˀel *ha:ha:r* ***wayhi:*** ***mo;še*** ***ba:ha:r*** ***ˀarba:ˤi:m***
to the-mount WAYY:be:3SG:MASC Moses in-the-mount forty
yo:m ***wˀarba:ˤi:m*** ***la:yla:***
day and-forty night
'Moses entered the cloud, and went up into the mountain; **there he stayed forty days and forty nights.**' (Ex. 24:18)

As a subcategory of holistic function we may find the verb *hyy* to report a "summary" of years. Such "summaries" of years are found in a small group of cases (four occurrences in our sample), usually not in a regular narrative, but as a part of a genealogy discourse. Consider the following list of genealogy:

(66) 3. *wayḥi:* *ˀa:d̲a:m* *šlo;ši:m* *u:mˀat̲* *ša:na:*
WAYY:live:3SG:MASC Adam thirty and-hundred:of year
wayyo:led̲ *bid̲mu:t̲o:* *kṣalmo:* *wayyiqra:*
WAYY:beget:3SG:MASC in-likeness-his as-image-his WAYY:call:3SG:MASC
ˀet̲ 4. *šmo:* *še;t̲* *wayyihyu:* *yme:* *ˀa:d̲a:m* *ˀaḥᵃre:*
ACC name-his Seth WAYY:be:3PL:MASC days:of Adam after
ho:li:d̲o: *ˀet̲* *še;t̲* *šmo;ne* *meˀo;t̲* *ša:na:*
INF:beget-he ACC Seth eight:FEM:of hundreds year
wayyo:led̲ *ba:ni:m* *u:b̲a:no:t̲* 5. *wayyihyu:* *kol*
WAYY:beget:3SG:MASC sons and-daughters WAYY:be:3PL:MASC all:of
yme: *ˀa:d̲a:m* *ˀᵃšer* *ḥay* *tšaˤ* *me:ˀo:t̲* *ša:na:*
days:of Adam that ?:live:3SG:MASC nine:FEM:of hundreds year
u:šlo;ši:m *ša:na:* *wayya:mo;t̲*
and-thirty year WAYY:die:3SG:MASC

'3. Adam had lived one hundred and thirty years, and begot a son in his likeness and image, and named him Seth. 4. After the birth of Seth he lived eight hundred years, and had other sons and daughters: 5. He lived nine hundred and thirty years, and then he died.' (Gen. 5:3-5)

The two occurrences of *wayyihyu:* (as well as the occurrence of *wayḥi:* 'lived') do not report two holistic states but rather indicate the number of years which passed in Adam's life when the events took place (the event of the birth of the sons and the daughters and the event of Adam's death). We also have similar cases with "summaries" of the number of people, soldiers, wounded, dead, etc., as in the following example:

(67) 45. *wayyihyu:* *kol* *pqu:d̲e:* *b̲ne:* *yiśra:ˀe;l...*
WAYY:be:3PL:MASC all:of numbered:of sons:of Israel
46. *wayyihyu:* *kol* *happqud̲i:m* *še;š* *me:ˀo:t̲*
WAYY:be:3SG:MASC all:of the-numbered:people six hundreds
ˀelep̄ *u:šlo;šet̲* *ˀala:p̄i:m* *waḥame;š* *me:ˀo:t̲* *waḥamišši:m*
thousand and-three:of thousands and-five hundreds and-fifty
'45. The total number of Israelites... 46. recorded in the lists of fathers' families was six hundred and three thousand and five hundred and fifty.' (Num. 1:45-46)

There are also unexplained cases (very small in number, though) of *hyy* in the narrative discourse denoting containment situations, as in the following example:

(68) 23. *wayyo;mer* *ha:ˀa:d̲a:m...25. wayyihyu:*
WAYY:say:3SG:MASC the-man WAYY:be:3PL:MASC
šne:hem *ˤaru:mmi:m* *ha:ˀa:d̲a:m* *wˀišto:* *wlo;*
two:of-them:MASC naked:PL:MASC the-man and-wife-his and-NEG
yitbo;ša:šu:
YIQ:ashamed:3PL:MASC
'23. And the man said...25. Now they were both naked, the man and his wife, but they had no feeling of shame.' (Gen. 2:23-25)

It is not likely that 'were naked' in verse 25 will be interpreted as denoting a situation obtaining after the event denoted in 23, but rather as containing it. It is surprising that the nominal *qotel* or the perfect *qatal* form was not used here.

In our corpus another use of *hyy* as a part of the predicate found is its function as an auxiliary to denote certain aspects.[11] Firstly it combines with the verb *hlk̲* 'go' where the latter denotes a process. In such cases the verb *hyy* denotes the time of that process. This combination, widely used in MH, is found in a few cases in the Bible, as in examples (69a-b) below:

(69) a) *whammayim* *ha:yu:* *ha:lo:k̠* *wḥa:so:r...*
and-the-water QAT:be:3PL INF:go and-INF:decrease
'The water continued to recede...' (Gen. 8:5)

b) *wayhi:* *qo:l* *haššo;p̄a:r* *ho:le;k̠*
WAYY:be:3SG:MASC voice:of the-trumpet QOT:go:SG:MASC
wḥa:ze;q *mʔo;d̠;...*
and-QOT:strengthen:SG:MASC very
'and the sound of the trumpet grew even louder.' (Ex. 19:19)

Since BH does not mark the time of a situation (which can be inferred from the combinations of the parameters and/or the context), the examples in (69) consist of exceptional cases. Usually a development of a process is expressed by the verb *hlk̠* only, e.g.,:

(70) *...wd̠a:wid̠* *ho;le;k̠* *wḥa:ze;q* *u:b̠e:t̠*
and-David QOT:go:SG:MASC and-QOT:strengthen:SG:MASC and-house:of
ša:ʔu:l *ho;lk̠i:m* *wd̠alli:m*
Saul QOT:go:PL:MASC and-QOT:weaken:PL:MASC
'...David was growing steadily stronger while the house of Saul became weaker and weaker.' (SamII 3:1)

Another penetration of a later stage (but see FN 11) is seen in the occurrences of *hyy* verbs denoting habitual events. While in Mishnaic Hebrew this is the primary means of denoting habitualities, in BH the forms *yiqtol-wqatal* are used for this purpose. Therefore, as said above, we can regard the (small number) of the phrases consisting of *hyy* with another verb to denote habituality in past or future time, as penetrations from a later stage of the language, as in the following example:

(71) *wayyo;mer* *ʔᵃdo;ni:-b̠ezeq* *šib̠ʕi:m* *mla:k̠i:m* *bho;no:t̠*
WAYY:say:3SG:MASC Adoni-Bezek seventy kings thumbs:of
yd̠e:hem *wrag̠le:hem* *mquṣṣa:ṣi:m*
hands-their:MASC and-feet-their:MASC QOT:cut-off:PL:MASC
ha:yu: ***mlaqqṭi:m*** *taḥat̠* *šulḥa:ni:...*
QAT:be:3PL QOT:gather:PL:MASC under table-my
'Adoni-bezek said, I once had seventy kings, whose thumbs and great toes were cut off, **picking up the scraps from under my table...**' (Jud. 1:7)

2.2.3.2 *The segmentational function of wayhi: and wha:ya:*

As shown in Tables (2.3a) and (2.3b) above, most of *wayhi:* and *wh:aya:* occurrences (69% and 59.5% respectively) do not function as predicates. This finds support in the fact that only in the predicative occurrences do *wayhi:* and *wha:ya:* agree in gender and number with the subject NP: It is *wayhi:* or *wha:ya:* only in 3rd person singular masculine; in other persons they are conjugated as any other verb: *watthi:* (or *wha:yta:*) for 3rd person singular feminine (as in example 62b above), *wayyihyu:* (or *wha:yu:*) for third person plural masculine (as in example 67), etc. When they function as segmentation particles *wayhi:* and *wha:ya:* do not agree in person, gender or number; it is always *wayhi:* (or *wha:ya:*) regardless of the NP-subject's gender and number. Compare, e.g., (72a) where the NP-subject is in singular masculine with (72b) where it is in plural:

(72) a. *wayhi: ki: he;ḥe;l ha:ˀa:d̲a:m la:ro;b̲ ˤal*
wayhi: that QAT:start:3SG:MASC the-man to-INF:increase on
pne: ha:ˀᵃd̲a:ma:...
face:of the-earth
'When mankind began to increase and to spread all over the earth...' (Gen. 6:1)

b. *wayhi: he;m qo;b̲ri:m ˀi:š...*
wayhi: they:MASC QOT:bury:PL:MASC man
'When they were burying a dead man...' (KingsII 13:21)

In table 2.3 the segmentational function of *wayhi:* has been subcategorized as "temporal" (54.5%) and "other" (14.5%) segmentation. The modal *wha:ya:*, however, functions only in temporal segmentation.[12]

Partee (1984), Dowty (1986) and others claim that in what Partee calls a "simple linear progression" the R-time lies 'just after' the preceding event.[13] But when the sentence is modified by a frame adverbial (see Bennett & Partee 1978 [1972] for this notion), such as "on Tuesday", "at three o'clock", "in June" or a **when**-clause, the R-time is determined according to that adverb. Partee calls this phenomenon "updating the R-time". To appreciate the different relations of R-times compare (73a) to (73b):

(73) a) John bought a bunch of newspapers, and went to the beach.
b) John bought a bunch of newspapers. Two hours later he went to the beach.

In (73a) as well as in (73b) the situation reported in the second clause follows the situation reported in the first, i.e., they bear the sequentiality relation.

However, the more specific relations between the R-times in each sentence are not the same: in (73a) R_2 is 'just after' R_1 (see note 13 for the definition of the notion), but in (73b) they have a "gap" between them. This difference can be presented in the diagrams in (74) below, where (74a) represents (73a) and (74b) represents (73b):

(74) a) $[_{R1}E_1][_{R2}E_2]$
b) $[_{R1}E_1]...[_{R2}E_2]$

The dotted line between R_1 and R_2 in (74b) is to represent the interval of two hours separating them. The gap between the R-times in (74b) is specified as being two hours long, but the gap can also be unspecified, and then it may be understood from the context or remain vague. This is the situation with, e.g., **when** clauses. Consider the following example taken from Partee (1984: ex.16):

(75) Mary turned the corner. When John saw her, she crossed the street.

The gap interval between the first and the second R-time is not specified, and furthermore in this particular case the context does not imply its length. Partee claims that in cases such as (75) the (preposed) **when** clause triggers the movement of the R-time forward. Partee's theory requires the R-time in such cases to override the current R and establish a new R, which **must** follow the last R. The important role of R-time updaters is further demonstrated in Partee (1984) by the comparison she makes between the anomalous discourse (76a) and the normal discourse (76b) (hers: 19-20):

(76) a) People began to leave. The room was empty and the janitors came in.
b) People began to leave. When the room was empty the janitors came in.

Partee explains that (76a) is anomalous because "we don't expect the state of the room being empty to hold 'just after' people beginning to leave" (p.262). (76b), on the other hand, is normal because the **when**-clause signals an introduction of a new, later, R-time, "and we interpret 'the janitors came in' with respect to a time which is after people began to leave and just after the room became empty". But while I accept this analysis of (76) I do not, however, accept her claim that (76a) would not be anomalous if its second sentence did not express a state. Her claim is that we need a **when**-clause in (76a) because "sentences expressing states cannot by themselves move the action forward". But an event-clause without a connector "when" would also generate an unacceptable discourse. Compare modifications (77a) and (77b):

(77) a) People began to leave. The last person left and the janitors came in.
b) People began to leave. When the last person left, the janitors came in.

As with example (76a) of Partee, (77a) is anomalous although its second clause denotes an event, since here, too, we do not expect the last person to leave 'just after' people started to leave, and we need a **when** introduction to update the current R-time. Hence the normal discourse (77b).

In BH, R-time updating phrases are always prefixed by a *wayhi:* (or *wha:ya:*) particle when they are sentence initial. When the R-time "jumps" forward, away from the current R-time, it is marked by *wayhi:*, and the adverbial phrase is preposed (except for a very small number of counter-examples — see examples 83-84 below), as in examples (78) and (79) below:

(78) 1. *wayyaške;m yho:šu$_a$ˤ babbo;ker wayyisˤu:*
WAYY:get-up:3SG:MASC Joshua in-the-morning WAYY:travel:3PL:MASC
me;haššiṭṭi:m wayya:bo;ˀu: ˤad hayyarde;n hu: wkol
from-the-Shittim WAYY:come:3PL:MASC until the-Jordan he and-all:of
bne: yiśra:ˀe;l wayya:linu: ša:m ṭerem yaˤabo;ru:
sons:of Israel WAYY:sleep:3PL:MASC there before YIQ:pass:3PL:MASC
2. ***wayhi: miqṣe; šlo;šet ya:mi:m*** *wayyaˤabru:*
wayhi: from-end:of three:MASC:of days WAYY:pass:3PL:MASC
haššo;ṭri:m bqereb hammaḥane...
the-officers inside:of the-camp
'Joshua rose early in the morning, and he and all the Israelites set out from Shittim and came to the Jordan, where they encamped before crossing the river. **At the end of three days** the officers passed through the camp...' (Jos. 3:1-2)

In (78) there is a specified gap interval — three days long — between the event reported in the clause preceding the *wayhi:* phrase and the event reported in the clause following the phrase. In (79) below the gap is not specified:

(79) *wayhi: ˀaḥare:-ke;n wayyišˀal da:wid bayhwh le;mo;r...*
wayhi: afterwards WAYY:ask:3SG:MASC David in-God to-INF:say
'After this David inquired of the Lord, saying...' (SamII 2:1)

The *wayhi:* phrase in (78-79) cannot be interpreted as reporting an event, but as an obligatory particle for the preposed adverbials, signaling a new updated R-time. The claim that *wayhi:* is a marker of an updated R-time can be supported by the fact that it may appear with no adverbial at all, as in example

(72b) above, still moving the story line to a "distant" R-time. For this reason it can also be attached to a *qatal* clause:

(80) 19. *wattkal* *lhašqo;to:* *watto;mer* *gam*
WAYY:finish:3SG:FEM to-INF:water-him WAYY:say:3SG:FEM also
ligmalle:ka: *ʔešʔa:b* *ʕad* *ʔim* *killu:*
to-camels-your:SG:MASC YIQ:draw:1SG till if QAT:finish:3PL
20. *lišto;t* *wattmahe;r...* *wattišʔab* *lkol*
to-INF:drink WAYY:haste:3SG:FEM WAYY:draw:3SG:FEM to-all:of
gmalla:w 21. *wha:ʔi:š* *mišta:ʔe;* *la:h*
camels-his and-the-man QOT:wonder:SG:MASC to-her
mah^{a}ri:š *la:daʕat* *hahiṣli:$_{a}$ḥ* *yhwh*
QOT:silence:SG:MASC to-INF:know QUE-QAT:succeed:3SG:MASC God
darko: *ʔim* *lo:* 22. ***wayhi:*** ***kaʔ^{a}šer*** ***killu:*** ***haggmalli:m***
way-his if NEG *wayhi:* when QAT:finish:3PL the-camels
lišto:t *wayyiqaḥ* *ha:ʔi:š* *nezem* *za:ha:b...*
to-INF:drink WAYY:take:3SG:MASC the-man nose-ring gold
'19. She finished giving him a drink and said, I will draw water for your camels too until they have had enough 20. She hurried up... and watered all the camels 21. The man was watching quietly to see whether or not the Lord had made his journey successful 22. **When the camels had finished drinking** the man took a gold nose-ring...' (Gen. 24:19-22)

The boldfaced clause in verse (22) cannot move the R-time forward, because the *qatal* form is a perfect aspect, which is a "parasitic" aspect concerning R-time (see ch. 5 for details). However, we still understand the situation reported in this clause as moving the R-time forward. This is due to the *wayhi:*. We can explain, in a similar way, infinitivals preceded by a *wayhi:*:

(81) 12. *wayyagge;d* *yaʕ^{a}qo;b* *lra:he;l* *ki:* *ʔ^{a}ḥi:* *ʔa:bi:ha:*
WAYY:tell:3SG:MASC Jacob to-Rachel that brother:of father-her
hu: *wki:* *ben* *ribqa:* *hu:* *watta:roṣ* *wattagge;d*
he and-that son:of Rebecca he WAYY:run:3SG:FEM WAYY:tell:3SG:FEM
13. *lʔa:bi:ha:* ***wayhi:*** ***kišmo;$_{a}$ʕ*** ***la:ba:n*** ***ʔet*** ***še;maʕ*** ***yaʕ^{a}qo;b***
to-father-her *wayhi:* as-INF:hear Laban ACC report:of Jacob
ben ***ʔ^{a}ḥo;to:*** *wayya:roṣ* *liqra:to:* *wayḥabbeq*
son:of sister-his WAYY:run:3SG:MASC towards-him WAYY:hug:3SG:MASC
lo: *waynašššeq* *lo:* *waybi:ʔe;hu:* *ʔel*
to-him WAYY:kiss:3SG:MASC to-him WAYY:bring:3SG:MASC-him to
be:to:...
house-his
'12. Jacob told Rachel that he was her father's kinsman, and Rebekah's son. She ran and told her father. 13. **When Laban heard the news of his sister's son Jacob**, he ran to meet him, embraced him, kissed him, and welcomed him to his house...' (Gen. 29:12-13)

The boldfaced infinitival phrase in verse (13) can be interpreted as a **when**-clause, and preceded by *wayhi:* it updates the R-time.[14] Partee (1984) emphasizes that only preposed **when**-clauses update the R-time. Her claim finds support in the BH *wayhi:* expressions. It is indeed the case that **when**-clauses preceded by *wayhi:* always precede the main clause, where **when**-clauses which are not preceded by *wayhi:* cannot be preposed, and do not update the R-time. Consider the following example:

(82) 1. *wyaˤᵃqo;ḇ* *ha:laḵ* *lḏarko:* *wayyip̄gˤu:* *ḇo:*
and-Jacob QAT:go:3SG:MASC to-way-his WAYY:meet:3PL:MASC in-him
2. *malˤᵃḵe:* *ʔᵉlo;hi:m* *wayyo;mer* *yaˤᵃqo;ḇ* ***kaʔᵃšer***
angels:of God WAYY:say:3SG:MASC Jacob when
ra:ʔa:m *maḥᵃne;* *ʔᵉlo;hi:m* *ze...*
QAT:see:3SG:MASC-them:MASC camp:of God this:MASC
'1. Jacob went on his way, and the angels of God met him. 2. Jacob said **when he saw them**: This is the company of God...' (Gen. 32:1-2)

The underlined **when**-clause is subordinated to the main clause preceding it, and hence it is not preceded by a *wayhi:* particle. Since it has a *qatal* verb, which cannot introduce its own R-time, this clause does not update the R-time.[15] Moreover, when a **when**-clause or a gerundive phrase are preposed they are always preceded by a *wayhi:*, except for a very small number of counter-examples, e.g.,:

(83) ***kišmo;ₐˤ*** ***ˤe;ša:w*** ***ʔeṯ*** ***diḇre:*** ***ʔa:ḇi:w*** *wayyiṣˤaq*
as-INF:hear Esau ACC words:of father-his WAYY:cry:3SG:MASC
ṣˤa:qa: *gḏo;la:* *u:ma:ra:* *ˤaḏ* *mʔo;ḏ* *wayyo;mer...*
cry big:SG:FEM and-bitter:SG:FEM till very WAYY:say:3SG:MASC
'When Esau heard what his father said, he gave a loud and bitter cry and said...' (Gen. 27:34)

However, this might not be evidence, since an adverb must be also preceded by a *wayhi:* as noted above, and the following case is also an exceptional:

(84) *baḥo;ḏeš* *haššli:ši:* *lṣe;ṯ* *bne:* *yiśra:ʔe;l*
in-the-month the-third to-INF:leave:of sons:of Israel
me;ʔereṣ *miṣra:yim...*
from-land:of Egypt
'In the third month after Israel had left Egypt...' (Ex. 19:1)

In view of the above discussion it is not surprising to find in Gesenius the comment that new narrative segments start with *wayhi:* when the connection with the previous segment is "loose". When a new frame of time is established it is usually detached from the current discourse topic. This assumption finds support in the claim of Sanford & Garrod (1981) that a "jump" in time is a kind of segmentation, or to put it in their terms, a shift in time (and a shift in place and topic) causes a switch in the scenario. Similarly, Moens (1987:86, & Steedman 1988:22) claims that preposed *when*-clauses behave like phrases that are used to explicitly change topic.

The function of *wayhi:* as a segmentation marker is even more salient in the cases I have labelled "other segmentation" function of *wayhi:*. Consider example (85) below:

(85) *wayhi: ra:ˁa:ḇ ba:ˀa:reṣ wayye;reḏ ˀaḇra:m*
wayhi: hunger in-the-land WAYY:descend:3SG:MASC Abram
miṣrayma: la:ḡu:r ša:m ki: k̲a:ḇe;ḏ ha:ra:ˁa:ḇ
Egypt-to to-INF:live there because heavy:SG:MASC the-hunger
ba:ˀa:reṣ
in-the-land
'When there was a famine in the land Abram came down to Egypt to live there because the famine was severe.' (Gen. 12:10)

The phrase *wayhi:* is not followed by a temporal expression, and cannot be identified easily as opening a new frame of time. It is usually analysed (e.g., by Gesenius 1909) as the **verb** *hyy* describing a state. Such an analysis has to account for the form — *wayyiqtol* — used here, instead of a nominal clause or a *qatal* form. But if it was in one of these two forms it would be interpreted wrongly as a state containing (also) the situations reported in the previous clauses. Therefore we can interpret the particle either as denoting an inchoative situation (as done by the English translator of *The New English Bible*), and interpret the whole verse as saying "Famine broke out and Abram went down to Egypt", or as updating the R-time by picking up one subinterval of the interval of time at which the state of famine obtained. However, consider example (86):

(86) *wayhi: ˀi:š ˀeḥa:ḏ min ha:ra:ma:ṯayim ṣo:p̄i:m me;har*
wayhi: man one:MASC from the-Ramathaim Zophim from-mountain
ˀep̄ra:yim u:šmo: ˀelqa:na: ben yro;ḥa:m ben ˀᵉli:hu:
Ephraim and-name-his Elkanah son:of Jeroham son:of Elihu
ben to;hu: ḇen ṣu:p̄ ˀep̄ra:ṯi:
son:of Tohu son:of Zuph Ephrathite

'There was a man from Ramathaim, a Zuphite from the hill country of Ephraim, named Elkanah son of Jeroham, son of Elihu, son of Tohu, son of Zuph an Ephraemite.' (Sam.I 1:1)

It is not likely that the *wayhi:* clause in this case is interpreted as denoting an inchoative situation. It is also difficult to analyse it as picking up an interval (of Elkanah's existence?).[16]

Let us consider now the temporal segmentation function of the modal *wha:ya:*.

(87) ***wha:ya: kbo;*** ***mo;še ha:ˀo;hela:*** *ye;re;d*
wha:ya: as-INF:come Moses the-tent-to YIQ:descend:3SG:MASC
ˁammu:d heˁa:na:n wˁa:mad *petah ha:ˀo;hel*
pillar:of the-cloud WQAT:stand:3SG:MASC entrance:of the-tent
wdibber *ˁim mo;še*
WQAT:speak:3SG:MASC with Moses
'When Moses entered the tent, the pillar of cloud came down, and stayed at the entrance to the tent and spoke with Moses.' (Ex. 33:9)

(88) *yo;mar* *na:* *ˀado;ne;nu:* *ˁaba:deka:*
YIQ:say:3SG:MASC please master-ours servants-yours:SG:MASC
lpa:ne:ka: *ybaqšu:* *ˀi:š yo;de:$_a$ˁ*
to-front:of-you:SG:MASC YIQ:search:3PL:MASC man QOT:know:SG:MASC
mnagge;n *bakkinno:r* ***wha:ya: bihyo:t*** ***ˁa:le:ka:***
QOT:play:SG:MASC in-the-violin *wha:ya:* in-INF:be on-you:SG:MASC
ru:$_a$h ***ˀelo;hi:m*** ***ra:ˁa:*** *wnigge;n* *bya:do:*
spirit:of God bad:SG:FEM WQAT:play:3SG:MASC in-hand-his
wto:b la:k
?:good to-you:SG
'why do you not command your servants here to go and find some man who can play the harp? — then, **when an evil spirit from God comes on you** he can play and you will feel better.' (SamI. 16:16)

The boldfaced clauses in (87) and (88) are preposed **when**-clauses, which function as adverbials for the matrix sentences, updating the R-time. In this sense the particle wha:ya: is sometimes attached to an **if**-clause — *wha:ya: ˀim* — meaning, roughly, 'if and when'. Consider the following examples:

(89) a. *wayyo;mer* *ˁe;li: lišmu:ˀe;l* *le;k*
WAYY:say:3SG:MASC Eli to-Samuel IMP:go:2SG:MASC
ška:b ***wha:ya: ˀim yiqra:*** ***ˀe;le:ka:***
IMP:lie:2SG:MASC *wha:ya:* if YIQ:call:3SG:MASC to-you:SG:MASC
wˀa:marta:...
WQAT:say:2SG:MASC

‘Eli said to Samuel, Go lie down and, **If he calls again**, say...’ (SamI 3:9)

b. *wayye;d̲aˤ* *ˀo:na:n* *ki:* *lo;* *lo:* *yihye*
WAYY:know:3SG:MASC Onan that NEG to-him YIQ:be:3SG:MASC
hazza:raˤ ***wha:ya: ˀim ba:*** ***ˀel ˀe;šet̲ ˀa:ḥi:w***
the-seed *wha:ya:* if ?:come:3SG:MASC to wife:of brother-his
wšiḥe;t̲ *ˀarṣa:...*
WQAT:spill:3SG:MASC ground-to
‘Onan knew that the issue would not be his; (so) **whenever he slept with his brother’s wife** he spilled his seed on the ground...’ (Gen. 38:9)

2.2.4 *The Non-Sequential Forms*

The above discussion has shown that *wayyiqtol* and *wqatal* verbs may appear, indeed, only in a sequence. The findings presented in table 2.1 also show that other forms cannot comprise a sequence. The non-sequential forms *qatal* and *yiqtol* may appear in sequence only at the beginning of a subnarrative and a direct speech where it functions to mark the transition from the main to the subordinate discourse. This is discussed further in chapter (5) below.

However, 1% of the *qatal* and 0.65% of *yiqtol* verbs in our sample do appear in clauses reporting sequential situations, although not at the beginning of a subnarrative or a direct speech. But in most of the cases where such verbs appear in sequential clauses they are attached to a conjunction such as *wˀaḥar* ‘and then’, which suggests that the verb itself does not move the R-time forward — see discussion in ch.(5) below.

There is also a small number of puzzling cases where a clause with a *qotel* verb bears the sequentiality relation to the neighboring clause(s) (which happened not to be in our sample). But those clauses are all in dream reports, and may be interpreted as a vivid description (such as a game report in a radio or a television broadcast) — this will be illustrated and discussed in ch. (3). We also have a number of cases where a non-modal sequential clause has a *yiqtol* verb. This violates not only the SEQ but also the MOD parameter. Consider examples (90) and (91) below:

(90) *ˀa:z* *ya:šir* *mo;še* *u:bne:* *yiśra:ˀe;l* *ˀet̲* *hašš:ira:*
then YIQ:sing:3SG:MASC Moses and-sons:of Israel ACC the-song
hazzo;t̲ *lyhwh* *wayyo;mru:* *le;mo;r...*
the-this:FEM to-God WAYY:say:3PL:MASC to-INF:say...
‘Then Moses and the Israelites sang this song to the Lord saying...’ (Ex. 15:1)

But this case might be regarded as violating only the MOD parameter, since in what follows we do not have a narrative discourse, but rather a poetry section. The following example is more problematic:

(91) *ˀa:z ta:b̲o;na: štayim naši:m zo;no:t̲ ˀel hammelek̲*
then YIQ:come:3PL:FEM two:FEM women prostitutes to the-king
wataˁamo;d̲na: lp̄a:na:w
WAYY:stand:3PL:FEM to-front:of-him
'Then came to the king two women who were prostitutes and stood before him.' (KingsI 3:16)

It is interesting that the conjunction denoting the sequentiality is different from the conjunction attached to qatal verbs. It is the particle *ˀaz* which has two meanings: 'at that time' and 'and then'. In our cases, it is usually interpreted as the latter only. The combination of *ˀaz yiqtol* was regarded by some of the scholars of the historical-comparative approach as a demonstration of the origin of *wayyiqtol*. Bauer (1910), for example, regards the *yiqtol* in these cases as a remnant of the original form (see the survey in the introduction). Other scholars, explaining the Dagesh Forte in *wayyiqtol* as a remnant from the particle *wˀaz*, find support in these cases.

2.2.5 *The Biblical Hebrew Forms and Tense Interpretation*

As claimed in chapter (1) the BH forms do not denote tenses. Thus we find *wqatal*, *qatal*, *yiqtol* and *qotel* in clauses reporting events in either one of the three possible spheres of time. However, *wayyiqtol* clauses are always interpreted as reporting situations in the past. This is not a coincidence, i.e., it is not the case that the text just happens to have *wayyiqtol* verbs only in clauses interpreted as denoting past situations. The interpretation of *wayyiqtol* in the past sphere only is entailed from the combination of its features [+SEQ] [-MOD]. First consider the possibility of *wayyiqtol* clauses reporting situations in the future. As will be shown in chapter (4), future is one of the modals. Being non-modal, therefore, *wayyiqtol* cannot be interpreted in the time sphere of future. Present time situations may be non-modal as in "John is eating an apple". But they also may report generic situations such as "Cows eat grass" or habituals such as "John eats an apple every day". It will be shown in chapter (4) that generics and habituals are both modals. Now sequential clauses in present time may be interpreted only as generics or habituals, as in "(Every Friday) John buys a bunch of newspapers, goes to the beach, reads for a while and goes back home to shower". A string of clauses in the present which does not report habitual events cannot be interpreted as reporting successive events, as in "John is eating an apple and reading the newspaper" (note that in English the only way to report non-modality in the present is by the progressive). In other words, sequence in the present time sphere is necessarily modal. Now since *wayyiqtol* is a sequential form, and since it cannot report generics or habituals for being non-modal, it follows that it cannot be interpreted as reporting situations in the present time. So by definition *wayyiqtol* may appear only in non-modal sequential clauses, but by elimination it can appear only in clauses which report past time situations.

NOTES

1. Modern Hebrew lacks aspect altogether, and therefore the past may even be interpreted as an anterior event (where English would use the past perfect), as in (i) and (ii) below (all the verbs are in past tense):

(i)	*šatiti*	*rak*	*kafe*	*haboker*	*ki*	*kamti*	*me'uxar*
	drink:PAST:1SG	only	coffee	the-morning	because	get-up:PAST:1SG	late

'I had only coffee this morning, because I had got up late.

(ii)	*kšemiryam*	*higi'a*	*gamru*	*kvar*	*'et*	*kol*	
	when-Miriam	arrive:PAST:3SG:FEM	finish:PAST:3PL	already	ACC	all	
	ha'oxel.						
	the-food						

'When Miriam arrived, they had already finished all the food'.

2. a. In this work I follow those linguists who use the German term 'aktionsart' (plural: 'aktionsarten') for the semantic distinctions irrespective of how they are lexicalized. I am aware of the fact that the term is used in a different way by Slavonic linguists who use it only as lexicalisation of the relevant distinctions provided that the lexicalisation is by means of derivational morphology. (See Comrie 1976 FN 4 on p.6.)

   b. The following overview summarizes the issue only briefly; the interested reader can find excellent overviews in Hinrichs (1985) and Binnick (1991). Another updated survey is Verkuyl (1993) who also suggests critical analyses for each approach.

3. For example, Bach (1981) adopts Vendler's classification, but suggests a different terminology. Mourelatos (1978,1981), on the other hand, maintains the terminology, but suggests a different subcategorization (although he ends up with the same four groups as those of Vendler). Similarly, Moens (1987, & Steedman 1988) uses the same distinctions with different terminology, but also adds a fifth group labeled "point".

4. The difference between the subgroups, according to Vendler's characterization, is continuity vs. non-continuity.

5. It is interesting that all these scholars "feel" the same about this property, even though they work within different frameworks. E.g., Parsons (1990) is a neo-Davidsonian event-based theory (a modification of Davidson 1967), and therefore sees "culmination" as a property of the events themselves rather than of their intervals. (I will not discuss the event based approach here. The interested reader is referred to Verkuyl 1993 who discusses logical problems analysed by Lascarides 1988, and linguistic ones analysed by himself.)

6. The overview I offer for Verkuyl's analysis is obviously an extreme oversimplification, which leaves out many of the subjects he analyses. For instance, I do not discuss why directional PPs such as "to the store" assign the property [+SQA] to a predicate, but directional PPs such as "towards the store" do not (see section 13.6 in Verkuyl's book for this particular subject). I shall not go into these subjects here because this would force us into a detour through many intricacies of the localist theory of Jackendoff.

7. Comrie (pc) claims that this is only a pragmatic inference. He compares (16a) to (i) below:

   (i) I read "War and Peace".

   As he correctly claims, (i) does not entail that I am not now again reading it. However, note the adverb "again" indicates that it is a *different* event, another event of reading "War and Peace". In contrast, (16c) may mean that the *same* state of being at home continues.

8. As discussed in the Introduction, not all scholars analyze the forms in terms of sequentiality. The *waw*-conversive theory of the Jewish scholars in the Middle-Ages, the historical-comparative theory scholars (e.g., Bauer 1910) and the more recent study of Washburn (1994) do not analyze the forms as necessarily denoting sequential events. Bauer, e.g., opposes this analysis, arguing that eleven books in the Bible start with a *wayyiqtol* verb (see survey in the introduction for further details).

9. Note that sentences like (47b) would be ruled out as ungrammatical in languages such as (modern) English which require the transitive verb "requested" to take a direct object. My colleagues Mohammad Mohammad and Chauncy Chu suggested to check the hypothesis whether BH allows omitting of the object in other cases too. This, indeed, seems to be the case, as noticed also by Sternberg (1982). It seems that when the information is understood from the context, the narrator may not add the direct object, as in (47b) and in (i) below.

(i) 6. *wrib̲qa:* *ˀa:mra:* *ˀel* *yaˁaqo;b̲* *bna:*
and-Rebecca QAT:say:3SG:FEM to Jacob son-her...
9. *lek̲* *na:* *ˀel* *haṣṣo;n* *wqaḥ* *li:*
IMP:go:2SG:MASC please to the-flock and-IMP:take:2SG:MASC to-me
miššam *šne:* *gd̲a:yey* *ˁizzi:m* *ṭo;b̲i:m...*
from-there two:MASC:of kids:of goats good:PL:MASC
14. *wayye;lek̲* *wayyiqaḥ* *wayyab̲e:* *lˀimmo:...*
WAYY:go:3SG:MASC WAYY:take:3SG:MASC WAYY:bring:3SG:MASC to-mother-his
'and Rebecca said to Jacob her son... Go to the flock and pick me out two fine young kids... So Jacob went to the flock, fetched two kids and brought them to his mother...' (Gen. 27:6-14)

The second and the third clauses 'fetched' and 'brought' in verse (14) are not followed by their respective objects. Omitting the object in these clauses is permitted since the clause in verse (9) has the object 'fine young kids', providing the information for the clauses in verse (14), too. However, omitting recoverable information might be merely an option, as illustrated in (ii) below, where the narrator mentions the object even though its information is recoverable from the context:

(ii)	*wayyimṣa:*	*d̲u:d̲a:ˀi:m*	*baśśa:d̲e*	*wayya:b̲e;*
	WAYY:find:3SG:MASC	mandrakes	in-the-field	WAYY:bring:3SG:MASC

ˀo;t̲a:m	*ˀel*	*le;a:*	*ˀimmo:...*
them	to	Leah	mother-his

'He found mandrakes in the field and brought them to his mother Leah.' (Gen. 30:14)

10. A second look to this paragraph reveals that there are other problems, in addition to this one. First, it has several reports for the same situations, e.g., there are four reports for the fact that the sons of Israel left their God and worshipped other gods. Secondly, the situations reported are habitual and hence they would be expected to be depicted by modal clauses, with modal verb forms. Indeed, in verse 18 the text switches to the modal forms. Therefore, it is possible that the whole paragraph is a late addition to the text, when the verbal system had been collapsed. But it should be emphasized that whether this is indeed a late text or not should be determined by other independent phenomena such as vocabulary. Note also that this text is of the same kind of the text in ex. 56, i.e., it seems to be a chronicle rather than a narrative text.

11. It is probably a penetration from a later stratum of the language, since this use of *hyy* is found largely in Mishnaic Hebrew, and only in a small number of cases in Biblical Hebrew. However, this assumption must be supported by other, independent, phenomena, especially since the examples cited are usually attributed to an earlier era of the language.

12. It is not clear to me if it is merely a coincidence that we do not find texts with *wha:ya:* marking "other" segmentation, or if it is not possible to have such text.

13. Partee accepts the formal characterization of her notion 'just after' suggested to her by Ewan Klein: E' is just after E iff E' is after E and there is no contextually relevant E'' between E' and E (see her note 28). When discussing **when** clauses she mentions a suggestion made to her by Remko Scha (note 35), who requires that the end of E be included in E'. I think we can combine the two suggestions, and assume that R' is just after R iff the final point t_n of R is the initial point t_1 of R'.

14. Although I have not investigated them methodologically, as said in chapter (1), we may assume that infinitival phrases do not move the R-time forward, as they are not independent clauses. In cases such as our example they function, it seems to me, as gerundives, which cannot have their own R-time, although they denote events.

15. However, it is possible for an adverb such as "in the morning" to appear in the final position of the clause, and still update the R-time, as in example 78. This supports Partee's suggestion that time adverbs, unlike **when**-clauses update the R-time not only when they are sentence initial. Note that we have derived the same conclusions, although having a different theory in general.

16. But a second look in the paragraph in which this clause appears reveals that there are other questionable uses of the verb forms, e.g., the forms in verse 4 of the chapter:

(i) *wayhi: hayyo:m wayyizbaḥ ʔelqa:na: wna:ṯan*
wayhi: the-day WAYY:sacrifice:3SG:MASC Elkanah WQAT:give:3SG:MASC
lip̄ninna: ʔisto: u:lḵol ba:ne:ha: u:ḇno:ṯeha: ma:no:ṯ
to-Penninah wife-his and-to-all:of sons-her and-daughters-her portions
'On the day when Elkanah sacrificed, he gave several shares of the meat to his wife Penninah with all her sons and daughters'

The time expression *hayyo:m* 'the day' is preceded by *wayhi:* indicating a specific non-modal R-time. The following verb form is correctly in a non-modal form — *wayyiqtol*, but the verb following it is in the modal form *wqatal* instead of being also in *wayyiqtol*. Other problems of this kind are scattered throughout the whole chapter, which might indicate that this chapter was written or edited in a period when the aspect system was not clear to the author. I would suggest that it is from a later period, when the aspect system had collapsed, but there is other evidence which relates it rather to an earlier period of the language.

Chapter 3

Inclusion: The Progressive Aspect

A situation is inclusive if it includes its R-time (and, as a result, it usually includes other situation(s), especially when it appears in a narrative discourse). But this is an oversimplification which will be rectified in section 3.1 below. Such situations cannot move the R-time forward since they do not meet the basic requirement of the definition of SEQ — namely that the situation has to be contained in its (independent) R-time . We have seen, in chapter 2 above, that states usually include their R-time, but they, however, can be delimited by an adverb such as "(for) three days" and then be contained in their R-time (and hence appear on a sequence). In other words, languages have devices to restrict the number of the intervals of stative situations, i.e., to bound their duration and force them to be contained in their R-time, which enables them to be candidates for a sequence. In this chapter we will see that languages can, furthermore, "undelimit" events (which are delimited by definition to a one single interval), which causes them to include their R-time and become unable to form a sequence. I will term such situations **inclusive**. The device languages usually use for "undelimiting" events is the aspect system, where the progressive functions to indicate inclusion, as the participial form '-ing' in English, the imparfait in French (in one of its uses), and the participial *qotel* form in BH.[1] In the first part of this chapter I will examine the INC(lusive) relation, i.e., the prog(ressive) aspect in general, demonstrating it mainly through the English progressive, since most of the literature on the subject is on English. In the second part of the chapter I will discuss in details the INC parameter in the prose of BH.

The '-ing' form in English (just like the *qotel* in BH and in MH — see section 3.2 for illustrations) is used not only in predicate phrases, but also as a part of a noun-phrase, as in the phrase "promising author" where the participial "promising" functions as an adjectival, and in nominalization NP's as "the taking of the letters" where "taking" functions as the head of a nominal.

When it is a part of an NP, the participial does not have a role in the temporal interpretation. Therefore, in the following discussion I will take into account only predicative uses of this form, as illustrated in (1) below, including gerundive clauses as in example (2) taken from Comrie (1976):

(1) At five o'clock we were eating supper.

(2) Going down the street, I met Harry.

3.1 Definition of The Progressive Aspect

The traditional approach, represented also by modern linguists as Leech (1968), analyzes the prog(ressive) in English in terms of the speaker's perspective. According to this approach, the difference between sentences in simple-past such as "John ate supper" and sentences in prog such as "John was eating supper" is whether the speaker sees the situation of eating as complete (finished), or as continuing. However, such an approach is not very explanatory and fails to capture the temporal relations holding between situations in the narrative discourse. Another line of analysis found already in Leech (1969) but developed mainly in Goldsmith & Woisteschlaeger (1982) indicates a temporary component of the meaning of the progressive sentence. Analyses within this approach are taken to explain the difference between (3) and (4) below:

(3) The statue stands at the corner.

(4) The statue is standing at the corner.

Moens (1987:61) shows that the temporary reading of sentences such as (4) is only a relative notion, and Kearns (1991:13) shows it to follow by mere implicature. Moreover, this analysis cannot explain the ungrammaticality of (5) below:

(5) *I was remembering his name, but I forget it.

Another approach was developed in Vlach (1981), followed by others (e.g., Parsons 1990, Moens 1987, Moens & Steedman 1988, Kearns 1991, Kamp & Reyle 1993). Vlach comes to the conclusion that progressive sentences denote states. Examining prog sentences we can, indeed, see that they share many properties with states. First, they are also distributive — if John was building a house (say in the year 1976) then he was building a house in every subinterval of 1976.[2] This claim is supported by the logical entailments suggested by Reinhart (1986) and Dowty (1986), which are common to both prog and states (see ch. 2 for more details):

(6) a) John was at home. ~ → ~ John is at home.
b) John was drawing a circle. ~ → ~ John is drawing a circle.
c) John drew a circle. → ~ John is drawing the same circle.

The state in (6a) as well as the situation denoted by the prog sentence in (6b) do not entail that the situation is not continuing now. (Vlach draws some more analogies between states and prog, and Mittwoch 1988 adds to them some more points, but as the analogies seem to be relevant specifically to the English prog rather to the inclusive aspect in general I will not deal with them in this discussion.) However, although I accept the analyses above, the comparison both draw between states and prog is wrong. Firstly, although they share the distributive property, prog and states differ in some crucial respects, and secondly they can interact with each other. Recall that states can be modified by delimiters such as "(for) three days" which restrict their duration and enable them to appear on a sequence. By contrast, prog sentences, as demonstrated in Mittwoch (1988), cannot appear with delimiters and hence can never appear in a sequence. Compare the grammaticality of (7a) with the ungrammaticality of (7b):[3]

(7) a) John slept (for) ten hours.
b) *John was sleeping (for) ten hours.
c) *John was drawing a circle for ten hours.

This can be demonstrated also by delimiters such as "three times":

(8) a) John was sick three times this winter.
b) *John was dancing three times this week.
c) *John was drawing a circle three times yesterday.

The count adverb yields a well-formed sentence when combined with a stative predicate, but an ungrammatical sentence when it modifies a prog sentence. As mentioned above, states may interact with prog, which shows further that they are not identical. This will be discussed in section 3.1.2 below. There are (at least) two other inadequate analyses, namely the agentive and the "dynamic" approaches. These analyses will both be dealt with in section 3.1.2.

More promising is the truth-conditional approach, represented by Dowty (1977,1979), Taylor (1977), Bennett (1981), Vlach (1981), Bach (1980), Mittwoch (1988) and others. The truth conditions stipulated for sentences in the prog all relate to the fact that sentences such as (1) and (2) above are to be evaluated at some subinterval of the situation denoted by it. This subinterval, translated into the terms of this work, is the R-time (included in the prog situation), as shown in the following examples of Mittwoch (1988):

(9) a) I am working.
b) At 5 o'clock I was working.
c) When you came in I was working.

In (9a) the R-time included in the interval of working is R_S (and hence the speech-time itself is also included in that interval), in (9b) it is the adverbial and in (9c) it is the R-time of the other event (and hence the event itself, naturally). The requirement for the prog to contain an R-time explains the difference in grammaticality between (10a) and (10b):

(10) Yesterday John was a. building a house.
b. *eating supper.

In (10a) the R-time "yesterday" is understood as included in the situation of the house building, since we know that building a house takes more than one day. The same R-time in (10b) with the "shorter" activity — eating supper — yields an ill-formed sentence as it is understood as including rather than being included in the situation. If we add an R-time of a more delimited duration to this sentence it will be well-formed:

(11) {At 5 o'clock / When the bomb exploded} yesterday John was eating supper.

Now the prog clause has an R-time (5 o'clock or the bomb explosion) included in it, and therefore (11) is well-formed. This also shows, as König (1980) and Mittwoch (1988) claim, that the R-time of the prog is not determined independently but by the context.[4] Scott (1970), Montague (1970), Bennett & Partee (1978 [1972]), McCawley (1981) and others claim that the subinterval evaluating the prog (i.e., the R-time) should be a momentary interval.[5] However, Dowty (1977) shows that the R-time of the prog can also be an extended interval, as in his following example:

(12) John was wearing sunglasses when I had lunch with him.

Dowty's analysis departs again from that of Bennett & Partee on another important point. Bennett & Partee stipulate that the R-time included in the interval of the prog must not be the initial or the final endpoint of that interval. Hence, they argue, the interval of the prog sentence must begin before and continue after the R-time. (Cf. Moens & Steedman 1988:18.) This requirement reflects the framing effect of the prog noted by Jespersen (1933). Jespersen claims that the prog sentence denotes a situation which functions as a temporal frame encompassing something else, the R-time in our framework, as it begins before that R-time and does not stop after it. However, Kearns (1991) shows that the temporal frame reading is merely an implicature, and Jespersen himself acknowledges the possibility that the prog might stop after the R-time. Dowty finds this observation to support his departure from Bennett & Partee. Like them, he requires the R-time to be a non-final subinterval of the prog interval. However, he argues that some of the prog interval may hold in some other possible world other than our actual one. Consider his example (19) given here under (13):

(13) John was watching television when Bill entered the room.

Dowty agrees that the television watching probably extended at least a few moments after Bill entered the room, but he explains this only as an invited inference. To see this he compares (13) with (14 - his:20) below:

(14) John was watching television when he fell asleep.

The interval of the television watching in (14) cannot be understood as continuing after the event of falling asleep in the actual world, but only in some other possible world. In other words, Dowty considers progressive sentences as involving a modal meaning, which poses many difficulties. Since Dowty has developed this line of explanation mainly to account for the interaction of the prog aspect with accomplishment predicates, I postpone the discussion of the issue to section 3.1.2. For the present discussion, I merely want to note that we should not incorporate a modal component to the progressive, as done by Dowty, and I, therefore, completely abandon the requirement that the prog interval must continue (either in the actual or in some other possible world). It is sufficient to stipulate that it has to include the R-time, which can also be a final subinterval of the prog situation. Mittwoch (1988) furthermore, claims that the subinterval included in the prog does not have to begin before the prog situation either. She illustrates this by (12) above and by other examples. Mittwoch's conclusion, is therefore, that the R-time can be either a proper or non-proper subinterval of the situation denoted by the prog sentence. Note also that a prog can include more than one R-time as in (15):

(15) When John was eating supper, somebody broke in and started to scream.

We can conclude, therefore, that:

(16) $\exists$ at least one R-time, $R \subseteq$ PROG-situation.

Prog can also appear in modal sentences, as in the following example:

(17) John should be eating supper at 5 o'clock.

Prog, furthermore, is not limited to semelfactive (=non repetitive) meaning only. As Jespersen (1933), Mittwoch (1988) and others show, prog can appear in habitual sentences too, as in the following sentence (Jespersen 1933:182):

(18) I am (was) writing every morning at the time when he usually comes (came).

Jespersen notes that examples as (18) are possible if the 'framing' is repeated each time. Intuitively, what he means is that in (18) the speaker indicates two habituals where one (his coming) is always included in the other (my writing). That is, the prog habitual situation includes the habitual event. For the purpose of this chapter this intuitive description is sufficient, but see chapter 4 for a formal analysis.

3.1.1 *Inclusion and the Narrative Discourse*

If the above analysis of the prog is adequate we should predict that prog sentences will not appear in a sequence, since the definition of R-time movement requires that the situation be included in its R-time (see discussion in chapter 2.1 above). Consider the sentences in (19) below:

(19) a) *Ruth was eating supper, and then {took / was taking} a shower.

b) *Ruth was eating supper, but before {she took / was taking} a shower.

c) Ruth was eating supper when Dina {took / was taking} a shower.

d) Ruth was eating supper when {the phone rung. / she suddenly heard a scream.}

As predicted, (19a) and (19b) are bad, because the clauses added to the progressive sentence have precedence adverbials denoting that the situation of the prog sentence precedes and follows the situation in the following clause respectively. By contrast, when the sentences in prog combine with clauses denoting situations included in the prog interval they generate good sentences, as in (19c) and (19d). Moreover, the prog is *needed* in cases such as (19d).

Kamp & Rohrer (1983) analyze the relationship of the imparfait with its R-time in DRS (=the discourse representation structure — see section 2.1 for this notion). As they show, a clause in imparfait introduced into the narrative discourse always includes the current R-time, and since this R-time includes the event reported in the previous clause, the imparfait situation includes that event, too. Only when the imparfait clause contains an adverb, they claim, does it not include the previous event. Their example is given below under (20):

(20) *Le docteur entra chez lui et vit sa femme debout. Il lui sourit.* ***Un moment après elle pleurait.***
'The doctor came in (his house) and saw his wife standing. He smiled at her. **A moment later she was crying**'.

As they argue, the crying does not include R_3 of the event "he smiled at her" and hence does not include that event which is contained in it as well. In section 2.2.3.2 we analyzed adverbs such as the one in (20) as updating the R-time. We can conclude, then, that an INC clause introduced into the discourse includes the current R-time, unless it is updated. Recall that **when**-clauses also update the R-time in the discourse, and, indeed, a prog sentence prefixed by "when" does not have to include the current R-time. Consider:

(21) John made supper. When he was eating his meal he (suddenly) heard a scream.

Seemingly, (20) and (21) are counter-examples to the claim that an INC clause does not move the R-time forward. However, note first that what allows the movement of the R-time in these cases is the adverb. Secondly, the R-time movement in (20) and (21) is only an invited inference (due to conversational rules). In other words, it is not a necessary logical inference, as demonstrated in (22) below (suggested to me by Reinhart):

(22) At 5 o'clock John was lying on the bed and at 6 o'clock he was (also) smoking a cigarette.

The adverb "at 6 o'clock" in (22) updates the R-time (which was 5 o'clock) and the prog sentences can be understood as successive situations. However, they can also be interpreted as holding an overlapping relationship, and when "also" is added to the second one they are necessarily interpreted as overlapping (where the first starting before the second). Dowty (1986), who also analyzes prog sentences as counter-sequential, discusses apparent counter-examples of prog sentences without an updating R-time. Consider the following example:

(23) In the darkness, John felt his way up the stairway of the dilapidated old house. Halfway up, there was a loud cracking noise under his feet, and suddenly he was falling through space. (Dowty 1986; ex. 37)

Dowty, correctly, analyzes the underlined prog sentence in this and similar examples as denoting a situation which begins prior to the protagonist's perception of the situation. This means that the situation succeeding the previous event is the implicitly reported perception, i.e., "suddenly" modifies the implied clause "he felt that...". In other words, the situation of the prog sentence does *not* follow the previous situation, but includes it. This line of explanation may account for similar examples given in Hinrichs (1986 [1982]) and for the French example of Kamp & Rohrer (1983):

(24) Jean *tourna l'interrupteur. La lumière éclatante* ***l'éblouissait***.
'John turned the switch on. The sparkling light **dazzled** (was dazzling?) him.'

From the fact that INC situations include the current R-time in the narrative discourse it follows that two or more INC situations in succession must be interpreted as simultaneous. Consider the following fragment of narrative:

(25) John opened the door and turned on the light. Two people were sitting at the table and the cat was scratching the window nervously.

When the first prog sentence is introduced into the discourse, the current R-time is the one including the event of John's turning on the light, and hence the situation of the people sitting at the table includes this R-time. But since this situation did not introduce a new R-time, the next prog situation (the cat scratching the window) includes the same R-time (i.e., the R-time of the event), and necessarily overlaps the prog situation denoted by the previous clause. Note that, in this case, the two prog situations (probably) include, in addition to the current R-time, the R-time preceding it (i.e., the event of opening the door too). As represented by (15) above INC situations can include more than one R-time; as a matter of fact, the number of the R-times included is not limited, and it is determined syntactically and/or pragmatically.

3.1.2 *The Interaction of the Progressive Aspect with the Aktionsarten*

Dowty (1977,1979), Vlach (1981), Moens (1987) and others treat the prog as an operator applied to a sentence (or as Bach 1980 and Hinrichs 1985, to a predicate). To illustrate the approach consider the logical form (26b) of sentence (26a) analyzed in Dowty (1977:45-46):

(26) a) John was drawing a circle.
b) PAST[PROG[JOHN DRAW A CIRCLE]]][6]

In general it is represented as PROG[A] where [A] is the base predicate (or sentence). It has been claimed that to capture the truth conditions of a sentence in prog it is not sufficient to observe that it must contain an R-time; account must also be taken of the Aktionsarten of the base predicate, crucial for logical inferences. Consider the sentences in (27) (analyzed in Dowty 1977):

(27) a) John was drawing a circle.
b) John was pushing a cart.

In (27a) the base predicate is an accomplishment (draw a circle), while in (27b) it is an activity (push a cart). Observe now the entailments (27') of these two sentences:

(27') a) John drew a circle.
b) John pushed a cart.

As argued by Dowty, the inference in (27'a) does not follow (27a), while the inference (27'b) from (27b) is valid. The difference in the entailments is due to the difference between the Ak' of the base predicates.[7] Dowty, labelling it **the imperfective paradox**, explains the failure of (27'a) as a result of the "collision" between the meaning of the acc' and of the prog. An acc' verb phrase as "draw a circle" involves completion, or in Dowty's terms, it involves "the coming about of particular states-of-affairs". In our example, the verb-phrase "draw a circle" involves the coming into existence of a circle. However, a sentence in prog does not entail a completion of the circle drawing (as noted also by Jespersen 1933). To account for the imperfective paradox Dowty stipulates in his truth conditions of the prog that the circle, e.g., will be completed in all inertia worlds. These are possible worlds that are exactly like the actual world up to R-time. After that time the most natural course of events is supposed to take place. The progressive of a sentence is true if its non-progresssive counterpart is true in all the worlds in which the situation proceeds "normally". In the example "John was drawing a circle at ten PM" this would mean that the sentence is true at ten PM, if in any normal course of events John would finish drawing the circle some time after ten PM. Dowty's analysis is motivated also by progressives with an activity in their scope, as they may continue beyond the R-time, as discussed above (see example 13). However, as mentioned there, the incorporation of a modal component into the prog analysis raises many difficulties. Firstly, it cannot differentiate between modal prog clauses such as (17) and (18) above and non-modal ones such as (27). Secondly, Parsons (1990) and Moens (1987) point to some difficulties concerning the notion of inertia worlds. Parsons (pp. 169-170) argues that it seems to be the case that the things in our actual worlds progress in the most compatible way, and that even if there is only one such case that shows that our actual world is one of inertia worlds. This, argues Parsons, will require the progressive sentence to be false, unless the non-prog version actualizes later in time, which revives the imperfective paradox. Similarly, Moens (1987) shows that it is impossible to determine where the actual world ends and the set of inertia worlds starts. Moens discusses the following example given by Dowty:

(28) Max was crossing the street when he was hit by a truck.

According to Dowty this sentence is true if in every inertia world where events progress "normally" Max will cross the street. However, Moens shows this analysis to be inadequate. Since the evaluating time (i.e., R-time) is given in the "when"-clause, says Moens, it means that the actual world is taken to extend up to the point where Max gets hit, and hence he will not cross the street in any inertia world and the prog sentence will come out false, counter-intuitively. If, alternatively, claims Moens, one "freezes" a world where Max is crossing the street a fraction of a second before he gets hit by a truck, then in any normal extension of the world he will still get hit, and the prog sentence will again come out as false. "The truck hitting Max", says Moens, "is not an interruption of the natural course of events; it *is* the natural course of events" (p. 67). However, realizing that it is yet an interruption of something, Moens claims that it is the interruption of Max's plans. A similar analysis is given in Kamp & Reyle (1993) who claim that what we can conclude from a sentence such as "Mary is writing a letter" is that "what is going on in present is the sort of thing that *would* result in a complete letter, if things *were* to continue as planned" (p. 576). However, as they themselves admit, it is not clear what this counterfactual exactly means. Parsons (1990:170) argues, correctly, that intent cannot be part of a general analysis of the prog, for such an analysis will falsify sentences such as "The river is undercutting the bank".

The most persuasive argument against Dowty's analysis is found in Mittwoch (1988). Mittwoch shows that Dowty's analysis cannot account for sentences which can denote only completed events and hence cannot appear in prog as the ungrammaticality of the following sentence shows:

(29) *John was drinking three cups of tea (when I arrived).

As she notes, (29) cannot mean that John was at the middle of one out of what later turned out to be three cups of tea (the sentence can be grammatical only in special interpretation, e.g., as a futurate prog). Mittwoch, too, therefore, rejects this part of Dowty's analysis. She adopts instead the approach, proposed by Vlach (1981), Bennett (1981), ter-Meulen (1984) and others, which regards acc' base sentences like **John build a house** as having, in addition to their event reading, at least the potential for a process reading — the process leading up to the endpoint, where the prog sentence, **John was building a house** means 'John was in the process of building a house'. In other words, the PROG operator applies to the process reading only. This line of analysis is found in a more consistent way in Moens (1987, & Steedman 1988). Moens claims that the progressive is a function which requires its input to denote a process, and therefore when the base predicate is a culminated process (= acc') it may take the prog only if we "strip off" the culmination point, turning the acc' into a process (=activity). Kamp & Reyle (1993:558), although suggesting an analysis which gives the prog an intent component (as discussed above) also claim that the prog refers to the preparatory phase of the acc'. Similar analyses are given in Binnick (1991:207) and Verkuyl (1993: 321). (Kearns 1991 goes as far as claiming that the simple and the prog sentences have two different predicates. But she, too, agrees that while the predicate "build a house" denotes an event, the predicate "building a house" is true of processes.)

Although it is more difficult, this approach explains PROG when applied to achievement predicates, too. Vendler (1967) claims that achievements cannot occur in prog, but Dowty (1977,1979), Mourelatos (1978), Vlach (1981), Moens (1987, & Steedman 1988) and others pointed out that it is not true of all achievements that they fail to appear in prog. Vlach provides some examples:

(30) a) The ship be arriving
b) Max be dying
c) Mary be winning

Vlach explains (30a-b) as representing processes where the parallel simple-tense sentences represent a completion of some accomplishment. (30a), as he claims, may be to say that the ship has entered the harbor, or that it has begun procedures for docking or something of the sort. (30b), which is more problematic, may be understood as denoting a gradual failure of the body's natural functions. Vlach, however, has difficulties in explaining (30c) where it is difficult to see what process leads to Mary's winning. Vlach suggests interpreting it as a futurate prog, similar to:

(31) The Celtics are playing tomorrow.

Parsons (1990:36) suggests that "is winning" is simply "is ahead". Another possible interpretation of such sentences is the iterative meaning as in:

(32) John was kicking the ball (when I arrived).

The use of the prog in (32) represents that John gave a number of kicks to the ball (compare 32 with "John kicked the ball"). Another possible explanation may be in the line of Moens' explanation for the following example (his:244):

(33) John was reaching the top.

Moens, as mentioned above, requires progressive to be applied only to processes, and if the base predicate is not a process, it should be coerced into process meaning. The way he does it for ach' like (33) is by first turning the predicate into a culminated process (=acc') by focusing on the preparatory process which ends in culmination (of being at the top). Then the culmination point is "stripped off", allowing the prog to describe the preparatory process as ongoing. According to this analysis, "Mary was winning the race" describes the preparatory process of winning, but not necessarily the winning itself.

The interaction of prog with stative verbs has given even more attention in the literature. Vendler claims that stative verbs may not take the prog. This claim is found in many works which take the Vendlerian categories into their basic account. Vlach (1981), who believes prog sentences to report states (as mentioned above), claims that the PROG operator is used by speakers to turn events into states, or in his words, "this is what the PROG is FOR". Bach (1981), accepting this claim, takes it as an explanation for the incompatibility of the prog with states (Cf. also Leech 1969, Bennett & Partee 1978 [1972]). However, there is firm evidence in the literature that prog may combine with stative predicates (Binnick 1991:282, Verkuyl 1993:36, Kearns 1991:163, to name the most recent works), as shown in the following example from Binnick (1991:282):

(34) I'm feeling rather ill.

Moens (1987), realizing the empirical data, allows the prog operator to apply to stative verbs. However, being consistent with his requirement that the prog may take as input only processes he requires stative verbs to turn into processes first before taking the auxiliary prog. Moens believes that turning statives into processes "only involves thinking of the state as being restricted in time" (p. 59). However, it seems to me that thinking of states as restricted in time does not, intuitively speaking, turn them into processes. But Moens also suggests two criteria for turning states into processes, namely agentivity and dynamism. As he claims, a predicate such as "unaware" cannot be interpreted as agentive, and therefore it cannot be combined with a progressive auxiliary. However, he himself cites the example "The baby is resembling his father more and more" (ex. 126Fii) which is not agentive. He attributes the ability of having the prog in such cases to the "more & more"-structure. Moens argues that this structure provides the sentence with the "dynamic" property, which expresses different stages of the situation (rather than a homogeneous one as in the case of the sentence without the "more & more" modifier). Verkuyl (1993) shows both criteria to be invalid. In Table 2 on p. 37 he provides examples of progressive sentences which bear, indeed, both or one of the properties, but also the sentence "Small things are mattering" which bears neither agentivity nor "dynamism" (or "progress in time" in Verkuyl's terms). Moens himself admits the fact that he cannot account for all stative verbs in progressive as turning into process first (p. 98). However, he claims that there is still a crucial difference between processes and states concerning the contexts in which they take the progressive. As he shows, correctly, one cannot utter (35a; his:252)) below but needs to utter (35b; his:253)), in a state of affairs where they see a man walking in the park:

(35) a) ?The man who walks over there (is president of GM).
b) The man who is walking over there (is president of GM).

In contrast, Moens claims, states do not have to take a prog as shown in (36; his:254) below:

(36) a) That man is president of GM.
b) That music sounds like Mozart.
c) What you see here is one of my granny's teeth.

Moens is right in accepting (35b) but not (35a) in the state of affairs he describes. The difference in grammaticality between the sentences, I claim, is due to the fact that R_S is included in the situation, and therefore the sentence requires the prog. However, I disagree with Moens that statives may choose between the progressive and the non-progressive sentence in similar contexts. I argue that not only may the prog be applied to stative predicates, but furthermore it *must* be applied to them when the speaker utters an inclusive situation. This is shown by the difference in grammaticality between (37a) and (37b) below:

(37) a) I was living in the states when Reagan was elected.
b) *I lived in the states when Reagan was elected.

Since the event of being elected functions (also) as the R-time of the situation of living in the states, and since it is included in that situation, the prog is required. Only a small group of stative verbs do not appear in prog (and can have inclusive meaning nevertheless). This group includes the verb 'be' and verbs such as 'know', 'love', 'hate' and the like which I will label here as **mental state verbs**.[8] It is interesting that these verbs do not come in the BH inclusive form as well, as will be shown in next section. (However, they do appear in the imparfait in French, probably because the other alternative, i.e., the passé-simple, would give them an inchoative meaning). The verbs offered by Moens in examples (36) belong to this group, and that is why they do not come in prog. The sentence in (36b), furthermore, is interpreted not as inclusive, but like a generic (or habitual), meaning that that music *usually* sounds like Mozart (it seems to me peculiar to think of it as sounding like Mozart only now at R_S).

To conclude, the progressive aspect is **not** identical to states, but functions to denote inclusive situations, regardless of the Ak' of the predicate base.

3.2 Inclusion in Biblical-Hebrew

BH has a special form, parallel to the English '-ing', to denote inclusive situations — the participial *qotel* form. As in the case of the English progressive, this form does not appear with the verb 'be' and with mental state verbs such as 'know'. When a mental state or the state of being is denoted, the perfect *qatal* form is used. There is only a very small number of counter-examples where a mental state verb appears in *qotel* (see ex. ii in FN 9 below for illustration).

In what follows I will demonstrate these claims and deal with some apparent counter examples.

The form *qotel* is usually treated in the literature as a nominal or an adjectival, leaning on the behavior of the *qotel* as a part of a noun phrase. As a noun, it can appear with the determiner *ha* 'the' as in *hayyo;ṣˀi:m* 'the leaving people' (Gen. 9:18); it can form a compound-noun (called *smixut*-construction in Hebrew) as in *yo;de̲;ₐˁ ṣayid̲* 'knowing (of) hunt' (= 'hunt knower' = 'hunter') (Gen. 25:27),[9] *šo;p̄e;k̲ dam* 'shattering of blood' (Gen. 9:6). As an adjective, the *qotel* is conjugated only according to gender and number (not to person as a "normal" verb form). However, as Gesenius and others show, the *qotel* shares some syntactic and semantic properties with verbs. For example, it can govern a noun phrase as its object, as in *ḥo;b̲eṭ ḥiṭṭi:m* '(he was) threshing wheat' (Jud. 6:11). In such cases the *qotel* functions as a predicate just like any verbal form and has a role in the temporal system. In the discussion below, therefore, I will take into account only the cases where the *qotel* is predicative. I, furthermore, will refer to the qotel forms as verbs, for reasons that will be given below.

The role of the *qotel* in the temporal system in BH has been discussed by many Hebraists. Kimchi (1545), the *waw-conversive* theory in the Middle

Ages and Schroeder (1766) labelled the *qotel* as *benoni* 'middle' or *ˤomed* 'standing', claiming that it is a part of a three-place paradigm of tense where the *benoni* denotes the present tense (a middle tense between past and future). Gesenius and Bergsträsser claim that the *qotel* mostly denotes simultaneous situations. However, simultaneity is not sufficient for characterizing the *qotel* form. *Qatal*, too, may appear in simultaneous clauses (see ch. 5). I will show that the *qotel* denotes not just that a situation is simultaneous with another situation in the discourse, but more specifically that it includes it, as it has to contain an R-time. Consider the following example:

(38) *wayya:ḇo; malˀaḵ yhwh wayye;šeḇ taḥaṯ ha:ˀe;la:*
WAYY:come:3SG:MASC angel:of God WAYY:sit:3SG:MASC under the-oak
ˀᵃšer bˤop̄ra: ˀᵃšer lyo:ˀa:š ˀᵃḇi: ha:ˤezri: ***wg̲iḏˤo:n bno:***
that in-Ophrah that to-Joash father:of the-ezrite and-Gideon son-his
ḥo;ḇe;ṭ ḥiṭṭ:im baggaṯ *lha:ni:s mippne:*
QOT:thresh:SG:MASC wheat in-the-winepress to-INF:hide from-face:of
miḏya:n
Midian
'The angel of the Lord came and sat under the terebinth at Ophra which belonged to Joash the Abiesrite. **His son Gideon was threshing wheat in the winepress**, to hide it from the Midianites.' (Jud. 6:11)

The boldfaced clause has a *qotel* verb *ḥo;ḇe;ṭ* 'threshing', and in fact the situation denoted by it contains the R-time of the events (and hence the events themselves) of the angel coming and talking to Gideon. That is, the situation denoted by the *qotel* clause contains at least the event reported in the preceding clause, as required by the definition of INC clauses in the narrative (in this case it includes in addition other events preceding the last reported event, and probably some of the events reported in the clauses following the *qotel* clause). However, as predicted, when the R-time is updated, the situation of the *qotel* clause is understood as including the event denoted in the following clause (but does not determine if it also includes the event denoted in the previous clause). Consider the following example:

(39) 20. *wayya:moṯ ˀᵉli:ša:ˤ wayyiqbruhu: u:g̲ḏu:ḏe:*
WAYY:die:3SG:MASC Elisha WAYY:bury:3PL:MASC-him and-troops:of
mo:ˀa:ḇ ya:ḇo;ˀu: ḇa:ˀa:reṣ ba: ša:na:
Moabite YIQ:come:3PL:MASC in-the-land ?:come:3SG:MASC year
21. ***wayhi: he;m qo;ḇri:m ˀi:š*** *whinne: ra:ˀu: ˀeṯ*
wayhi: they:MASC QOT:bury:PL:MASC man and-alas QAT:see:3PL ACC

haggdu:d *wayyašli:ku:* *ʔet* *ha:ʔi:š* *bqeber* *ʔeli:ša:ʕ...*
the-troop WAYY:throw:3PL:MASC ACC the-man in-grave:of Elisha...
'20. Elisha died and they buried him. Year by year Moabites raiders used to invade the land. **Once some men were burying a dead man** when they caught sight of the raiders. They threw the body into the grave of Elisha...' (Kings2 13:20-21)

The boldfaced *qotel* clause is in a preposed *wayhi:* clause, which means that it updates the R-time (see a discussion on *wayhi:* in section 2.2.3 above). Therefore, the R-time included in it is not the R-time of the last mentioned event but the R-time of the event reported in the following clause. Another group of *qotel* clauses which do not include the R-time of the last mentioned event is in direct speech, where such a clause contains R_S, i.e., the R-time of the speech event. Consider:

(40) *watto;mer* ***mippne:*** ***śa:ray*** ***gbirti:*** ***ʔa:no;ki:***
WAYY:say:3SG:FEM from-face:of Sarai mistress-my I
bo;rahat
QOT:escape:SG:FEM
'She said, **I am running away from Sarai, my mistress.**' (Gen. 16:8)

The boldfaced clause reports a direct speech of Hagar, and its R-time, therefore, is not the current R-time of the discourse, but the R_S in which the speech-event of Hagar is included.

The *qotel* form is used to denote inclusive relation in modal clauses, too:

(41) *wayyo;mer* ***lammo:ʕe;d*** ***hazze*** ***ka:ʕe;t*** ***ḥayya:***
WAYY:say:3SG:MASC to-time the-this:MASC now next-year
ʔat ***ḥo;beqet*** ***be;n...***
you:SG:FEM QOT:hug:SG:FEM son
'He said, In due season, **this time next year, you shall be embracing a son**.' (KingsII 4:16)

(42) ***hinne;*** ***ʕo:da:k*** ***mdabberet*** ***ša:m*** ***ʕim-hammelek***
hinne while:still-you:SG:FEM QOT:speak:SG:FEM there with-the-king
waʔani: *ʔa:bo:* *ʔaḥarayik* *u:mille;ti:*
and-I YIQ:come:1SG after-you:SG:FEM WQAT:support:1SG
ʔet *dba:ra:yik*
ACC speech-yours:SG:FEM
'**Then while you are still speaking there with the king**, I will follow you in and tell the whole story.' (KingsI 1:14)

In the promise reported in (41) the *qotel* clause denotes a situation which is said to take place in the future time, and the R-time 'this time next year' is supposed to be included in it. (42) reports a future planning. Natan the prophet plans with Bat-Sheva to talk King David into handing the crown to her son Solomon. Natan tells Bat-Sheva to go to the king and talk to him about it, and then, while she is still talking to him, Natan will come in and support her. That is, the event of his coming in will be included in the activity of her talking to the king, and hence the event is in the modal form *yiqtol* and the activity is in the *qotel*.

The claim that *qotel* verbs can appear only in inclusive clauses finds support in their interaction with adverbials. As in the case of the progressive in English, they do not interact with precedence adverbials, which refer only to restricted situations which are included in their R-time. Nor do they combine with delimiters which restrict the situation and force it to be contained in its R-time. By contrast, they appear either with frame "short" adverbials included in them as in (41), or with containment adverbial such as *(b)ˤo:ḏ* 'while yet', *ˀaz* 'at the same time',[10] *bayym:mi:im ha:he;m* 'in those days', *ba:ˤe;ṯ hahi:* 'at that time' and the like. Examples (42) above and (43) below demonstrate the use of the adverbial *ˤo:ḏ* (with 2nd. and 3rd. person suffixes respectively):

(43)	*wayyip̄nu:*	*miššа:m*	*ha:ˀᵃna:ši:m*	*wayye;lḵu:*		
	WAYY:turn:3PL:MASC	from-there	the-people	WAYY:go:PL:MASC		
	sḏo;ma:	***wˀaḇra:ha:m***	***ˤo:ḏennu:***	***ˤo;me:ḏ***	***lip̄ne:***	***yhwh***
	Sodom-to	and-Abraham	yet-he	QOT:stand:SG:MASC	to-face:of	God

'The men turned and went towards Sodom, **and Abraham remained standing before the Lord**.' (Gen. 18:22)

The adverb *ˀa:z* (in the sense of 'at that time') is not common in the Bible, but in the three cases in which it occurs, the associated verb is in *qotel* form, as in:

(44)	*wayhi:*	*ri:ḇ*	*be:n*	*roˤe:*	*miqne;*	*ˀaḇra:m*
	WAYY:be:3SG:MASC	fight	between	herdsmen:of	cattle:of	Abram
	u:ḇe:n	*ro:ˤe:*	*miqne;*	*lo:ṭ*	***whakknaˤᵃni:***	
	and-between	herdsmen:of	cattle:of	Lot	and-the-Canaanite	
	whapprizzi:	***ˀa:z***	***yo;še;ḇ***	***ba:ˀa:reṣ***		
	and-the-Perizzite	then	QOT:sit:SG:MASC	in-the-land		

'There were quarrels between Abram's herdsmen and Lot's. **And the Canaanites and the Perizzite were then dwelling in the land.**' (Gen. 13:7)

(The containment adverbials do not combine with other forms, which demonstrates further that *qotel* is the only inclusive form, but this will be discussed later.) The claim that all and only *qotel* clauses denote inclusive situations is also supported by a statistical analysis. Table 3.1 below presents the findings of this analysis for the INC parameter, as performed on the clauses constituting our sample (described in ch.1, section 1.2 above). The table summarizes all the occurrences of inclusive clauses, excluding only those cases in which the text itself cannot independently determine whether the clause in question is inclusive, but only whether the interpretation of inclusiveness is possible. To make the results stronger these cases were not included (however, see FN 6 in ch. 1 above). In other words, the questionable cases, mentioned under the question mark '?' in the table, are not counter-examples, as they can be inclusive. The following example illustrates a questionable case:

(45) 9. *wayyaṣmaḥ* *yhwh* *ˀᵉlo;hi:m* *min* *ha:ˀᵃd̲a:ma:* *kol*
WAYY:plant:3SG:MASC God God from the-earth every:of
ˤe;ṣ *neḥma:d̲* *lmarˀe* *wṭo:b̲* *lmaˀᵃk̲a:l* *wˤe;ṣ*
tree nice:SG:MASC to-sight and-good:SG:MASC to-food and-tree:of
haḥayyi:m *bt̲o:k̲* *hagg:an* *wˤe;ṣ* *haddaˤat̲* *ṭo:b̲*
the-life inside the-garden and-tree:of the-knowledge good:SG:MASC
wa:ra:ˤ 10. ***wna:ha:r*** ***yo;ṣe;*** ***me;ˤe;d̲en*** ***lhašqo:t̲***
and-bad:SG:MASC and-river QOT:leave:SG:MASC from-Eden to-INF:water
ˀet̲ ***hagga:n*** *u:mišša:m* *yippa:re;d̲*
ACC the-garden and-from-there YIQ:separate:3SG:MASC
wha:ya: *lˀarba:ˤa:* *ra:ši:m*
WQAT:be:3SG:MASC to-four:MASC heads
'9. The Lord God made trees spring from the ground, all trees pleasant to look at and good for food; and in the middle of the garden he set the tree of life and the tree of the knowledge of good and evil. 10. **There was a river flowing from Eden** to water the garden, and when it left the garden it branched into four streams.' (Gen. 2:9-10)

It is not clear if the situation denoted by the boldfaced *qotel* clause in (45) includes an R-time. However, it is possible to understand it as including one or more of the events denoted in the preceding and/or the following clauses. Cases such as (45), as said above, were deleted from the total number of the occurrences as represented in table 3.1, and only the rest, represented under the raw 'clear' were calculated. Another point to be discussed before representing the findings is the distinction between what I call verbal and nominal *qotel*. Since, as discussed above, the *qotel* is not a pure nominal nor a pure verb, it is usually called by Gesenius and others **participial** and by contemporary Hebraists, e.g., Berman (1978), **the Benobi** 'middle', to reflect its nature as standing at the middle between a noun and a verb. It is not my concern in this work to determine if the *qotel* is a verb, a nominal or neither, but nonetheless I refer to it as a verbal form, to distinguish it from what I call here **nominal qotel**, referring to inclusive clauses which would have a verb ‘be’ in *qotel* could it appear in this form. The **verbal qotel** (henceforth: VQ) has been illustrated in the examples given so far. The “nominal qotel” (henceforth: NQ) is demonstrated in example (46) below:

(46) *wayya:b̲o;ˀu: b̲ne: yiśra:ˀe;l bt̲o:k̲ hayya:m bayyabba:ša:*
WAYY:come:3PL:MASC sons:of Israel inside the-sea in-the-land
whammayim la:hem ḥo:ma: mi:mi:na:m
and-the-water to-them wall from-right-their:MASC
u:miśśmo;la:m
and-from-left-their:MASC
‘and the Israelites went through the sea on the dry ground, **while the waters were a wall for them to right and to left.**’ (Ex. 14:22)

In the group of NQ I include also qotel forms which Gesenius labels “passive participial” as the participial *šlu:p̄a:* ‘drawn’ in the following example:

(47) *watte;re ha:ˀa:t̲o:n ˀet̲ malˀak̲ yhwh niṣṣa:b̲*
WAYY:see:3SG:FEM the-ass ACC angel:of God QOT:stand:SG:MASC
badderek̲ wḥarbo: ***šlu:p̄a:*** *bya:d̲o:...*
in-the-way and-sword-his QOT:drawn:SG:FEM in-hand-his
‘The ass saw the angel standing in the road with his sword **drawn**...’ (Num. 22:23)

Now let us present Table 3.1 and discuss the findings. (The table does not include the 59 cases of *qatal* in verb ‘be’ or in one of the mental states verbs, although we tend to interpret them as inclusive situations, for reasons mentioned above, and discussed in detail in chapter 5.)

Table 3.1. The inclusive aspect and the verb forms in BH

FORM	VQ	NQ	YIQTOL	WAYYIQTOL
TOTAL	253	425	1121	2445
?	N = 51	N = 28	N = 13	N = 3
	20%	6.6%	1.1%	0.1%
REST	N = 202	N = 397	N = 1108	N = 2442
[+INC]	N = 175	N = 397	N = 14	N = 1
	87%	100%	1.26%	0.04%

In what follows I will discuss first the findings of the *qotel* clauses and then deal with the other forms.

There is a dramatic difference between the two kinds of *qotel.* While 13% of the VQ clauses are not inclusive, i.e., they are counter-examples to the claim that *qotel* clauses denote inclusive situations, there is no counter example to this claim concerning the NQ clauses. In other words, while all the situations denoted by NQ clauses include at least one R-time (usually the one including the previous event) there are VQ clauses (27 in our sample) which report situations which do not contain an R-time. These cases can be grouped into three classes, as summarized in Table 3.2 below (where one of the groups is not represented in our corpus).

Table 3.2. ***qotel*** *and the inclusive aspect*

TOTAL	[+INC]	[–INC]			
		FUTURATE	PERCEPTION	HABITUAL	OTHER
N = 202 100%	N = 175 87%	N = 14 7%	N = 0 0%	N = 9 4%	N = 4 2%

The largest group of the counter-examples is the "futurate *qotel*". The *qotel* clauses in this group denote future events without an R-time included in them, parallel to the futurate progressive in English (see discussion in secton 3.1.2 above). Consider the following examples:

(48) 10. *wayṣaw* *yho:šu$_a$ˁa* *ˀeṯ* *šo;ṭre:* *ha:ˁa:m*
WAYY:order:3SG:MASC Joshua ACC officers:of the-people
11. *le;mo;r* *ˁiḇru:* *bqereḇ* *hammaḥ^{a}ne*
to-INF:say IMP:pass:2PL:MASC inside the-camp
wṣawwu: *ˀeṯ* *ha:ˁa:m* *le;mo;r* *ha:ḵi:nu:*
and-IMP:order:2PL:MASC ACC the-people to-INF:say IMP:prepare-2PL:MASC
la:ḵem *ṣe;ḏa:* ***ki:*** ***bˁo:ḏ*** ***šlo;šeṯ*** ***ya:mi:m***
to-you:PL:MASC provision because in-more three:MASC-of days
ˀattem ***ˁo;ḇri:m*** ***ˀeṯ*** ***hayyarde;n*** ***hazze***
you:PL:MASC QOT:pass:PL:MASC ACC the-Jordan the-this:MASC
la:ḇo: *la:rešeṯ* *ˀeṯ* *ha:ˀa:reṣ* *ˀašer* ***yhwh***
to-INF:come to-INF:inherit ACC the-land that God
no;ṯe:n ***la:ḵem*** ***lrišta:h***
QOT:give:SG:MASC to-you:PL:MASC to:INF-inherit-her

'Joshua ordered the officers saying, Pass through the camp and order the people saying, Get food ready to take with you; **for within three days you are crossing the Jordan** to come occupy the country which the **Lord your God is giving you** to posses.' (Jos. 1:10-11)

(49) ... *watto;mer* *ha:ˀišša:* *ˀel* *yo:ˀa:ḇ* ***hinne;*** ***ro;šo:***
WAYY:say:3SG:FEM the-woman to Joab *hinne;* head-his
mušla:ḵ ***ˀe;le:ḵa:*** ***bˁaḏ*** ***haḥo:ma:***
QOT:thrown:SG:MASC to-you:SG:MASC through the-wall
'The woman said to Joab, '**Here is his head being thrown to you over the wall.**' (Sam II 20:21)

The boldfaced clauses in (48)-(49) all denote future events. Nonetheless, they all have *qotel* verbs. Sternberg (1982) explains (49) as follows: the woman promises that Joab can see his enemy's head as if it has already been thrown. This explanation is supported by the fact that most of the futurate *qotel* are said by God or one of his prophets, and then they can be understood as performative speech acts.

The second group, which I labelled "perception" has no representatives in our corpus, but as it appears in the Bible it should be dealt with. All the examples in this group appear in dreams, as in the following stretch of discourse:

(50) 5. *wayyi:ša:n* *wayyaḥ^{a}lo;m* *še;ni:ṯ* ***whinne;*** ***šeḇaˁ***
WAYY:sleep:3SG:MASC WAYY:dream:3SG:MASC again *whinne:* seven
šibb^{o}li:m ***ˁo;lo:ṯ*** ***bqa:ne*** ***ˀeḥa:ḏ*** ***bri:ˀo:ṯ***
ears QOT:rise:PL:FEM in-stalk one:MASC healthy:PL:FEM
wṭo;ḇo:ṯ 6. ***whinne;*** ***šeḇaˁ*** ***šibb^{o}li:m*** ***daqqo:ṯ***
and-good:PL:FEM whinne; seven:FEM ears thin:PL:FEM
u:šḏu:p̄o;ṯ ***qa:ḏi:m*** ***ṣo;mḥo:ṯ*** ***ˀaḥ^{a}re:hen***
and-shrivelled:PL:FEM east-wind QOT:grow:PL:FEM after-them:FEM
7. *wattiḇlaˁna:* *haššib^{o}li:m* *haddaqqo:ṯ* *ˀe:ṯ*
WAYY:swallow:3PL:FEM the-ears the-thin:PL:FEM ACC
šeḇaˁ *haššib^{o}li:m* *habbri:ˀo:ṯ* *whammle:ˀo:ṯ;*
seven:FEM:of the-ears the-healthy:PL:FEM and-the-full:PL:FEM
wayyiqaṣ *parˁo:* *whinne;* *ḥ^{a}lo:m*
WAYY:wake:3SG:MASC Pharaoh *whinne;* dream
'5. He fell asleep again and had a second dream: **he saw seven ears of corn, full and ripe, growing on one stalk**. 6. **Growing up after them were other seven ears, thin and shrivelled by the east wind.** 7. The thin ears swallowed up the ears that were full and ripe. Then Pharaoh woke up and knew that it was a dream.' (Gen. 41: 5-7)

As a preliminary to a discussion of (50) we need to deal first with the particle *(w)hinne*; 'alas' or 'behold'. Sternberg (1982,1985) and Berlin (1983) show that BH has devices for changing perspective from the narrator's to one of the characters' and vice versa. Speeches and thoughts of the characters can be reported either from the narrator's or the characters' perspectives. When they are from the narrator's perspective, they are reported indirectly as in the following example (analyzed by Sternberg 1982, example 2):

(51) *wayye;lku:* *bne:* *da:n* *ldarka:m;* *wayyar*
WAYY:go:PL:MASC sons:of Dan to-way-theirs:MASC WAYY:see:3SG:MASC
mi:ka: *ki:* ***ḥ**a**za:qi:m*** ***he;mma:*** ***mimmennu:***
Micah that strong:PL:MASC they:MASC from-him
wayyip̄en *wayya:šob* *ˀel* *be:to:*
WAYY:turn:3SG:MASC WAYY:return:3SG:MASC to home-his
'The Danites went on their way and Micah, **seeing that they were too strong for him,** turned and went home.' (Jud. 18:26)

The perspective of the character is represented either by a direct speech, quoting the character's words, or by what Sternberg identifies as a free indirect discourse, representing his thoughts and content of perception as he is experiencing them. A verb of saying is used to indicate the direct-speech (see section 2.2.2 above for illustrations), and the particle *whinne*; (which is a *waw* prefixed *hinne*; distinct from it as discussed in Sternberg — see below a summary of his discussion) is used for the "free indirect thoughts". Consider his examples (28) and (4a) given here under (52) and (53) respectively:

(52) ... *wayyašqe;p̄* *ˀabi:melek* *melek* *plišti:m* *bˁad*
WAYY:look:3SG:MASC Abimelech king:of Philistine through
haḥallo:n *wayyar* ***whinne;*** ***yiṣḥa:q*** ***mṣaḥe;q***
the-window WAYY:see:3SG:MASC *whinne;* Isaac QOT:play:SG:MASC
ˀe;t ***ribka:*** ***ˀišto:***
ACC Rebecca wife-his
'...Abimelech the Philistine king looked down from his window and saw **Isaac and his wife Rebecca playing together.**' (Gen. 26:8)

(53) *wayya:bo;* *yip̄ta:ḥ* *hammiṣpa:* *ˀel* *be:to:* *whinne;*
WAYY:come:3SG:MASC Jephthah to-Mizpah to house-his *whinne;*
bitto: ***yo;ṣe:t*** ***liqra:to:*** ***btuppi:m***
daughter-his QOT:come:out:SG:FEM towards-him with-drums
u:bimḥo;lo:t...
and-with-dances
'Jephthah came to his house in Mizpah, **and there was his daughter coming towards him with tambourines and dances** ...' (Jud. 11:34)

In (52) as well as in (53), the *whinne;* prefixed clause reports the content of the respective characters' perception, where in (52) there is also a verb of perception *wayyar* 'saw' indicating that the forthcoming clause reports some content of perception.[11] As Sternberg notes, most of the *whinne;* clauses are *qotel* ones, as they indicate situations simultaneous with the events of the character's perception. To be more accurate, it is clear that the event of perception, being punctual (intuitively speaking), is included in the *qotel* situation. Only in few cases does *whinne;* appear in *qatal* clauses, but this can be explained by the fact that a *qatal* verb usually denotes a state resulting from an event as in the case of the perfect aspect in English (see discussion in chapter 5). But not only *whinne;*, the particle *hinne;* (without the *waw*) is also used to coincide perception with some state. Sternberg shows that *hinne;* appears only in direct speech where the speaker deictically points out to some situation perceived by him. In the case of *hinne;*, therefore, we can conclude that it appears in clauses denoting situations which include R_S as their R-time. In the light of the understanding of *whinne;* let us consider now the dream of Pharaoh, given in (50) above. Pharaoh's dream is reported by *qotel* clauses prefixed by *whinne;*. The form of the report in this case is no different from other cases, and in fact, is identical to the form of other people's reports (see, e.g., the dreams of Joseph). It seems to me that dreams are treated in a way similar nowadays to radio or television sport reports which describe an ongoing game. That is, Pharaoh reports his dream (in our example) as if he is perceiving the events happening in front of his eyes, as the particle *whinne;* indicates. However, it continues with a *wayyiqtol* form *wattib̲laˁna:* 'swallowed' instead of *qotel* (prefixed by *whinne;*).

The third group of the counter-examples is the "habituals", where instead of a *yiqtol* verb the clause contains a *qotel*. Consider the following example:

(54)	*wayyitto;ṣ*	*ˀet̲*	*ba:te:*	*haqqd̲e;ši:m*	*ˀᵃšer*
	WAYY:demolish:3SG:MASC	ACC	houses:of	the-prostitutes:MASC	that

bb̲e:t̲	*yhwh*	*ˀᵃšer*	***hanna:ši:m***	***ˀo;rḡo:t̲***	***ša:m***
in-house:of	God	that	the-women	QOT:weave:PL:FEM	there

ba:tti:m	***la:ˀᵃše;ra:***
houses	to-the-Asherah

'He also pulled down the houses of the male prostitutes attached to the house of the Lord, **where the women wove vestments in honor of Asherah.**' (Kings2 23:7)

The verb "weave" is in *qotel*, although it indicates a habitual activity. This use of the *qotel* might be a penetration of a later stratum of the language where participial forms are used to denote habitual situations (in present tense, and in past and future tense when combined with the verb ‘be’ conjugated in the respective tense). This suggestion is supported by the fact that most of the examples appear with the verb ‘be’ as in Mishnaic and Modern Hebrew. The underlined clause in (55) below may illustrate this:

(55) *wayyo;mer* *ʔad̲o;ni:* *b̲ezeq* *šib̲ʕi:m* *mla:k̲i:m* *bho;no:t̲*
WAYY:say:3SG:MASC Adoni bezek seventy kings toes:of
yd̲e:hem *wraḡle:hem* *mquṣṣa:ṣi:m* ***ha:yu:***
hands-their:MASC and-feet-their:MASC QOT:cut-off:PL:MASC QAT:be:3PL
mlaqqṭi:m ***taḥat̲*** ***šulḥa:ni:***...
QOT:pick-up:PL:MASC under table-my
‘Adoni-bezek said, Seventy kings whose thumbs and great toes were cut off **used to pick up the scraps from under my table.**’ (Jud. 1:7)

It has been demonstrated so far that *qotel* clauses denote inclusive situations. Now let us examine the claim that other forms do not. Table 3.1 above shows that this claim is quite adequate, however with some counter-examples which deserve some consideration. First consider *yiqtol* verbs in such clauses:

(56) ... *wayyo;mer* *la:ra:ša:ʕ* ***la:mma:*** ***t̲akke***
WAYY:say:3SG:MASC to:the-guilty:MASC why YIQ:hit:2SG:MASC
re;ʕek̲a:
friend-your:SG:MASC
‘He asked the man who was in the wrong, ‘Why are you striking your friend?’ (Ex. 2:13)

(57) 9. ...*wayyo;mar* *qa:ḥem* *na:* *ʔe;lay*
WAYY:say:3SG:MASC take-IMP:2SG:MASC-them:MASC please to-me
10.*waʔab̲a:rk̲em* *wʕe:ne:* *yiśra:ʔe;l* *ka:b̲d̲u:*
WQAT:bless:1SG-them:MASC and-eyes:of Israel QAT:heavy:3PL
mizzo;qen ***lo;*** ***yu:k̲al*** ***lirʔo:t̲***
from-oldness NEG YIQ:can:3SG:MASC to-INF:see
‘9. He (Israel) said, Bring them to me, please, and I will bless them. 10. Now Israel’s eyes were dim with age, **and he could not see.**’ (Gen. 48:9-10)

The boldfaced clauses in (56) and (57) denote situations which include the R_S and the R-time of the preceding event respectively. However, the verbs in these clauses are not in *qotel*, but in *yiqtol*. But a second look at the occurrences of *yiqtol* in inclusive clauses reveals that most of them are in questions (see in addition to example 56, also Jud. 19:17, 21:18, Sam1 1:8,13 and Kings1 3:9). Could it be that questions are treated as modals which explains the phenomenon just described? (See chapter 4 for discussion.) However, as shown above (e.g., 41-42), *qotel* verbs can also appear in modal assertions, and therefore this line of explanation is unsatisfactory. (But see further discussion on these and similar examples in ch. 4.) On the other hand, as shown in table 3.1, inclusive clauses with *yiqtol* verbs are very small in number (14 in our sample — 1.3% of all the *yiqtol* occurrences).

The number of inclusive clauses with *wayyiqtol* verbs is even smaller: 1 occurrence in our sample (0.04%), which was given under (ii) in FN (9), repeated here under (58):

(58) ***wayyeˀᵉhab̲*** ***yiṣḥa:q*** ***ˀet̲*** ***ˁe;śa:w*** *ki:* *ṣayid̲*
WAYY:love:3SG:MASC Isaac ACC Esau because hunt
bp̄i:w *wrib̲qa:* *ˀo;heb̲et̲* *ˀet̲* *yaˁᵃqo;b̲*
in-mouth-his and-Rebecca QOT:love:SG:FEM ACC Jacob
'Isaac favored Esau because he kept him supplied with venison, but Rebecca favoured Jacob.' (Gen. 25:28)

As mentioned in the discussion in FN (9), the verb *wayyeˀᵉhab̲* 'love' cannot be understood as inchoative 'fall-in-love', but nevertheless it is in *wayyiqtol* instead of *qatal* form. As noted there, too, the verb 'love' in the second clause is also in an unexpected form, which suggests that this verse is in general irregular.

NOTES

1. Modern Israeli Hebrew, too, uses the *qotel* for this purpose, but in a very limited way (see Hatav 1977); the more usual way are expressions such as "at the middle of the conversation".

2. Vlach does not accept the analysis of the progressive as being distributive, since if John took a vacation during 1976 and did not work, say in June of that year, we still say that "John was building a house" in 1976. Moens (1987:62) discussing a similar argument in Gabbay & Moravcsik (1980) shows it to be inadequate, claiming that it depends on the predicate whether we can allow gaps in progressive sentences or not; (i) given by Gabbay & Moravcsik (ex. 136 in Moens) does not allow gaps, (ii) (Moens':137) does.

   (i) Rosanne was reading a book when the phone rang.
   (ii) John was building a house when his father died.

   Recall, moreover, that any distributive situation may allow gaps, as discussed in ch. (2) above (ex. 6).

3. As mentioned in ch. (2), Comrie (pc) and Kearns (1991) disagree with Mittwoch's claim. Comrie provides example (i) below as a good sentence:

(i) I was just snoozing for a couple of minutes when the boss walked in.

Kearns argues that a "for"-adverbial modifies the R-time (frame time, in her terminology) in the prog sentences, but she requires the context to recover the R-time, whose length is determined by the "for"-phrase (p.181). If accepting Kearns' claim we would have to explain the presence of the "for"-phrase when it appears with a frame adverbial in sentences such as "John slept for two hours yesterday". However, recall that when presenting some tests for Ak' identification I mentioned the fact that the "for"-test is not as reliable as the "in"-test. This might suggest that "for"-phrases could modify events too, but in a limited way (which is to be determined). This may explain examples such as (i) where "for a couple of minutes" is not interpreted to be modifying the prog situation (snoozing), but rather the event of walking, which is the R-time of the prog sentence. However, this is only a possible line of explanation which needs to be investigated further.

4. Comrie (pc) claims that the time adverbial does not have to be explicit, it can be understood, e.g. (10b) in answer to (i):

(i) What is John likely to be doing at 7 in the evening?

However, note that the time adverbial IS explicit, though in the question. I.e., The R-time "7 o'clock in the evening" of (10b) is recoverable from the (linguistic) context.

5. McCawley (1981) uses the iota operator to bound this moment as represented by his analysis (b) of sentence (a) (his: 11.3.10):

a) When Tom entered Agnes's office, she was writing a letter.
b) (ιt: R_t(Tom enter Agnes's office)($\exists$I:tεI)R_I(Agnes write a letter)

R_t and R_I indicate that the expressions they are combined with are true at the indicated time.

6. a) I am ignoring in this discussion the tense operator.
b) If the PROG is taken to be an operator applied to a predicate, the semantic presentation would be slightly different (as illustrated in Hinrichs 1985):

John [PAST[PROG[DRAW A CIRCLE]]]

7. Dowty (1979) even uses this difference as a test for determining if a given predicate is reporting an event or a distributive situation.

8. I am ignoring the problem raised by Leech (1969), Smith (1983), Bach (1981), Goldsmith & Woisteschlaeger (1982) and others, who show that sometimes mental state verbs appear in prog, as in the following example taken from Smith (1983):

(i) I'm hating zoology class.

The analyses given for such sentences usually indicate a temporary component of the meaning of the state. I discussed the shortcoming of this line of analysis in section 3.1 above.

9. Note that when it functions as a nominal, the *qotel* form can appear with mental verbs too, as in this particular example. This behavior is also common to the *qotel* in Hebrew and the '-ing' form in English; compare the example from BH with the English phrase "a loving husband". But, as noted above, there is also a small number of examples where the *qotel* appears in predicative clauses, too. Consider the following examples:

(i) ... ***yhwh hu: yo;de;ₐʕa*** *wyiśra:ʔe;l hu: ye;da:ʕ...*
God he QOT:know:SG:MASC and-Israel he YIQ:know:3SG:MASC
'The Lord, he knows, and Israel must know...' (Jos. 22:22)

(ii) *wayyeʔehab yisha:q ʔet ʕe;śa:w ki: sayid*
WAYY:love:3SG:MASC Isaac ACC Esau because hunt
bp̄i:w ***wribqa: ʔo;hebet ʔet yaʕaqo;b***
in-mouth-his and-Rebecca QOT:love:SG:FEM ACC Jacob
'Isaac favoured Esau because he kept him supplied with venison, **but Rebecca favoured Jacob.**' (Gen. 25:28)

In (i) the verb 'know' appears in *qotel* and in (ii) the verb 'love'. Note that (ii) has another non-regular use of the verb — the first occurrence of 'love' appears in *wayyiqtol* — *wayyeʔehab* — although it does not denote an inchoative situation, which suggests that this verse is exceptional.

10. Note that there are two lexicals *ʔaz*, one of which means 'then' and appears only in clauses denoting successive situations.

11. Kogut (1986) claims that due to *(w)hinne*; the verb of seeing is understood as indicating perception. This suggestion seems to be inadequate, as the inchoative meaning is acquired by 'see' through its form — *wayyiqtol* — see discussion in chapter 2 above.

Chapter 4

Modality

One of the puzzles of the BH aspect system is that seemingly unrelated functions such as future and past generic have the same form — *yiqtol* or *wqatal* (which are distinguished in the SEQ parameter, as discussed in Chapter 2). The solution to the "riddle" lies in the fact that these and other functions, such as conditionals, habituals, etc., are all semantically related. It will be shown that they indicate some modality. Seeing this requires an examination of some major findings of modal semantics.[1] In its traditional analysis, modality has to do with the notions of **necessity** and **possibility**. I will, therefore, start my discussion with these two notions and with the related ideas of **possible worlds** and **branching time**. Then I will analyze the different kinds of modality and the temporal relations holding between modal statements. In the second part of this chapter I will analyze the modal forms in BH.

4.1 Necessity and Possibility

Logicians distinguish between propositions asserting that they **happen** to be true as (1) below (contingent sentences), propositions which are necessarily true as in (2), and propositions which express possibility as in (3):

(1) John went to the beach.

(2) a) A bachelor is an unmarried man.
b) No one can move faster than light.
c) If a man is in Rhodes, he is not in Athens.
d) John must go to the beach.
e) Fritz must be taken to the vet.

(3) a) This fragile glass might break if it falls down.
b) John may go to the beach.
c) John is allowed to go to the beach.

The sentences in (2a-e) illustrate different kinds of necessity. (2a) is a famous example of a logical (also called "alethic") necessity; (2b), taken from Hugh & Creswell (1968), is claimed to be necessary by what we **know** about the laws of physics; (2c), taken from Heim (1982) is necessarily true by what we **know** about the geographical facts of our world. Since the necessity in (2b-c) is knowledge-based it is usually labelled **epistemic**. (2d) has two readings: It can either be interpreted as "from what we know we state that it is necessary that John goes to the beach", i.e., as an epistemic necessity, or as "John is obliged to go", which is usually labelled **deontic** necessity. (2e), taken from Heim (1982), is known as **moral** necessity. Similarly, we find different kinds of possibility.[2] (3a), e.g., demonstrates an epistemic possibility, (3b) is ambiguous between epistemic and deontic modality and (3c) is clearly a deontic modality. The sentences in (2a-e), therefore, can be paraphrased as "it is necessary that A" and the sentences in (3a-c) as "it is possible that A", where A is the proposition which is claimed to be necessary (or possible). Logicians see "it is necessary that" and "it is possible that" as modal operators on propositions.[3] Analyses of these two operators in modal logic, especially since the influential work of Kripke (1959), interpret them as quantifications over possible worlds. A necessary proposition is analyzed as being true in every possible world, and a possibly true proposition is true in some possible worlds. However, the notion of possible worlds raises many ontological difficulties. Kripke (1972) provides a comprehensive explanation for this notion. He states that a possible world is not a far-fetched world, lying in some far star, but can be regarded as a possible state or history of the (actual) world. However, McCawley (1981), Lewis (1973), Heim (1982), Kratzer (1981b) and others, claim that when evaluating a necessary or possible proposition it makes more sense to relate not to every possible world, but only to those which resemble our world.[4] This relation among worlds is called **accessibility**, and worlds that resemble each other are called accessible worlds. The worlds that resemble the actual world, then, are said to be accessible to the actual world, and a necessarily true proposition is true in every world accessible to the actual world. However simple it might seem, the notion of accessibility has raised many difficulties in modal logic, as it requires the definition of resemblance amongst worlds, which is problematic.

(See Hugh & Creswell 1968 and the more recent linguistic studies of Kratzer 1981b and Heim 1982 for the possible interpretations of this notion.) Another related problem is the principle of cross-world identity which requires individuals to be the "same" in all the worlds that are accessible to each other, e.g., sentence (2d) (John must go to the beach) involves the individual named John, who should be the same person across all the worlds in which he goes to the beach. However, as pointed out in the literature, e.g., by McCawley (1981), it is not clear how we can make sure that all the Johns are the same individual, even if we have evidence that they share the same properties. Of all the attempts to solve the problem, semanticists seem to accept the one suggested by Scott (1970) (see, e.g., Dowty, Wall & Peters 1981). However, I will not examine the problems of accessibility and cross-world identity any further, since they do not arise in the framework adopted in this work. Although many of the arguments presented in this chapter have been developed from works done within the framework of possible-worlds semantics, the framework adopted here is that of the tense logicians who assume the notions of **branching time** and **possible futures** introduced by Kripke (1958 — as summarized in Prior 1967 — Prior does not mention the reference), adopted by the tense logicians of the time and later also by Thomason (1970), McCawley (1981), Dowty (1979) and others. In this approach, time is considered as non-linear, branching towards the future, where the different branches are thought of as alternative futures. Thomason makes it clear that for any given time, regardless of its relation with the speech time, there may not be merely a single future course of time, but multiple alternative possible futures. That is, from *every* index of time t_i — be it the time of speech t_0 or any other point preceding or following t_0 — the time branches to the "right", as illustrated in the following diagram:[5]

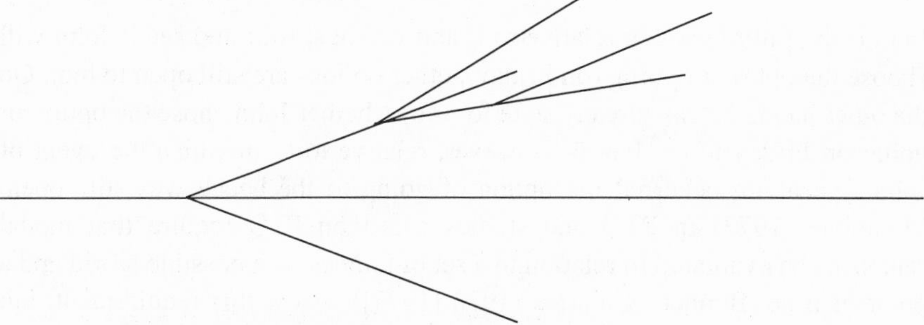

Figure 4.1. Time Branching

The idea of allowing time to branch from every point-of-time, including the times preceding the time-of-speech t_0 might seem problematic, as we conceive only the "real" future to be open, while the past is not, for we already know which course of events has been taken place. (Cf. Tedeschi 1981 who allows time to branch only in time following the S-time.) However, this is known only post-factum, just as we know at t_2 which of the possible futures branching from t_1 had turned out to be the actual one. Since we are talking of possible futures in the past, too, the term itself might be confusing. In order to avoid confusion between future time and future tense on the one hand, and possible future on the other hand, it is better to use a less confusing term: **branching options.** (McCawley uses the term **time branches**, which I will use as an alternative term. I will also retain the term **possible futures** when the branches relate to future time). To get an intuitive sense of the notion, let me draw an example. Suppose John had finished school at some point t_{-2} (preceding t_0 of my utterance). He then had different options branching from t_{-2}: to go on holiday, to make some money, or to visit his parents. At t_{-2} all three options were still open, but only one, naturally, was realized — John chose to have a holiday. At t_{-1} (which follows t_{-2} but also precedes t_0) John faced other options, which were open to him as a result of his decision (a different decision would open different options): to go abroad, to join his friends in the country, to go to the beach or to stay home and rest. John chose to go abroad and now, at t_0 he has to choose between the following options: Spain or France. Only in the future, after he decides, will we know which of the options were realized. This can be illustrated further by the following sentences:

(4) a) John will go to the beach (on Friday).
b) John said (on Sunday) that he would go to the beach (on Friday).

In (4a) the future is open relative to t_0 and we must wait and see if John will choose the option of going (on Friday), other options are still open to him. On the other hand, we can already state for (4b) whether John chose the option of going on Friday to the beach. However, relative to t_{-1} in which the event of John's speaking occurred the option of going to the beach was still open. Montague (1973) in PTQ and studies based on PTQ require that modal sentences be evaluated in relation to a set of indices — a possible world and a point of time. Bennett & Partee (1978 [1972]) accept this requirement, but replace points-of-time with intervals (for reasons explained in ch.2 above). I will elaborate on this issue in the following sections. For the purpose of the present discussion it is sufficient to state that, basically, this approach is adopted in this study, but adjusted to its framework. That is, modal propositions are evaluated according to their quantification over branching options and to the relation of their R-time with R_S. Moreover, it will be shown that modality also interacts with aspects such as sequentiality and inclusion.[6]

This introduction provides a basis for the analysis of the different kinds of modality, and their interaction with tense and aspect.

4.1.1 *Epistemic "must" and "may"*

This section deals with the epistemic modalities expressed in (2d) and (3b) repeated here as (5) and (6). (For the deontic readings of these sentences see section 4.1.6 below.) In this section I will not discuss alethic modalities and general physical truths, since they are, as I will show, special cases of generic statements, and as such will be discussed in section 4.1.5.

(5) John must go to the beach.

(6) John may go to the beach.

As mentioned in the previous discussion, sentences such as (5) and (6) are treated in this study similarly to traditional analyses. They are analyzed as involving universal and existential quantification over branching options (=time branches), as shown in the truth conditions (7a) and (8a) below, respectively, accompanied by the logical forms (7b) and (8b) :

(7) a) "John must go to the beach" is true iff in every branching option "John go to the beach" is true.

b) $\forall O(O \text{ is a possible option} \rightarrow E \subseteq O)$

(8) a) "John may go to the beach" is true iff there is a branching option in which "John go to the beach" is true.

b) $\exists\, O(O \text{ is a possible option } \& \ E \subseteq O)$

(7a) and (8a) formulate the truth conditions for (5) and (6) respectively; (7b) and (8b) are general formulas for **must** and **may** propositions respectively. (NOTE: (7b) and (8b), as well as all the formulas presented in this work, are not parts of some formal language, but only illustrative shortenings of the corresponding English formalization, in this case (7a) and (8a).)

R-time and R_S are not part of the formulas, because they are not relevant for the definition of modal sentences. R-time and R_S play a role in determining truth conditions of modal sentences only via their interaction with tense and aspect. Like in the case of the non-modal statements, the relations of R-time with E-time and R_S determine the aspect and the tense respectively, not the modal component. E.g., while in (5) and (6) the R-time includes the E-time, in sentences such as "John must be watching television," it is the other way around, and hence the difference in their truth conditions. (See a more detailed discussion in section 4.1.3 below.) Note also that while the sentences in (5) and (6) are in present tense, the events they are reporting are understood to take place in the future. This, I claim, is because in modalities there are two different situations the speakers refer to. One situation is, indeed, the (modal) event of John's going to the beach. The other situation is the non-modal state of "being necessary/ possible A". The intuition that this is a state is given a formal analysis in Verkuyl (1993). Recall that according to Verkuyl if a sentence has an expression of the kind [-SQA], i.e., an NP which does not specify quantity, it will be distributive (durative in Verkuyl's terms). Thus while "John went to the beach" is non-distributive (terminative, non-durative in Verkuyl's terms), "John went to beaches" is durative because it has the bare plural NP "beaches" whose quantity is not specified. (See more details in chapter 2.) Accordingly, Verkuyl (p. 272) claims that when a sentence refers to one world it is terminative, but when it refers to a set of possible worlds it is durative. Applying Verkuyl's analysis to **must** and **may** sentences which refer to sets of possible worlds, we can say that sentences (5) and (6) are distributives, whose E-times are included in R_S. (The states' R-times may also precede or follow R_S. See discussion in section 4.1.3 below.) It is easier to appreciate this point by the modal sentence (9):

(9) John wants to go to the beach.

This sentence, analysed as deontic modal (see section 4.1.6 below), expresses two situations: The modal event of going to the beach, and the non-modal state of wanting. Hence it also involves two R-times: R_S which is the R-time of the state of wanting and some R-time in the future in which John (might) go to the beach.

4.1.2 *Future Statements*

It is well known that future-tense sentences are encoded in many languages as a category of mood. (English and BH are good examples.) Lyons (1977) points to the fact that in Proto-Indo-European languages there was no future-tense, but only modal forms expressing future propositions, too. Moreover, he shows that future tense sentences are sometimes used to express non-factuals as hypotheses, wishes, etc. These facts reflect the debate among philosophers whether to treat sentences in future as declarative statements like sentences in past-tense, or as modalized propositions. Lyons (1977), for instance, claims that a future-tense sentence must be analyzed as intentional, as a subjectively modalized utterance expressing a prediction rather than as a statement. However, Lyons himself shows that a future sentence can be embedded in a factive predicate as in (10) below:

(10) He knows that it will rain.

Another approach is discussed in Prior (1967) as the "Peircian" theory. According to this theory, a future sentence is no different from a **must**-proposition. That is, [FUTURE A] should be true iff A is true in every branching option following the S-time. In the Peircian theory, Prior points out, there is no mere "will be" but only "necessarily will be". Thomason (1970) rejects this theory on the ground that it entails that formulas such as [FUTURE A] V ~[FUTURE A] will be invalid, although they are tautologous and intuitively valid. Thomason (1983) requires the future to be contingent — true in some possible options and false in others (as with **may** statements). However, McCawley (1981) claims that this analysis of the future is too weak and that when speakers utter a sentence such as

(11) John will go to the beach.

they assert that at some time in the **actual** future John will go. McCawley finds support for his intuition in the ways one applies words like *right*, *wrong*, *true* and *false* in talking about previous statements about the future, as shown in example (12) below (his: 11.3.4):

(12) George said in June that Mary would finish her thesis by January, but he was wrong.

As he claims, the speaker is not attributing to George the proposition that Mary would not finish her thesis by January in any possible future; e.g., if Mary actually finished her thesis by January but was in danger of not finishing it by then, one could not say (12) to indicate that George made a rash assertion: (12) is a remark about the correctness of a statement about the actual future. This analysis seems to treat the future in exactly the same way that past sentences are treated, which means that it does not account for its modal component nor for the fact that it is usually conceived as open, unlike the past. However, its intuitive validity is obvious. Moreover, McCawley accounts for the "openness" property of the future by allowing the situation to hold in some other possible futures in addition to the actual one. I adopt the intuitive claim of McCawley, that the statements about the future are statements about the actual future, but at the same time require them to involve quantification over possible futures to account for their modal character. This will be done by adding a restrictive term to the set of branching options. Let us discuss this one example. Consider the truth conditions (13a) and the formula (13b) I suggest for the future sentence (11):

(13) a) "John will go to the beach" is true iff in every branching future which turns out to be the Actual Option (AO) "John go to the beach" is true.

b) $\forall O(AO \longrightarrow E \subseteq O)$

The universal quantification, then, is restricted by AO (which is the actual future), but leaving open the possibility for the event of John's going to the beach to occur in some, all or none of the other futures. The definition of AO in (13a) as the branch time which *will turn out to be AO* ensures that the future be open. A similar notion of AO was found in Kamp & Reyle (1993:535) who claim that "when someone uses the future tense, he is typically referring to *whichever way* the future *will turn out*". (Emphasis is mine.)

In classical logic, (13b) would be analysed in a Russellian way which would not presuppose the existence of an actual future in which the event occurs or the state obtains. According to this approach, if, e.g., right after uttering (11) the world explodes and there will be no actual future, the sentence is still true, since the universal quantifier may range over empty sets. However, Verkuyl (1993:106-107) attributed to De Jong & Verkuyl (1985) argues that there are two uses of "all": (a) a lawlike use as in "All ravens are black"; and (b) a contingent use as in "All the seats are taken". The former use corresponds to the classical use of the universal quantifier, and it may be true even if there are no ravens, since it attributes an analytic property of ravens. The latter use presupposes the existence of the seats, and therefore, following Strawson (1950), the sentence "All seats are taken" will be neutral (will have no truth value) if there are no seats. It seems to me that in the case of the future speakers use the contingent "all", i.e., they presuppose the existence of the (actual) future, and therefore sentence (11) will be neutral if the world explodes right after uttering it. Note, however, that speakers presuppose the existence of the future in a different way than the past. While the past is already determined, the future, as said above, is still open and "to a significant degree undetermined." (Kamp & Reyle p. 534).

In addition to the restrictive term AO there is (at least) one more difference between the future and other modals. In section (4.1.1) above I showed that modals such as **may** and **must** sentences report non-modal states in addition to the modal situation. The future, in contrast, seems to report only the situation which is said to take place in the future, i.e., it does not report in addition a non-modal state. (Moens 1987 takes the position that it does, however, without discussing it.) The difference, it seems to me, is due to the fact that the future refers to *one* possible future — AO — unlike other modals which refer to a set of possible options.

The fact that future sentences (usually only?) determine that $R>R_S$ indicates (at least in English) that the future form is used also as a tense marker, in addition to its modal meaning. When it interacts with other modalities it functions merely as a tense, and hence does not presuppose an actual future. Consider the following example, analyzed in McCawley (1981, ex. 11.3.1):

(14) It is possible that Bill will finish his novel.

The truth conditions formalized for the future are incompatible with the truth conditions of **may**-statements, and since (14) has a future indication ("will") as well as a **may** phrase ("it is possible"), it, seemingly, violates our rules. McCawley shows that there is no such contradiction, and explains (14) as saying that there is a time branch in which 'Bill finish his novel' is true at some future point on that time branch. In other words, he takes 'will' in this sentence to indicate tense. This analysis seems to me to be correct, and the 'will' in English (and possibly in other tensed languages), seems to be ambiguous between tense and modality. When there is a modal term, in addition to the future 'will' as in (14), it disambiguates the future form to indicate tense, and vice versa: when the sentence is conjugated in another tense combined with 'will' it disambigutes 'will' to indicate modality only, as in (4b) reproduced here under (15):

(15) John said that he would go to the beach.

When, on the other hand, it is not combined with any other modal term or tense form it functions both as a modal to denote future and as a tense to determine that R_S precedes the R-time of the event. (But these rules of thumb require a more subtle analysis in tensed languages.)

Allowing 'will' to function as a pure tense marker will account for other modals combined with 'will', such as:

(16) a) John will have to go.
b) John will probably go.

Sentences (16a-b) will have the truth conditions and the formulas formulated in (7) and (8) respectively, but with the specification that the R_S precedes the R-time of the states of being necessary and being possible. Similarly, these formulations apply to sentences such as (17) below with the specification that $R<R_S$:

(17) a) John had to go to the beach (yesterday).
b) John could go to the beach.

Note that we interpret the event (of going to the beach) in (17a), e.g., as also preceding the time of speech. However, this is only an implicature, as shown by the following example:

(18) A: Why is he leaving?
B: He had to leave; His boss fired him and gave him a two week notice.

4.1.3 *Conditionals*

Recent semantic studies, mainly Kratzer (1981a,1981b), followed by Heim (1982), analyze conditionals as modal sentences. According to this view, an **if...then** sentence involves a modal expression — either explicitly as in (19) and (20) or implicitly as in (21) (the examples are taken from Heim 1982):

(19) If John enters this room, he **might** trip the switch.

(20) If John is in Athens, he is **necessarily** in Greece.

(21) If John enters this room he will trip the switch.

The modal expression in (19) corresponds to **may**-propositions and in (20) to **must**-propositions. In (21), it is argued by Kratzer and Heim, there is an invisible modal of necessity, i.e., (21) is equivalent to (20). The logical form suggested by Kratzer is, therefore, common to (19)-(21):

(22) if α...then modal β

where the **if**-clause functions as a restrictive term which limits the set of the accessible worlds in which the event of the **then**-clause occurs. Heim (1982), accepting this analysis, formulates the truth conditions for the conditionals according to the kind of modal they involve on the one hand, and according to the restrictive term on the other. Hence, (20) and (21) will have the same truth conditions, involving universal quantification, and (19) will differ from them both, involving existential quantification. But all three will involve restriction on the accessible worlds over which the quantification ranges. (23) below represents the truth conditions for sentences as (19), and (24) for sentences as (20) and (21), proposed in Heim (where the notion of branching options has replaced that of accessible worlds):

(23) If M specifies the modal relation of possibility, then
"If S_1 then M+S_2" is true iff there is a branching option in which S_1 is true and S_2 is true.

(24) If M specifies the modal relation of necessity, then
"If S_1 then M+S_2" is true iff in every branching option in which S_1 is true, S_2 is also true.

Heim demonstrates the claim that sentences like (21) have an invisible necessity operator by applying the general truth conditions (24) to sentence (21):

(25) (21) is true iff for every branching option: if John enters this room in O', then John trips the switch in O'.

The formula for conditionals such as (25) will be as presented in (26), where (26a) is the specific formulation of (25) and (26b) is the general formula for such conditionals:

(26) a) ∀O(John enter the room in O → John switch the light in O)
b) $\forall O(E_1 \subseteq O \rightarrow E_2 \subseteq O)$

The relationship between the R-times of the events of the conditional and R_S is worth commenting on. Although it is more common that the R-times in conditionals follow R_S, it is not necessarily so. For example, the R-times of the (possible) events in (27a) below precede rather than follow R_S, and in (27b) the R-time shared by both events is identical to R_S:

(27) a) If John entered the room, he switched off the light.
b) If Mary is in the room, John is very happy.

Moreover, the different R-times in the conditionals may bear different relations with R_S. Consider:

(28) a) If John is swimming (now) he will be able to join the team (next week).
b) If John took swimming lessons, he is now participating in the competition.

In (28a), the R-time of the protosis is simultaneous with R_S while the R-time of the apodosis follows it; in (28b), the R-time of the protosis and the apodosis precede and are simultaneous with R_S, respectively.

The relations between the different R-times of the conditional may also vary. Although it is more usual to find conditionals with sequential relations, such as (26) (probably because the protosis is usually understood as the cause of the apodosis[7]), this is not a necessary condition. For example, in the following sentence the (possible) events of the conditional share the same R-time:

(29) If John leaves the party, Mary will leave with him.

This reflects a more general phenomenon of temporal relations holding in modal clauses. As said in chapters (1) and (2) and in section 4.1.1 above, two events in the future time or in **may**-statements may be sequential or simultaneous as in (30) and (31) respectively:

(30) a) Mary will buy a newspaper and (then) go to the beach.
b) Mary might buy a newspaper and go to the beach.

(31) a) John will sing while Mary dances.
b) John might sing and dance (at the same time).

As mentioned in section 4.1.1 above, the definitions of the temporal relations holding in modal clauses will be the same as in non-modal ones, i.e., as they are defined in chapters (2), (3) and (5). However, in modal clauses we must assume, in such cases, that the situations are contained in the same branching option(s). If they are not (or are not necessarily) included in the same option(s), many times we cannot assert a temporal relation between them, as in the following examples:

(32) a) John might go to Spain or to France (this summer).
b) John might go to Spain, but Mary will definitely go to Egypt.

In (32a) the interpretation imposed is that the first conjunct is in a different possible option than the second (assuming that John cannot be in two different places exactly at the same time). (32b) is ambiguous: John's going to Spain may be realized in the future, so that (at least) in the actual future the two situations take place, but it may also be not realized, so Mary's situation may be in the actual future without John's. Therefore, (32a) clearly indicates that the R-time of the two options is identical ("this summer"), while in (32b) it is not determined whether the R-time of the first clause is identical to the R-time of the second, or the R-times differ, and John may go to Spain in the actual future before, after or at the same time that Mary goes to Egypt. (This is further evidence that R-time is not relevant for analyzing modals.)

Let us now discuss conditionals with a possibility modal term. Reconsider (19) repeated here as (33):

(33) If John enters this room he might trip the switch.

According to the truth conditions stipulated in (23), the logical form for (33) should be as follows:

(34) $\exists O(E_1 \subseteq O \ \& \ E_2 \subseteq O)$

However, (34) does not reflect the fact that the **if**-clause in the sentence is a restrictive term, and simply requires that both events (reported in the antecedent and the consequent) occur. But then (34) is the logical form of modalized conjunctions such as (35):

(35) John might enter the room and trip the switch.

which differs in its truth conditions from (33). (35) (and its formula 34) requires that there be at least one branching option in which the two events both occur. In contrast, (33) allows the set of the options in which John enters the room to be empty, which allows John: (a) not to enter the room and hence not to switch off the light; and (b) not to enter the room and still switch off the light. Intuitively, what a condition such as (33) expresses is that the antecedent delimits the set of branching options in which the situation of the consequent may occur, and the consequent, in turn, picks up only some of those options. This intuitive description should be given the truth conditions in (36a) formalized as (36b):

(36) a) If M specifies the modal relations of possibility, then "If S_1 then M+S_2" is true iff for every branching option O in which S_1 is true, there is a branching option O' in which S_2 is true.

b) $\forall O(E_1 \subseteq O) \rightarrow \exists O'(E_2 \subseteq O')$

(36) reflects the fact that there might be an option in which E_2 occurs but not E_1, but not vice versa, i.e., there is no possible option in which E_1 occurs but not E_2. For our example: John might trip the switch even if he does not enter the room, but if he enters the room he will necessarily trip the switch (however, not necessarily in the same time branch).

4.1.4 *Counterfactuals*

Counterfactuals fall into several kinds:

(37) a) John should have gone to Jerusalem.
b) John could have been in Paris.

(38) a) If you had gone to Jerusalem you would have seen Mary.
b) If John had gone to Jerusalem he could have seen Mary.

In (37) there are "simple" counterfactuals and in (38) the sentences express counterfactual conditionals. Most of the works on counterfactuals, e.g., Lewis (1973) and Kratzer (1981c) deal only with conditionals. However, both kinds involve either a necessity term, as in the 'a' sentences or a possibility term as in the 'b's, which suggests that "simple" counterfactuals, too, should be treated as modalities. However, although they are treated as modalities in the literature, the counterfactuals do not behave in the same way as other modalities. They are expressed by past tenses, usually by the past perfect, as in English, Greek and Latin (see Palmer 1986), and creole languages (Bickerton 1976). In BḢ, too, as will be illustrated in section 4.2.2 and chapter 5 below, counterfactuals are not expressed by the modal forms, but by the (perfect) non-modal *qatal*. This peculiar phenomenon was pointed out by Palmer (1986) and others with no suggested solution. Since I, too, could not find a satisfactory explanation for this peculiarity I will leave the subject open for future investigation.

4.1.5 *Generics and Habituals*

Linguists do not usually distinguish between generic and habitual statements, and analyze generic sentences such as (39) and habitual sentences such as (40) below in the same way (Most of the examples are taken from Dahl 1975):

(39) a) Beavers build dams.
b) A dog has four legs.
c) Oil floats on water.
d) Two and two are four.
e) A dog might hate its master.

(40) a) John smokes.
b) John goes to the beach (every Friday).
c) The sun rises in the east.
d) John occasionally visits his uncle.

However, as Dahl (1975) shows, the sentences in (39) should be analyzed differently from those in (40). Although they all involve quantification over branching options, they differ in many respects. Firstly, we will see that the set of branching options over which the quantifier ranges is restricted in the case of the habituals to the actual option (as in the case of future statements), while in the case of the generics it is not restricted at all. Secondly, as we can see intuitively, habituals involve a quantification over intervals of time such as "every Friday" (in addition to the quantification over options), while generics must involve quantification over individuals. In order to demonstrate the claims more formally I first need to analyze each of the groups. Let me begin with generic statements.

McCawley (1981) accepts Carlson 1980 [1977])'s and Dahl (1975)'s claim that sentences such as (39) express properties. For example, (39a) is interpreted as saying that a property of beavers is to build dams. It is easy to see how Dahl (1975) and Heim (1982) conclude from such an observation that generic sentences involve a modal operator of necessity, and hence universal quantification over branching options. For example, (39a) will be analyzed as: for every branching option beavers build dams. This analysis seems to be identical to the interpretation of **must**-propositions, which suggests that generics are to be regarded in the same way as **must** propositions. However, they differ greatly in the quantification over the individuals in question. A generic sentence refers to species, groups of individuals, and hence the indefinite noun phrases in generic sentences, while a **must** proposition can refer to certain, definite individuals, and hence does not necessarily involve quantification over noun phrases. Compare the paraphrase (41a) for (39a) to (41b):

(41) a) Beavers (a beaver) must build (a) dam(s)
b) Our beaver must build (a) dam(s)

Both sentences in (41) assert that the building of a dam occurs in every branching option, but in (41a) the building is done by all beavers, and in (41b) by one particular beaver (and by conversational rules we infer that in 41a, unlike 41b, there are many events of buildings). Moreover, (41a) does not require beavers to exist, i.e., if, say, ten thousand years from now beavers will vanish, (41a) will be still true (but see the remarks at the end of this discussion). This well known fact is reflected in the logical forms given to generic sentences, which have the form of an implication. If we add to this classical formulation the requirement of quantification over branching options, the logical form for (39a) will simply be:

(42) ∀O ∀ x(possible-option O and beaver x) → (x build dams in O)

A similar analysis is given in Heim (1982). She claims that sentences with an indefinite NP are, sometimes, to be interpreted as conditionals, e.g., a sentence such as (43a) can be paraphrased as (43b):

(43) a) A cat that has been exposed to 2,4-D goes blind.
b) If a cat has been exposed to 2,4-D, it goes blind.

However, it might be argued, that while sentences with indefinite NPs are, indeed, to be regarded as generics, not every generic has to involve an indefinite NP. (Note also that not every indefinite NP is generic, as in "a student walked in".) Consider the following sentences:

(44) John speaks Arabic.

(45) This car goes twenty miles per an hour.

The sentence in (44) is ambiguous: it can be interpreted either as expressing how John communicates (always or sometimes) with people, or as asserting that John has the property of being able to speak Arabic (but never has the chance to perform his potentiality). The first interpretation is the habitual reading which will be discussed later. The second interpretation is usually said (e.g., by Dahl 1975) to be a generic statement about John. But it seems to me that we need to distinguish between sentences such as (44) and the generic sentences in (39). (44) may be paraphrased by a **may** sentence:

(46) John can speak Arabic.

and may be also analyzed as such. This is the way Kratzer (1981a) analyzes the sentence in (45). She gives paraphrase (47) for this sentence, which involves an explicit modal term of a **may** proposition:

(47) This car can go twenty miles per an hour.

The noun phrase "this car" in (45) and (47), however, may also be interpreted as an indefinite NP (this make of car), and then has the generic reading. This suggests that generics can, sometimes, involve existential quantification over possible options. The logical analysis for the generic reading of (45) will then be:

(48) $\forall x(\text{car } x) \rightarrow \exists O(\text{possible-option } O \;\&\; x \text{ go 20 miles per an hour in } O)$

Before leaving the subject of generics there are two important remarks to be made. First, I accept the approach adopted by Dahl (1975), Heim (1982) and others to one of the most discussed problems, namely the quantifier ranging over individuals in generic sentences. They claim that generics such as (39b) (a dog has four legs) will be true and the quantifier ranging over the NP "dog" should be universal, even if there are some freak dogs with three legs only. (For objections to this approach see Carlson 1980 [1977] who points out its shortcomings and suggests a different analysis.) Another issue is the R-time of generic situations. Edit Doron (personal communication) argues that if, for example, beavers stop building dams in some future time, formula (42) is false. But if she is right, then we cannot say that building dams is a property of beavers. In other words, the analysis depends on our definition of beavers. If beavers will not be called beavers anymore if they stop building dams (or dogs will stop being called dogs if in the course of evolution they start walking on two legs only, etc.), then (42) is correct. However, if we still call them beavers even after they stop building dams, then we should add a condition which determines the R-time in which this behavior of the beavers holds. For example, if beavers build dams only in this century, then we should add the condition that the R-time of the situation is 'this century'.

The analysis of habituals seems to be more complicated than that of generics. I will start with the simplest case. Consider first the following habitual sentence:

(49) John goes to the beach every Friday.

At first sight it is not easy to see the modal operator in habituals such as (49), but if we think of their logical entailments we see that they involve a necessity modal term:

(50) John goes to the beach every Friday. → a) John will go on Friday.
→ b) John went on Friday.

The entailments show that habituals should be true in our actual option, as the analysis of the future tense involves restriction to the actual future (see section 4.1.2 above) and the past tense sentence asserts something about the actual option preceding the time of speech. (Recall that by "branching option" I refer not only to a possible course of events that may take place after the speech time, but also to courses of events preceding it, including the actual one.) (50) does not entail anything about branching options other than the actual realized one. Hence, we can conclude that, like the case of future, habitual statements involve restriction to the actual option. The difference between them is that habituals also have undelimited quantification over intervals of time. Future statements may have quantification over intervals, but only in a way that restricts the E-time. Compare the quantification of (50) to the following:

(51) John will go three times to the theater.

In (51) there is a quantifier (three) determining the number of the intervals in which John will, in the future, go to the theater, but this quantifier functions as a delimiter (see chapter 2 for this notion and its behavior). The quantifier "every Friday" in (50), on the other hand, does not delimit the situation of John's going to the beach. (A sentence such as "John will go to the beach every Friday" is also a habitual, but in future time). Verkuyl (1993:326) shows that this affects habituals to have the distributive property. The distributive characteristic of habituals was observed by other linguists, too. Dowty (1986), Moens (1987) and Smith (1991) claim that habituals report states, Kearns (1991) argues that they are activities, and Depraetere (1995) characterizes them as unbounded-atelic situations. This explains the time expressions appearing in the following examples:

(52) a) Last year John used to go to the beach (every Friday).
b) This year John goes to the beach (every Friday).
c) Next year John will go to the beach (every Friday).

It is not plausible to interpret the adverbs "last year", "this year" and "next year" in (52a-c) respectively as modifying the R-times of each of the events of John's going to the beach, but as modifying the series of those events. Such series are not bound, and hence the situation they compose is distributive. Dowty (1986) shows that the definition of states applies to habituals. For example, in (52a) it is true in every subinterval of last year that "John goes to the beach every Friday". Note, furthermore, that (52a) does not entail that John did not go to the beach (every Friday) two years ago or that he does not still have that habit. The stative nature of habituals is their non-modal part, like any other modal. However, they express what kind of habit the individual is involved in, e.g., going to the beach every Friday. (Note that the duality of expressing two kinds of situations provides further evidence for the modal nature of habituals.) The question arising now is of the nature of the repeated event "go to the beach" and of the quantified adverb "every Friday". The first intuitive feeling is that the adverb "every Friday" is the R-time in which each of the events is included. (This seems to be the line of analysis taken by Kamp & Reyle 1993:635-6, although they use the notion of "location time" instead.) However, in Hatav (1993) I argue that since it is a quantified expression, "every Friday" cannot serve as a referential term. It is widely acknowledged that quantified noun phrases such as "every man" are not referential expressions, as opposed to "the man" (and under certain circumstances to "a man"). By analogy, a quantified NP indicating time such as "every Friday" cannot be referential, as opposed to referential expressions such as "last Friday", "The Friday before Christmas (of this year)", etc. This explains the difference in grammaticality between (53a) and (53b) below:

(53) a) John was building his house last winter.
b) *John was building his house every winter.

In chapter (3) we saw that the progressive demands an explicit R-time to be included in the situation time. (53a) provides such an R, "last winter", and hence it is grammatical. The only time expression appearing in (53b), on the other hand, is quantified, and therefore it cannot serve as an R-time for the sentence, hence the ungrammaticality. So if it is not an R-time, what is "every Friday"? Hornstein (1977) and others claim that adverbs and other time expressions may modify either the R-time of the sentence or the E-time. Since they cannot serve as R-times, quantified time expressions, I argue, may modify only the E-time. However, recall that events such as "go to the beach" are to be included in some R-time, and since "last year" in (52a) serves as the R-time of the whole series of the events (i.e., of the habitual state), it cannot serve also as the R-time of each of the occurrences of John's going to the beach. A related problem is that habituals, like other modals, may express temporal relations between the quantified events, i.e., aspects, such as sequentiality, inclusion and perfect, as in the following example (mentioned in ch. 1, too):

(54) John goes to the beach (every Friday), buys a bunch of newspapers, reads for a while and goes back home (to rest and take a shower).

Since sequences such as (54) should be represented in terms of R-times, and since R-times cannot be quantified, how would (54) be represented? The solution to both problems may be found in Verkuyl (1993). First recall that Verkuyl perceives predicates expressing events in terms of odometer, providing natural numbers. It is easy to see how the quantified expressions in habitual sentences are thought of in terms of natural (cardinal) numbers. This finds support in the fact that if we do not perceive a quantified expression in terms of natural numbers it does not trigger the habitual-effect, as shown in the following example:

(55) The weather in this town is always pleasant.

Now recall that Verkuyl takes the underlined interval of real time to be the relevant factor for tense and aspect. To account for the tense (and the aspect) of a habitual sentence Verkuyl suggests that tense operates on each of the *actual* occurrences of the habitual. This analysis accounts first for the eventive reading of the habit. In analyzing the habitual sentence "Judith ate (=used to eat) three sandwiches (at breakfast)" (ex. 294 on p. 325) Verkuyl says that the presence of the delimiting term (three sandwiches) does not trigger the effect of specified quantity for the whole sentence (which is distributive), but "gives an interpretation in which *each actualization* of an event in which Judith ate three sandwiches would be terminative" (p. 326; emphasis is mine). In other words, the eventive interpretation of "go to the beach", is due not to the potential but to the *actual* event and its R-time. This naturally accounts also for sequentiality and other aspectual relations which require (actual) R-times for their interpretation. The fact that once a habitual is actualized it is no longer habitual shows the irrelevance of aspect and hence R-time in characterizing habituals (like other modals). Hence we state the truth conditions for (50) as follows:

(56) a) "John goes to the beach every Friday" is true iff for every possible option which turns out to be the actual option AO, and for every Friday included in AO "John goes to the beach" is true.

b) $\forall O\ \forall E(AO\ \&\ \text{Friday}\ E) \rightarrow (E \subseteq O)$

Hornstein does not provide an analysis to account for the relation of the adverb modifying E-time and E-time itself. The truth conditions in (56a) and the general formula in (56b) express (my) intuitive understanding only. I would like here also to note that, like in the case of generics, I follow the approach which argues that even if John failed to go to the beach one Friday (for being sick or out of town), sentence (50) is still true.

The quantified E-time in a habitual situation is not always explicit as in the case of example (50). Consider the following example:

(57) John smokes/drinks.

All the analyses given to sentences such as (57) argue that they have an invisible adverb of quantification (see, e.g., Smith 1978, Kasher & Manor 1980 and others). In other words, when speakers utter (57) they mean that John smokes (or drinks) at certain times. The question is what do we mean by "certain"? Kasher & Manor (1980) show that the answer is not unambiguous, and depends on pragmatic considerations. For example, if John is in a society where they drink wine every meal, then John will not be considered a drinker if he drinks (only) at every meal. However, if John's society forbids drinking, then (57) will be appropriate even if John drinks only once a year for a special occasion. For a further demonstration, Kasher & Manor compare the following two sentences:

(58) a) Russell serves his wife.

b) Russell serves his country.

The stretches of time between which Russel serves his wife should be shorter than those of Russel serving his country. In other words, the relevant interval for habituals without an explicit frequency adverbial can be only determined contextually, and therefore cannot be spelled out in the logical form. The formula in (59) will be the closest way to describe in general sentences such as (58):

(59) $\forall O\ \forall E(AO\ \&\ \text{relevant } E) \rightarrow (E \subseteq O)$

The "regular" habituals usually involve universal quantification over intervals of times, but there are uses of habituals with existential quantification, as in the following examples:

(60) a) Caesar seldom awoke before dawn. (Lewis 1975)
b) John visits his uncle occasionally.
c) Mary goes sometimes (on some Fridays) to the beach.
d) Rachel is often/seldom in Jerusalem.

Intuitively, what the sentences in (60) assert is that there are some intervals (at least) in the actual option in which Ceasar gets up at dawn, John visits his uncle, etc. The number of the intervals is not determined and may be determined by pragmatic considerations, but in any case it must be bigger than one. This, however, is a more general problem of NP quantification (see, e.g., Barwise & Cooper 1981). The best we can do, then, is to assert that $E > 1$, bearing in mind that it is not sufficient. The formulation of the intuition would be:

(61) $\exists O\ \exists E(AO\ \&\ \text{relevant } E,\ E > 1\ \&\ E \subseteq O)$

The formula in (61) is similar to the formula of **may**-propositions, differing from it in the requirement that at least one of the branching options be the actual realized one.

Note that there are sentences which are generics **and** habituals, as the sentences in (62) below:

(62) a) The skin of the snake sheds several times a year.
b) Bears hibernate in cold winters.

The sentences in (62) involve universal quantification over branching options and over individuals (snakes and bears respectively), which show their generic characterization, and, in addition, also involve universal quantification over intervals of time (several times every year and every cold winter respectively), which makes them habituals.

4.1.6 *Deontic Modality*

Deontic modality deals with obligation and permission, as in the sentences (63a) and (63b) respectively:[8]

(63) a) John is obliged to go to the beach.
b) John is permitted to go to the beach.

As such, deontic modality deals with speech acts such as commands, requests and the like, called in the literature **directives** (see, e.g., Lyons 1977). It will be shown that these speech acts share the same properties with other speech acts such as wishes, hopes, warnings etc. (as far as the semantics of modality is concerned). Like alethic and epistemic modality, deontic modals involve necessity or possibility operators. (63a) is a demonstration of necessity and (63b) of possibility. Thus, sentences such as (63) have usually been analyzed within the framework of possible worlds semantics. However, it has been realized that the notion of possible worlds alone is not sufficient to account for deontic modals. Let me demonstrate this claim by some examples analyzed in Heim (1982):

(64) a) If a cat has been exposed to 2,4-D, he must be taken to the vet.
b) Felix must be taken to the vet.

Sentences such as (64a) express normative, law-like statements which, as claimed by Dahl (1975) and others, may be broken. Sentences such as (64b) express obligations which may not be obeyed. In other words, the usual analysis of the necessity modal term is not adequate for obligations, since the situations denoted by them need not obtain in every possible world, or even in every world accessible to ours. Therefore, Montague in *Pragmatics* (1974: 110) adds an extra condition to deontic modalities. He adds the notion of "better (or preferable) worlds". Then sentences such as (64) are true in a world when the cat is taken to the vet in all the better worlds accessible from that world. Kratzer (1981a), followed by Heim (1982), uses the notion of **ideal worlds** as a restriction on the set of possible worlds and adds the relation of **ordering source** which defines a relation of relative closeness to an ideal world. The ideal world of (64) is the world in which pets are treated properly, and the truth conditions stipulated for (64b) are as follows (it is a simplification of Heim 1982:177):

(65) (64b) is true iff in all possible worlds accessible to our actual world and which are the closest to the ideal world (in which pets are treated properly) Felix is taken to the vet.

The question now arises: how do we account for "ideal worlds" in the framework of branching options? It seems to me that we can adopt the idea by restricting the set of branching options, in the case of deontic modals, where the defined ideal world serves as a restrictive term. I suggest doing that by using the same means as in the case of conditionals, futurates and habituals. This can be done by reducing deontic modal statements to conditionals, whose **if** clauses will define the "ideal options". For example, (64b) will be paraphrased as follows:

(66) If pets are treated properly then Felix will be taken to the vet.

We now have a conditional sentence whose logical form is:

(67) $\forall$O(pets be treated properly in O $\rightarrow$ Felix be taken to the vet in O)

It seems that, the "ordering source" or the "ideal world" defined in the antecedent of the implication is due to pragmatic considerations. Kratzer lists examples of such sources: the law, what my father provides in his last will, what is good, etc. The same means of analysis will be adopted for all the directives (requests, demands, etc.) and for the other deontics, e.g., hopes, wishes and the like. Let us look at one more example:

(68) John hopes that Mary will visit him.

The logical form for (68) will be:

(69) $\forall$O(J's hopes are fulfilled in O $\rightarrow$ M visits J in O)

4.1.7 *Negation and Interrogatives*

Dowty (1986), Moens (1987), Verkuyl (1993) and others show that negative assertions are distributives (see ch. 5 below for a discussion). This should block negative assertions from appearing in sequence, unless modified by a delimiter like a "for"-phrase. However, consider the following example:

(70) John fell from the Empire-State building and/but did not get killed.

We have the feeling that the "non"-event in the second conjunct of (70) is in sequence with the event in the first. I suggested explaining this feeling as compatible with some other possible option in which the falling causes the death, since this is what we expect. Dorith Ben-Shalom suggested to me that this expectation is manifested in the contradiction implicated in (70), which can have an explicit contradiction word such as 'but'. That is, the "sequentiality" in (70) is inferred not from the negative component, but from the contradiction.[9] The thesis that there might be a contradiction inference in negative assertions finds support in Verkuyl (1993). Consider two of his examples (71a) and (71b) below (his: 331 and 339 respectively):

(71) a) Two girls did not eat five sandwiches
b) Not Judith ate three sandwiches

These and other cases, claims Verkuyl, should be explained in terms of contrastivity, and their predicates should be corrected as follows:

(71') a) ... but they ate FOUR sandwiches.
b) ... but Mary.

Interrogatives are usually regarded by linguists as directives. Palmer (1986) reports that there are languages in which the interrogative is part of the modal system. To analyze questions as modals we have to show how they involve quantification over branching options. This task is easy in the case of rhetorical questions. Consider:

(72) Would a cat/Mimi leave its/her kittens?!

The question in (72) can be paraphrased as saying that a cat (or Mimi) would never leave its kittens. In other words, it is only superficially a question (semantically speaking), and hence its formula should be of the indicative mood of the paraphrase:

(73) ~ ∃O(Mimi leave its kittens in O)

The data in Biblical Hebrew, as will be shown, support the claim that rhetorical questions are a kind of modals. As for "regular" questions the analysis is more problematic, as demonstrated by the fact that in BH they behave differently — their verb forms are due to the possible answer — if it is modal then the verb in the question will have a modal form, but if the possible answer is non-modal then the question will have a non-modal verb (see section 4.2.2 for illustration). Therefore I will not discuss interrogatives any further. (The interested reader may consult Lappin 1982 for a detailed discussion on the interrogative mood.)

4.2 Modality in Biblical Hebrew

The study of BH demonstrates that the unified analysis for modality in the previous sections is valid, for the same two forms *yiqtol* and *wqatal* function to denote each of the modals discussed above (except counterfactuals to which I will return in section 4.2.2). But although these two forms seem to be sufficient, Hebraists distinguish a group of modal forms which, it has been claimed, constitute a suppletive paradigm for directives:[10] The *short yiqtol* which is called the **jussive** (the Latin term for the mood of command) according to its function, the *long yiqtol* which is labelled **cohortative** (the Latin term for the mood of request) and the **imperative**. Another deontic modal form is the *waw* prefixed *wyiqtol*. It is reasonable, then, to refer to these forms by the general term **modal**. Furthermore, the forms *qatal* and *qotel* are also used in modal statements, **but** only under certain circumstances: the *qotel* is used in inclusive clauses and the *qatal* in perfect clauses and in counterfactuals. *Qatal* and *qotel* will be labelled **non-modal** forms, along with *wayyiqtol*.

The statistical counts in our sample show clearly that *yiqtol*, *wqatal* and the directives are indeed modal forms, while the other forms are not (see section 1.2 in chapter 1 for the description of the sample). Table (4.1) below summarizes the statistical findings, where the directives (including *wyiqtol*) are put in one row labelled 'DIR' (they will be detailed later). As usual, the row labelled '?' summarizes the questionable cases where the text itself cannot independently determine whether the clause in question is modal, but where the interpretation of modality is possible. To make the results non-controversial these were not included (but see FN 6 in chapter 1); that is, the calculated percentage in the row '+MOD' is based on the occurrences mentioned in the row labelled 'REST', which excludes the questionable cases.

Table 4.1. Modality in BH

	yiqtol	wqatal	DIR	qatal	qotel	wayyiqtol
TOTAL	N=788	N=396	N=483	N=1190	N=678	N=2445
?	N=33	N=9	N=0	N=29	N=48	N=7
	4%	2%	0%	2.4%	7%	0.3%
REST	N=755	N=387	N=483	N=1161	N=630	N=2438
+MOD	N=734	N=372	N=483	N=27	N=52	N=5
	97%	96%	100%	2.3%	7.7%	0.2%

In what follows I will discuss the findings presented in the table. In section 4.2.1 I will discuss the modal forms, and deal with the counterexamples in non-modal sentences, and in section 4.2.2 I will deal with the non-modal forms *qotel* and *qatal* in modal clauses. There is also a (very) small number of *wayyiqtol* verbs in modal clauses. They, too, will be dealt with in section 4.2.2.

4.2.1 *The Modal Forms*

Since the general forms used to denote modality are *yiqtol* and the sequential *wqatal*, I will begin my discussion with these two.

Until the nineteenth century scholars regarded *yiqtol* and *wqatal* as indicating future tense statements (while *wayyiqtol* and *qatal* expressed past time). But although this observation is partially correct it does not reflect the whole picture, since these forms also function to indicate, *inter alia*, generics, habituals and other modals, and specifically, in these cases it can report past events. To account for the use of the generics, some scholars regard them as denoting (extended?) present (e.g., Lee 1827) or present-future (e.g., the *waw* inductive theory and Bauer 1910). But neither of the approaches can explain habituals and other modal uses in the past. The aspect-oriented approach in the nineteenth century, e.g., Ewald (1827) and Driver (1874) was developed to account for this problem too. The theories in this approach analyze the two forms as indicating imperfective or incomplete situations. As shown in chapter (1) above, these theories suffer from many difficulties, but they do capture the intuition that the forms under discussion cannot be explained only as indicating future. The intuitions of both approaches can be explained if we observe that the two forms denote modal statements. The diversity in intuitions is a result of the puzzling fact that *yiqtol* and *wqatal* are used in all kinds of modalities (except counterfactuals which are denoted by *qatal*). Since in the previous sections I have already discussed the semantics of the different modals, it will suffice here merely to illustrate them through the two forms.

The tense-oriented theories, as mentioned above, observed that the forms *yiqtol* and *wqatal* appear in **future** clauses. Consider one example:

(74) *bˤo:d̲* *šlo;šet̲* *ya:mi:m* *yiśśa:* *p̄arˤo;* *ˀet̲*
in-more three:MASC:of days YIQ:lift:3SG:MASC Pharaoh ACC
ro;šek̲a: *wahᵃši:b̲k̲a:* *ˤal*
head-yours:SG:MASC WQAT:restore:3SG:MASC-you:SG:MASC on
kannek̲a: *wna:t̲ata* *k̲o:s* *parˤo:* *bya:d̲o:...*
post-yours:SG:MASC WQAT:give:2SG:MASC glass Pharaoh in-hand-his
'Within three days Pharaoh will raise you and restore you to your post, and then you will put the cup into Pharaoh's hand...' (Gen. 40:13)

The context makes it clear that the clauses in (74) report future situations (note also the futurate adverbial 'within three days'). Hence, the verb in the first clause is in *yiqtol* and the two verbs in the following clauses are in the sequence form *wqatal*. This example illustrates the use of the forms in clauses which denote future situations in relation to the S-time (or more precise, to R_S). But the two forms may also report future situations relative to other points of time. Consider the following examples:

(75) a) *wayyiṣer* *yhwh* *ˀᵉlo;hi:m* *min* *ha:ˀᵃd̲a:ma:* *kol*
WAYY:create:3SG:MASC God God from the-earth all:of
ḥayyat̲ *haśśa:d̲e* *wˀe;t̲* *kol* *ˤo:p̄* *hašša:mayim*
animal:of the-field and-ACC all:of bird:of the-sky
wayya:b̲e; *ˀel* *ha:ˀa:d̲a:m* *lirˀo:t̲* ***ma***
WAYY:bring:3SG:MASC to the-man to-INF:see what
yyiqwra:ˀ ***lo:***
YIQ:call:3SG:MASC to-him
'God formed out of the ground all the wild animals and all the birds of heaven, and brought them to the man to see **what he would call them**.' (Gen. 2:19)

b) *wˀᵉliša:ˤ* *ḥa:la:* *ˀet̲* *ḥolyo:*
and-Elisha QAT:sicken:3SG:MASC ACC sickness-his
ˀᵃšer ***ya:mu:t̲*** ***bo:***
that YIQ:die:3SG:MASC in-him
'Elisha fell ill with an illness of which **he would die**.' (Kings II 13:14)

In both examples the clauses with the *yiqtol* verbs report situations which are in the future in respect to some point in the past. In (75a), the event of Adam's calling the names lies in the future time relative to the event reported in the previous clause, and in (75b) the event of dying is in the future time with respect to the event of falling sick.

For the **generic** and the **habitual** uses of *yiqtol-wqatal*, consider the following examples:

(76) *ʕal-ke;n yaʕᵃzob̲ ʕi:š ʕet̲ ʕa:b̲i:w wʕet̲ ʕimmo:*
therefore YIQ:leave:3SG:MASC man ACC father-his and-ACC mother-his
wd̲a:b̲aq bˀišto: wha:yu: lb̲a:śa:r ˀeḥa:d̲
WQAT:stick:3SG:MASC in-wife-his WQAT:be:3PL to-flesh one
'That is why a man leaves his father and mother and is united to his wife, and the two become one flesh.' (Gen. 2:24)

(77) 39. ... *watthi: ḥo;q byiśra:ˀe;l* 40. *miyyami:m*
WAYY:become:3SG:FEM law in-Israel from-days
ya:mi:ma: te;lak̲na: bno:t̲ yiśra:ˀe;l lt̲anno:t̲
to-days YIQ:go:3PL:FEM daughters:of Israel to-INF:lament
lb̲at̲ yip̄ta:ḥ haggilʕa:d̲i: ˀarbaʕat̲ ya:mi:m bašša:na:
to-daughter:of Jephethah the-Gileadite four:MASC:of days in-the-year
'39. ...It became a tradition that 40. the daughters of Israel should go year by year and commemorate the fate of Jephethah's daughter, four days in every year' (Jud. 11:39-40)

The clauses in (76) report a generic behavior of people, and hence the verbs in them are in *yiqtol* and *wqatal*. In (77) the second verse, (40), indicates a habitual event, and the verb in it is in *yiqtol*, as expected. In both cases the time referred to is the present, which seems to support the analyses of those who analyze the forms as indicating present general truth. However, as observed by several scholars, the forms *yiqtol* and *wqatal* also appear in generic and habitual situations whose time sphere is the past. Reconsider the following example:

(78) 2. ...*ki: min habbˀe;r hahi:ˀ yašqu: ha:ʕᵃd̲a:ri:m*
because from the-well the-she YIQ:water:3PL:MASC the-flock
wha:ˀeb̲en gd̲o;la: ʕal pi: habbˀe;r
and-the-stone big:SG:FEM on mouth:of the-well
3. *wneˀesp̄u: ša:mma: k̲ol ha:ʕᵃd̲a:ri:m wḡa:llu:*
WQAT:gather:3PL there all the-flock WQAT:roll:3PL
ˀet̲ haˀeb̲en me;ʕal pi: habbˀe;r whišqu: ˀet̲
ACC the-stone from-on mouth:of the-well WQAT:water:3PL ACC
haṣṣo;n whe;ši:b̲u: ˀet̲ ha:ˀeb̲en ʕal pi: habbˀe;r
the-flock WQAT:return:3PL ACC the-well on mouth:of the-well
limqo;ma:
to-place-her
'2. ...because from that well they used to water the flocks. Over the well's mouth was a huge stone, 3. and all the herdsmen used to gather there and roll it off the mouth of the well, water the flocks and put it back on its place over the well.' (Gen. 29:2-3)

The natural interpretation regards (78) as reporting habitual events in the past. However, it might be argued that this interpretation is not accurate, and that here the writer of the Bible indicates habitualities which still obtained in his time. To demonstrate our point, then, we need examples less ambiguous. Consider the following two:

(79) 4. *...wayyib̲ku: gam bne: yiśra:ˀe;l wayyo;mru:...*
WAYY:cry:3PL:MASC also sons:of Israel WAYY:say:3PL:MASC
5. *za:k̲arnu: ˀet̲ hadda:ḡa: ˀᵃšer* ***no;k̲al bmiṣrayim***
QAT:remember:1PL ACC the-fish that YIQ:eat:1PL in-Egypt
ḥinna:m...
for-free
'4. and the Israelites cried and said... 5. We remember the fish which **we used to eat in Egypt for free**...' (Num. 11: 4-5)

(80) a) *...ki: lanna:b̲i: hayyo:m* ***yiqqa:re;***
because to-the-prophet today YIQ:be-called:3SG:MASC
lp̄a:ni:m ha:ro;ˀe
beforetime the-seer
'...For what is nowadays called a prophet **used to be called a seer**.' (SamI. 9:9)

b) *bayya:mi:m ha:he;m ˀe:n melek̲ byiśra:ˀe;l*
in-the-days the-they:MASC NEG king in-Israel
ˀi:š hayya:ša:r bˤe:na:w yaˤᵃśe
man the-fine in-eyes-his YIQ:do:3SG:MASC
'In those days there was no king in Israel **and everybody did what was right in his own eyes**.' (Jud. 17:6, 21:25)

The verb 'remember' in (79) and the adverbials 'beforetime' and 'in those days' in (80a) and (80b) respectively force a past-time interpretation on the statements in these examples.

In **conditionals** it is common to find a *yiqtol* verb in the protosis and a *wqatal* verb in the apodosis, e.g.:

(81) *wayyo;mer yhwh ˀim ˀemṣa: b̲isd̲o;m ḥᵃmišši:m*
WAYY:say:3SG:MASC God if YIQ:find:1SG in-Sodom fifty
ṣaddi:qim bt̲o:k̲ ha:ˤi:r wna:śa:t̲i: lk̲ol hamma:qo:m
righteous inside the-city WQAT:forgive:1SG to-all:of the-place
baˤᵃb̲u:ra:m
for-them:MASC
'The Lord said, If I find in the city of Sodom fifty good men, I will pardon the whole place for their sake.' (Gen. 18:26)

The forms of the verbs in the conditional will be the *qatal* or the *qotel* if they refer to anterior or inclusive (modal) situations respectively. This result will follow from my system — see next section for more details. However, most of the cases are as in example (80), since it is more likely to express the protosis first and then the apodosis, and since the temporal relations holding between the situations expressed in the two parts of the conditional are usually that of sequence. The reason of having usually a yiqtol form in the protosis, although it opens a sequence, is that it also opens a direct-speech in most cases. (A direct-speech seems to behave like a sub-discourse, and therefore the first clause in a direct-speech serves to mark a transition to the sub-discourse and hence may not have a sequential form. See ch. 5 for discussion.) When the conditional statement does not open the direct-speech in which it appears, a *wqatal* verb is used in the protosis, instead of a *yiqtol* verb prefixed by the particle *ˀim* 'if'. (See ex. 83 below, which is discussed in this respect in section 5.1, ex. 37.) Ibn Janaḥ explains the *waw* of the *wqatal* in the protosis of such conditionals as indicating 'if'. But this is the form we expect when the clause opens a modal sequence.

In section (4.1.7) we have seen that **rhetorical questions**, as expected by their analysis, are always treated as modals and hence their verbs are in one of the modal forms. Qimron (1980), e.g., illustrates a *yiqtol* verb in a rhetorical question:

(82) *wayyo;mru:* ***hakzo:na:*** ***yaˤaśe*** ***ˀeṯ*** ***ˀaḥo:ṯe;nu:***
WAYY:say:3PL:MASC QUE-as-harlot YIQ:make:3SG:MASC ACC sister-our
'They said, **Is our sister to be treated as a common whore**?!' (Gen. 34:31)

But *wqatal* verbs may also appear in rhetorical questions, if they consist of sequences:

(83) 10. *wayyaˤan* *na:ḇa:l* *ˀeṯ* *ˤaḇde:* *da:wiḏ*
WAYY:answer:3SG:MASC Nabal ACC servants:of David
11. *wayyo;mer...* *wla:qaḥti:* *ˀeṯ* *laḥmi:* *wˀeṯ*
WAYY:say:3SG:MASC WQAT:take:1SG ACC bread-my and-ACC
me:may *wˀeṯ* *ṭiḇḥa:ṯi:* *ˀašer* *ṭa:ḇaḥti:*
waters-my and-ACC slaughter-my that QAT:slaughter:1SG
lgo;zza:y *wna:ṯati:* *laˀana:ši:m* *ˀašer* *lo;* *ya:ḏaˤti:*
to-shearers-my WQAT:give:1SG to-people that NEG QAT:know:1SG
ˀe: *mizze* *he;mma:*
where from they:MASC
'10. Nabal answered David's servants and said... 11. Am I to take my food and my water and the meat I have provided for my shearers and give it to men who come from I know not where?!' (SamI. 25:10-11)

So far we have demonstrated the uses of *yiqtol* and *wqatal* in alethic and epistemic modalities. But they are also used to indicate **deontic** modal statements. Consider the following examples:

(84) *watto;mer* *ha:ˀišša:* *ˀel* *hanna:ḥa:š* ***mippri:***
WAYY:say:3SG:FEM the-woman to the-snake from-fruit:of
ˁe;ṣ ***hagga:n*** ***no;ke;l***
tree:of the-garden YIQ:eat:1PL
'The woman said to the serpent, **We may eat the fruit of any tree in the garden**.' (Gen. 3:2)

(85) 13. *wayyo;mer* *qayin* *ˀel* *yhwh* *ga:do:l* *ˁᵃwo;ni:*
WAYY:say:3SG:MASC Cain to God big:SG:MASC punishment-my
14. *minśo:* *he;n* *ge;rašta:* *ˀo;ti:* *hayyo:m* *me:ˁal*
from-INF:bear so QAT:expel:2SG:MASC me today from-on
pne: *ha:ˀᵃda:ma:* ***u:mippa:neka:*** ***ˀessa:te;r***
face:of the-earth and-from-face-your:SG:MASC YIQ:hide:1SG
wha:yi:ti: ***naˁ*** ***wa:na:d*** ***ba:ˀa:reṣ***...
WQAT:be:1SG fugitive:MASC and-vagabond:MASC in-the-land
'13. Cain said to the Lord, My punishment is heavier than I can bear; 14. Since you have driven me today from the ground, I must hide myself from your presence, and I will have to be a vagrant and a wanderer on earth.' (Gen. 4:13-14)

Bergsträsser (1972) interprets, correctly, the utterance of the woman in (84) as denoting permission, i.e., the woman reports to the snake that God permits them to eat the fruits of the garden. Bergsträsser explains the first of the two boldfaced clauses in (85) as denoting obligation. It seems to me that the second clause, too, is to be interpreted as an obligation (or both clauses as an epistemic necessity).

Although there are explicit forms for the directives (the imperative, the jussive and the cohortative), the forms *yiqtol* and *wqatal* are also used to express these speech acts. Consider the following paragraph:

(86) 1. *wˀe;lle* *hammišpa:ṭi:m* *ˀᵃšer* *ta:śi:m* *lip̄ne:hem*
and-these the-laws that YIQ:put:2SG:MASC to-face-their:MASC
2. *ki:* *ṯiqne* *ˁeḇeḏ* *ˁiḇri:* *še;š* *ša:ni:m*
if YIQ:buy:2SG:MASC slave Hebrew:SG:MASC six:FEM years
yaˁaḇo;ḏ *u:ḇaššḇiˁiṯ* *ye;ṣe;*
YIQ:work:3SG:MASC and-in-the-seventh:FEM YIQ:leave:3SG:MASC
laḥop̄ši: *ḥinna:m* 3. *ˀim* *bḡappo:* *ya:ḇo;*
to-freedom for-nothing if in-body-his YIQ:come:3SG:MASC

b̲gappo: *ye;ṣe;* *ˀim* *baˁal* *ˀišša:* *hu:*
in-body-his YIQ:leave:3SG:MASC if husband:of woman he
wya:ṣˀa: *ˀišto:* *ˁimmo:...*
WQAT:leave:3SG:FEM wife-his with-him
'1. These are the laws you shall set before them: 2. When you buy a Hebrew slave, he shall be your slave for six years, but in the seventh year he shall go free and pay nothing. 3. If he comes to you alone, he shall go away alone; but if he is married, his wife shall go away with him.' (Ex. 21:1-3)

The paragraph in (86) is a small fragment of a long list of laws. All the verbs in this list, and in other similar lists, are either in *yiqtol* or in *wqatal*. The question which arises is why these forms rather than the explicit directives, are used here. Qimron (1980) and others suggest that maybe the directives here are habitual or generic. However, the first *yiqtol* verb in our paragraph is in a semelfactive (=non-repetitive, i.e., non-habitual) clause. There are even more examples of *wqatal* verbs in semelfactive imperatives. Consider the following example:

(87) 13. *wayyo;mer* *ˀᵉlo;hi:m* *lno;$_{a}$ḥ...* 14. *ˁᵃśe;*
WAYY:say:3SG:MASC God to-Noah IMP:make:2SG:MASC
lk̲a: *te;ḇaṯ* *ˁᵃṣe:* *go;p̄er* *qinni:m* *taˁᵃśe*
to-you:SG:MASC ark:of woods:of gopher rooms YIQ-make:2SG:MASC
ˀeṯ *hatte;ḇa:* *wk̲a:p̄arta:* *ˀo;ṯa:h* *mibbayiṯ*
ACC the-ark WQAT:pitch:2SG:MASC her from-house
u:miḥu:ṣ *bakko;p̄er*
and-from-out in-the-pitch
'13. God said to Noah...14. Make yourself an ark with ribs of cypress; cover it with reeds and coat it inside and out with pitch.' (Gen. 6:13-14)

The first command given to Noah uses the imperative form *ʕaśe;*, as expected. However, in the rest of the commands God uses either a *yiqtol* or a *wqatal* verb. These uses cannot be interpreted as habituals or generics, as God expects Noah to build only one ark to escape the flood. The phenomenon of the unmarked modal forms to function in directives makes it impossible, sometimes, to determine whether the clause in question is a directive or a futurate. This may be solved on syntactic and/or pragmatic grounds. For example, in (87) the first verb in the series of commands is in imperative, which imposes its interpretation on the rest of the clauses. The context also indicates that these clauses are commands. However, this suggestion warrants a more thorough syntactic and pragmatic analysis of Biblical-Hebrew, than is possible in the present context.

The only modality which is not denoted by the modal forms is counterfactuality, which is (usually) denoted by the perfect aspect *qatal*. However, as said in section (4.1.4) this peculiar behavior of the counterfactuals is not limited to BH, but manifested in other languages, too. Counterfactuals will be illustrated in the next chapter, where the *qatal* is discussed.

The above discussion has shown that all the modals (except for counterfactuals) can be, and usually are, denoted by the two forms *yiqtol* and *wqatal*. However, although these two forms may be used to express directive speech acts, there are special forms for the different directives. These forms were presented together in Table (4.1). Let us now present their distribution:

Table 4.2. The Directives in BH

TOTAL	imperative	jussive	cohortative	wyiqtol
542	395	22	44	81

The largest group is of imperatives. However, since the imperatives constitute a suppletive paradigm with the other directives (as will be illustrated below), it makes sense to discuss them all together. Hebraists such as Gesenius (1909), Rubinstein (1980) and others claim that, although they form a different group within the modal forms, all the directives are connected to *yiqtol* not only in their semantics but also in form. The form of the jussive, which is also called the *short yiqtol* is very similar to the "regular" *yiqtol* (see Chapter 1 for discussion). In most of the verbs the difference between them is neutralized and can be seen only in two groups of verbs: a) In verbs with a *waw* or with a *yod* consonants in the second or the third root positions respectively, e.g., *yib̲en* (jussive) - *yib̲ne;* (*yiqtol*) 'build', *ya:qom* (jussive) - *ya:qu:m* (*yiqtol*) 'rise'; b) In verbs in binyan *hip̄ˤil*, where the jussive verbs differ from the *yiqtol* ones in the ultimate vowel — compare the following pairs where the first verb of each pair is the jussive form and the second the *yiqtol*: *yab̲de;l-yab̲di:l* 'differ', *yo:le;k̲-yo:li:k̲* 'make go'. The "mirror" form of the jussive is the cohortative. The cohortative is called a *long yiqtol* since it has the form of the *yiqtol* with an *a:* added to it as a suffix, e.g., *naʕb̲ra:* 'we pass', *ne;lk̲a:* 'we go', *ʔa:ši:ra:* 'I sing', etc. vs. the *yiqtol* forms *naʕab̲o;r*, *ne;le;k̲* and *ʔa:ši:r* respectively. Unlike the case of the jussive, the cohortative verbs are usually distinguished from the *yiqtol* ones, except for one group, namely verbs whose third root consonant is *yod*. For example, *ʔerʔe* 'I see' and *nište* 'we drink' are ambiguous between regular and long *yiqtol*. But not only the three forms of *yiqtol* are connected. The *waw* prefixed *wyiqtol* is clearly related to them and the imperative seems to be related, too (see e.g., Gesenius 1909 and Bergsträsser 1972 for details). But although they seem to be connected morphologically to *yiqtol*, the forms of the jussive, the imperative and the cohortative form a separate subcategory of the modals. As mentioned above, it is well acknowledged by Hebraists, e.g., Qimron (1980), that they form a suppletive paradigm of directives (and see FN 10), according to the person inflection. That is, they all function to utter some directive, and the choice of one of them is determined by the person in question. If the sentence expressing the directive is in second person the imperative (and sometimes the jussive) is used, if it is in first person it is in cohortative and if it is in third person it is in jussive. As a result of this, each form "specializes" in a certain directive. Cohortative and jussive statements are usually interpreted as requests and sentences in imperative as commands. The following examples illustrate the typical functions of each form:

(88) **imperative:**

wayyo;mer *yhwh* *ˀel* *ˀab̲ra:m* ***lek̲***
WAYY:say:3SG:MASC God to Abram IMP:go:2SG:MASC
lk̲a: *me;ˀarṣk̲a:*
to-you:2SG:MASC from-land-yours:2SG:MASC
u:mimmo:lad̲tk̲a: *u:mibbe:t̲*
and-from-homeland-yours:SG:MASC and-from-house:of
ˀa:b̲i:k̲a: *ˀel* *ha:ˀa:reṣ* *ˀᵃšer* *ˀarˀekka:*
father-yours:SG:MASC to the-land that YIQ:show:1SG-you:2SG:MASC
'The Lord said to Abram, Go from your country, your homeland, and your father's house, to the country that I will show you. (Gen. 12:1)

(89) **cohortative:**

26. *wa:ˀešlaḥ* *malˀa:k̲i:m* *mimmid̲bar* *qd̲e;mo:t̲* *ˀel* *si:ḥo:n*
WAYY:send:1SG messengers from-desert:of Kedemoth to Sihon
melek̲ *ḥešbo:n* *dib̲re:* *ša:lo:m* *le;mo;r* 27. *ˀeˁbra:*
king:of Heshbon words:of peace to-INF:say COH:pass:1SG
b̲ˀarṣk̲a:...
in-country-yours:SG:MASC
'26. I sent messengers out of the desert of Kedemoth to Sihon king of Heshbon with words of peace saying: 27. Let me pass through your land...' (Deot. 2:26-27)

(90) **jussive:**

wˤatta: ***ye;šeḇ*** *na:* *ˤaḇdḵa:* *taḥaṯ*
and-now YIQ:sit:3SG:MASC please servant-yours:SG:MASC instead:of
hannaˤar *ˤeḇeḏ* *laḏo;ni:* *whannaˤar* ***yaˤal*** *ˤim*
the-lad slave to-master-my and-the-lad JUS:go-up:3SG:MASC with
ˀeḥa:w
brothers-his

'Now **let your servant, please, remain** in place of the boy as your lordship's slave, and **let the lad** go with his brothers.' (Gen. 44:33)

In (88) God commands Abram to leave his country and go to a new one. The verb *leḵ* 'go' in the command clause is in imperative. In (89) Moses is requesting Sihon, the king of Heshbon, to let him pass with his people through his country. The verb indicating the request, in first person inflection, is in cohortative. (90) is an interesting example. The verse quoted here is part of a long speech of Judah to Joseph, begging him to let his little brother return home with them. It is clear, then, that (90) reports requests. The first request refers to the speaker himself (Judah), but the inflection of the verb denoting it is still in third person (had it been in first person, it would be in cohortative). However, superficially it is not in jussive form. It seems to me that this is a good example of the morphological neutralization of the jussive-*yiqtol* distinction. That is, while this is actually a jussive form, we cannot recognize it as such since it has exactly the same form of the *yiqtol*. This assumption is supported by the addition of the particle *na:*, which is added sometimes to requests, presumably parallel to the particle "please" in English.[11] The second verb *yaˤal* 'go-up' is clearly in jussive, since its root *ˤly* has a *yod* in the third position (its parallel *yiqtol* has a different form - *yaˤ*^{a}*le*). The function of the jussive in requests, usually addressed to a superior person such as God, explains its use in wishes and blessings. But although their functions are quite distinguished, the forms may "invade" each others areas. We find request clauses with verbs in imperative on one hand, and commands with jussive verb forms on the other:

(91) *wayyiṣˤaq* *mo;še* *ˀel* *yhwh* *le;mo;r* *ˀe;l* *na:*
WAYY:cry:3SG:MASC Moses to God to-INF:say God na:
rp̄a: ***na:*** ***la:h***
IMP:heal:2SG:MASC *na:* to-her

'Moses cried to God, saying, O Lord, please! **Heal her, please!**' (Num. 12:13)

(92) *wayyo;mer* *ˁelo;hi:m* ***yhi:*** ***ˁo:r*** *wayhi:*
WAYY:say:3SG:MASC God JUS:be:2SG:MASC light WAYY:be:3SG:MASC
ˁo:r
light
'God said, **Let there be light**, and there was light.' (Gen. 1:3)

The context makes it clear that in (91) there is a request, as it is not possible that Moses orders God. (Note also the addition of the particle *na:*.) Nonetheless, the verb is in imperative rather than jussive. The use of the imperative is appropriate since Moses is addressing God in the second person. Had he used the third person he would have used the jussive form. In (92) we have the opposite situation — God is ordering the light to be created. He is using the jussive form because he is not addressing the light in second person (maybe because the light had not yet been created?). The jussive may be used in second person (almost) only as a negative imperative to prevent someone from doing something.

In addition to the three forms discussed so far, there is, as mentioned above, another form which is used only in deontic modal clauses, namely the *waw* prefixed *yiqtol*. (It is not clear to me if, furthermore, it functions only in directives.) This form cannot be analyzed as the sequential counterpart for *yiqtol*. Firstly, unlike *yiqtol*, it is used only (or almost only?) in deontic modals, and secondly, the sequential counterpart for *yiqtol* is *wqatal*, as demonstrated in chapter (2) above (and see also Qimron 1986-1987). The only explanation which seems reasonable is that this form is not *wyiqtol*, but, is as a matter of fact, a *waw* prefixed jussive of those verbs with the neutralization of the morphological distinction between the jussive and the *yiqtol* forms. (There is, however, a small number of *wyiqtol* verbs in the groups which have retained the distinction, which of course, questions this hypothesis.) Another, somewhat weak, demonstration for this hypothesis is the fact that, like the other directives and contrary to *yiqtol* (and *wqatal*), the form *wyiqtol* has no counterexamples, as shown in table (4.1).

So far we have seen how the modal forms function to denote modalities. Table (4.1) shows that we can claim that they are used only in such clauses. The directives have no counterexamples to this claim, and the general modal forms have a very small number of occurrences in non-modal clauses — 3% of the *yiqtol* verbs and 4% of the *wqatal* verbs. Let me deal first with the yiqtol counterexamples. The non-modal clauses of the *yiqtol* verbs can be grouped in two classes: non-inclusive clauses whose expected verb forms are either *wayyiqtol* or *qatal*, and inclusive clauses whose expected verb forms are *qotel*. Many of the verbs in the first group are prefixed by the particle *ˀa:z* 'then'. Consider the following examples:

(93) a. *ˀa:z ya:ši:r mo;še u:b̲ne: yiśra:ˀe;l ˀet̲*
then YIQ:sing:3SG:MASC Moses and-sons:of Israel ACC
hašši:ra: hazzo;t̲ layhwh wayyo;mru: le;mo;r...
the-song the-this:FEM to-God WAYY:say:3PL:MASC to-INF:say
'Then Moses and the Israelites sang this song to the Lord saying...' (Ex. 15:1)

b. *ˀa:z yab̲di:l mo;še ša:lo;š ˤa:ri:m*
then YIQ:differentiate:3SG:MASC Moses three:FEM cities
bˤe;b̲er hayyarde;n mizrḥa: ša:meš
in-the-side:of the-Jordan east-to sun
'Then Moses set apart three cities on the other side of the Jordan river, in the east.' (Deut. 4:41)

In both examples the context makes it clear that the clauses report non-modal events — "Moses sang" and "Moses set apart the cities". As they are understood as occurring after the events reported in the previous section, the verbs denoting these events are expected to appear in *wayyiqtol* form. This problem is widely acknowledged. Scholars of the historical-comparative approach, e.g., Bauer (1910), see it as a demonstration of their claim that *yiqtol* used to be, *inter alia*, the narrative form. They assume that the particle *ˀa:z* has "saved" the original meaning of the *yiqtol* just like the prefixed *waw* has saved it in *wayyiqtol*. However, this particle may appear in front of *yiqtol* in modal clauses, too (e.g, Ex.12:44). On the other hand, there are non-modal *yiqtol* clauses which are not *ˀa:z* prefixed. Consider the following example:

(94) *wayyit̲qaˤ yo:ˀa:b̲ baššo:p̄a:r wayyaˤamd̲u:*
WAYY:blow:3SG:MASC Joab in-the-trumpet WAYY:stand:3PL:MASC
kol ha:ˤa:m ***wlo: yirdp̄u: ˤo:d̲ ˀaḥare:***
all:of the-people and-NEG YIQ:chase:3PL:MASC more after
yiśra:ˀe;l *wlo; ya:sp̄u: ˤo:d̲ lhilla:ḥe;m*
Israel and-NEG QAT:add:3PL more to-INF:fight
'Joab sounded the trumpet, **and all the people abandoned the pursuit of the men of Israel** and stopped fighting.' (SamII. 2:28)

The verb *rdp* 'chase' in (94) is expected to be in *qatal* form, since it reports a "negative" non-modal state (see chapter 5 for discussion) simultaneous to the event reported in the previous clause. Good evidence for this expectation is found in the following clause which also indicates a "negative" state. The verb *ya:sp̄u:* in this clause is in *qatal* form. The wrong form in our clause, and in similar cases, may be a result of corruption, as demonstrated by the fact that there are other versions of the Biblical text in which the verb *rdp* is, indeed, in *qatal* (as reported in Biblia Hebraica). The second group of non-modal *yiqtol* clauses denote inclusive situations, only some of which can be explained. Reconsider the following examples (discussed for the same reason also in ch. 3):

(95) 9. *...wayyo;mar* *qa:ḥem* *na:* *ʔe;lay*
WAYY:say:3SG:MASC IMP:take:2SG:MASC-them:MASC please to-me
waʔaḇa:raḵem 10. *wʕe:ne:* *yiśra:ʔe;l* *ka:ḇdu:*
WQAT:bless:1SG-them:MASC and-eyes:of Israel QAT:dim:3PL
mizzo;qen ***lo;*** ***yu:ḵal*** ***lirʔo:ṯ...***
from-old NEG YIQ:can:3SG:MASC to-INF:see
'9. ...Israel said, Take them to me, please, and I will bless them. 10. Now Israel's eyes were dim with age, and **he could not see**.' (Gen. 48:9-10)

(96) *wayye;ṣe;* *bayyo:m* *hašše;ni:* *whinne;*
WAYY:go-out:3SG:MASC in-the-day the-second:MASC and-behold
šne: *ʔana:ši:m* *ʕiḇri:m* *niṣṣi:m*
two:MASC:of people Hebrew:PL:MASC QOT:fight:PL:MASC
wayyo;mer *la:ra:ša:ʕ* ***la:mma:*** ***ṯakke***
WAYY:say:3SG:MASC to-the-guilty:SG:MASC why YIQ:hit:2SG:MASC
re;ʕeḵa:
friend-yours:SG:MASC
'He went out next day, and there were two Hebrews fighting together. He asked the man who was in the wrong, Why are you striking him?' (Ex. 2:13)

In (95) as well as in (96), the *qotel* seems to be the appropriate form for the verbs in the boldfaced clauses, as they both include their respective R-time. But the use of *yiqtol* in (95) can be explained on the grounds that it indicates a possibility (or more precisely, a lack of it). Furthermore, 'can' is a mental state verb which does not take the *qotel* form (see chapter 3 for discussion). However, regarding the latter point, the question is why the form of *qatal* is not used here? Secondly, why should the Bible use the verb "can" at all, as it could put the verb of seeing in *yiqtol* form to indicate the same situation? Thirdly, as pointed out to me by Comrie, the lexical item in question seems to mean 'be able', so for this to be further modalized the meaning would have to be 'be able to be able', which sounds odd, at least in English. But while we can find some explanation for the *yiqtol* form in (95), it is problematic to account for it in example (96). If we assume that the question word 'why' is responsible for the form, i.e., accept the approach that interrogatives are always modal, then we will have to explain why on the one hand there are cases such as (96) but without question words, and on the other hand, questions with a *qatal* verb as in example (97) or *qotel* verb as in (98), and even a *wayyiqtol* verb as illustrated also in (97):

(97)	*la:mma:*	*naḥbe;ṯa:*	*liḇro;$_{a}$ḥ*	*wattiḡno;ḇ*	*ˀo;ṯi:*
	why	QAT:hide:2SG:MASC	to-INF:flee	WAYY:steal:2SG:MASC	me

‘Why did you slip away secretly and steal away from me?’ (Gen. 31:27)

(98)	*...wˁatta:*	*la:mma:*	*ˀattem*	*maḥ^{a}ri:šim*	*lha:ši:ḇ*
	and-now	why	you:PL:MASC	QOT:silence:PL:MASC	to-INF:return
	ˀeṯ	*hammeleḵ*			
	ACC	the-king			

‘why are you last to bring the king back?’ (Sam.II 19:11)

Note, however, that the translation of (96) may also be “Why would you hit your brother?”, which has the modal “would”. English suggests that this clause might be interpreted as modal, and hence the *yiqtol* form.

The counterexamples of the *wqatal* verbs are even more difficult to explain. Some of them (5 out of 15 in our sample) are explained by Gesenius and Bergsträsser as corruptions. This hypothesis is supported by the fact that 3 of those 5 cases and 2 of the rest have the “right” form in other versions, as reported by Biblia Hebraica. Gesenius, furthermore, explains another 4 cases (of the 15) as the result of Aramaic influence.

4.2.2 *The Non-Modal Forms*

The modal forms *wqatal* and *yiqtol* cannot be used when the modality interacts with the perfect or the inclusive aspects. A verb in *wqatal* cannot indicate either of these aspects as entailed from its sequential character (see chapter 2). The form *yiqtol* cannot indicate inclusiveness because it is included in its R-time (see chapters 2 and 3 for discussion). It cannot be used as for denoting anterior situations either since it does not precede the R-time (see chapter 5 for discussion). It seems to be the case that it is used for simultaneous (modal) clauses (which may constitute a problem since *qatal* is used for simultaneity too — see ch. 5), or situations in different time branches, whose temporal relations are not specified (for illustration see discussion on example 48 in chapter 5).

Instead of the modal forms, then, inclusiveness in modal clauses is denoted by *qotel*, which is the general inclusive aspect, and modal clauses which bear the perfect aspect have verbs in *qatal*. For being non-modal forms, these two forms cannot appear in other modal clauses except under the circumstances just described. An exception is the counterfactuals which are denoted by *qatal* instead by one of the modal forms, but as mentioned more than once, this behavior of the counterfactual is not limited to BH, and needs a general explanation.

The following table summarizes the occurrence of *qatal* in modal sentences:

Table 4.3. Qatal in modal sentences

PERFECT N=7	COUNTERFACTUALS N=10	PERFORMATIVES N=2	UNEXPLAINED N=8

The function of *qatal* as a perfect aspect is not limited to modal situations. See chapter 5 below for discussion and illustration.

The second group, namely the counterfactual cases, is even larger in number. The particle *lu:* or its negative counterpart *lu:le:* is usually used to indicate counterfactuality. Consider the following example:

(99) *wayyilo;nu:* *ʕal mo;še wʕal ʔah^{a}ro;n kol bne:*
WAYY:complain:3PL:MASC on Moses and-on Aaron all:of sons:of
yiśra:ʔe;l wayyo;mru: ʔ^{a}le;hem kol ha:ʕe;da:
Israel WAYY:say:3PL:MASC to-them:MASC all:of the-congregation
lu: matnu: bʔereṣ miṣrayim ʔo: bammidba:r hazze
lu: QAT:die:1PL in-land:of Egypt or in-the-desert the-this:MASC
lu: matnu:
lu: QAT:die:1PL
'All the Israelites complained against Moses, and Aaron and all the community said to them **We wish we had died in Egypt or in this desert**.' (Num. 14:2)

In (99) the Israelites are clearly expressing a wish which cannot be fulfilled, and hence (99) expresses a "simple" counterfactual situation. The following example illustrates a counterfactual conditional. Note that here, too, the particle used is *lu:* (or *lu:le;*) which is the counterpart of the indicative *ʔim* 'if':

(100) ...*wayyo;mer* *la:hem* ***lu:le;*** ***ḥ^{a}raštem***
WAYY:say:3SG:MASC to-them:MASC if-NEG QAT:plough:2PL:MASC
b^{ʕ}eḡla:ṯi: ***lo:*** ***mṣ a:ṯem*** ***ḥi:ḏa:ṯi:***
in-heifer-my NEG QAT:find:2PL:MASC riddle-my
'...He said, If you had not ploughed with my heifer, you would not have found out my riddle.' (Jud. 14:18)

The last group comprises the two cases of performative clauses. Consider one example:

(101) *wayyo;mer* *yhwh* *yhu:ḏa:* *ya^{ʕa}le* ***hinne;***
WAYY:say:3SG:MASC God Judah YIQ:go-up:3SG:MASC *hinne;*
na:ṯatti: ***$^{?}$eṯ*** ***ha:$^{?}$a:reṣ*** ***bya:ḏo:***
QAT:give:1SG ACC the-land in-hand-his
'The Lord said, Judah shall attack. **I hereby deliver the country into his power**.' (Jud. 1:2)

As reflected in the English translation taken from *The New English Bible*, the boldfaced clause in (101) is a performative utterance, where God is giving Judah the power of conquering the land. The verb 'give' in this clause is in *qatal*. However, most of the performative speech acts in the Bible use the *qotel* form, as will be shown below. It is not clear to me if there is a complementary distribution between the *qatal* and *qotel* forms concerning performatives or if the speaker uses them in free variation. The explained occurrence of *qatal* in modal clauses reduces the number of counterexamples to 0.7% only. In the 8 unexplained occurrences, it seems the verbs in *qatal* can easily be replaced by *yiqtol*. Compare the verses in (102a) and (102b) below:

(102) a) 8. *wayyo;mer* *yhu:ḏa:* *$^{?}$el* *yiśra:$^{?}$e;l* *$^{?}$a:ḇi:w*
WAYY:say:3SG:MASC Judah to Israel father-his
šilḥa: *hanna^{ʕ}ar* *$^{?}$itti:...* 9... ***$^{?}$im*** ***lo;***
IMP:send:2SG:MASC the-lad with-me if NEG
h^{a}ḇi:$^{?}$o;ṯi:w ***$^{?}$e;leḵa:*** *whiṣṣaḡti:w*
QAT:bring:1SG-him to-you:SG:MASC WQAT:present:1SG-him
lp̄a:neḵa: *wḥa:ṭa:ṯi:* *lḵa:* *kol*
in-front:of-you:SG:MASC WQAT:sin:1SG to-you:SG:MASC all:of
hayya:mi:m
the-days
'8. Judah said to his father Israel, Send the boy with me... 9... **If I do not bring him back and restore him to you**, you shall hold me guilty all my life.' (Gen. 43:8-9)

b) *ki:* *ˁab̲dk̲a:* *ˁa:rab̲* *ˀet̲*
because servant-yours:SG:MASC QAT:become-surety:3SG:MASC ACC
hannaˁar *me;ˁim* *ˀa:b̲i:* *le;mo;r* ***ˀim*** ***lo;***
the-lad from-with father-my to-INF:say if NEG
ˀᵃb̲i:ˀennu: ***ˀe;lek̲a:*** *wḥa:ṭa:t̲i:* *lˀa:b̲i:*
YIQ:bring:1SG-him to-you:SG:MASC WQAT:sin:1SG to-father-my
kol *hayya:mi:m*
all:of the-days
'Your servant went surety for the boy to my father, saying **If I do not bring him back to you**, I shall hold me guilty towards my father all my life.' (Gen. 44:32)

The very same condition in (102a) and in (102b) have different verb forms in their protosis — in (102a) the verb is in *qatal* while in (102b) the same verb is in *yiqtol*. Could it be that in (102a) Judah is expressing a counterfactual in future, roughly meaning that it cannot be the case that he did not bring his brother back? A similar problem is faced in English. Compare (103a) with (103b) (suggested to me by Comrie) and also compare (103c) to (103d):

(103) a) If John stays we'll be happy.
b) If John stayed we'd be happy.
c) I will not leave until you have paid me.
d) I will not leave until you pay me.

Comrie believes that using the past tense in (103b) as opposed to the simple future in (103a) increases the hypothecality of the expression. This might be the difference between the use of the *yiqtol* vs. the *qatal* verbs in (102). A similar difference is manifested in (103c-d). The sentence in (103c) is in (present) perfect, while (103d) is in simple (present). It seems that the simple present is more common for conditionals in English. The two forms may differ in the degree of hypothecality. Mickey Schafer (pc) believes that (103c) has greater "emotional" content than (103d), indicating a promise, an obligation or even a threat. It seems to me that the same difference might explain when BH uses a *qatal* verb in the protosis of a conditional rather than a *yiqtol*. In (102a) Judah makes a strong promise to his father, hence using the form *qatal* for the verb 'bring'; in (102b) he reports the promise (to Joseph) rahter than making it, hence the form *yiqtol* of the same verb.

Now let us consider the *qotel* verbs in modal clauses. The *qotel* is more problematic concerning modality than *qatal*. First, the percentage of its occurrence is larger, as shown in table (4.1), although it is still relatively small (7.7% in our sample). Secondly, most of the occurrences are unexplained.

Table 4.4. qotel in modal clauses

INCLUSIVE	FUTURATE	UNEXPLAINED
9	14	29

Table (4.4) above summarizes the occurrences of the modal *qotel* in our sample. The only justified use of *qotel* to denote modal situations is when inclusive relation is reported — for discussion and illustration see chapter 3 above.

However, only 9 occurrences (1.3%) of the modal *qotel* appear in inclusive clauses. Fourteen (2%) occurrences are in futurate clauses, where a *yiqtol* verb is expected. The futurate *qotel* is also discussed in chapter 3. But most of the occurrences (4.3%) cannot even be grouped in a specific group like the futurate, but are used on many different occasions. Consider the following examples:

(104) *wayyeˀᵉhaḇ* *šlo;mo;* *ˀeṯ* *yhwh* *la:leḵeṯ* *bḥuqqo:ṯ*
WAYY:love:3SG:MASC Solomon ACC God to-INF:go in-laws:of
da:wiḏ *ˀa:ḇi:w* ***raq*** ***babba:mo:ṯ*** ***hu:*** ***mzabbe;ₐḥ***
David father-his only in-the-platforms he QOT:sacrifice:SG:MASC
u:maqṭi:r
and-QOT:burn-incense:SG:MASC
'Solomon loved the Lord, conforming to the precepts laid down by his father David; **only that he slaughtered and burnt sacrifices at the hill shrines**.' (KingsI 3:3)

(105) *wayyo;mer* *bilˁa:m* *la:ˀa:ṯo:n* *ki:* *hiṯˁallalt*
WAYY:say:3SG:MASC Balaam to-the-ass because QAT:mock:2SG:FEM
bi: ***lu:*** ***ye:š*** ***ḥereḇ*** ***bya:ḏi:*** *ki:* *ˁatta:*
in-me if QOT:EXIST sword in-hand-my that now
hᵃraḡti:ḵ
QAT:kill:1SG-you:2SG:FEM
'Balaam said to the ass, Since you have been making a fool of me, if I had had a sword in my hand, I should have killed you on the spot.' (Num. 22:29)

The boldfaced clauses in (104) report habitual events, and hence the verbs in them should have been in *yiqtol*, instead of *qotel*. In (105) the underlined clause is an apodosis of a counterfactual conditional, but nevertheless the verb appears in it is in *qotel* rather than in *qatal*.

The deviance of *wayyiqtol* where it is used in modal clauses is very small in number (0.2% in our sample). Moreover, one of the five occurrences

(KingsII 3:5) is probably a corruption, as demonstrated by the fact that there are versions in which the verb in question is in *wqatal* (see Biblia Hebraica), and another example (SamI 1:7) is found in a problematic chapter concerning the aspect system (see discussion on example 86 in chapter 2).

4.3 Conclusion

The study of the BH verbal system has clearly shown that what has been traditionally treated as modals are not the only clauses which appear with modal forms. It has also been shown that there is an interaction between aspect and modality. (The interaction between tense and modality, however, could not be manifested here, since BH is an untensed language.)

NOTES

1. a. It is not my intention to discuss all the issues concerning modality, but only those relevant to this chapter. The interested reader can find a comprehensive survey of modal logic in Hugh & Creswell (1968). For issues which are not covered there see Kratzer (1981a,b) and other works mentioned in this chapter.

   b. It should be emphasized again that the main concern of this work is semantic rather than pragmatic, and therefore pragmatic considerations will be incorporated only occasionally. For a comprehensive discussion of the pragmatic approach to modalities readers can consult Palmer (1986). He also provides a list of additional references, among which is Searle (1983), who treats modal propositions within the framework of speech acts.

2. The examples given here (for the necessary as well as the possible statements) are not an exhaustive list of the different kinds of modality. For such a list see Lyons (1977), Palmer (1986) and others. I take this opportunity also to note that since English is used here only as a meta language, I will not consider the ways in which it uses the different modalities, and will use them freely to demonstrate my points.

3. In formal logic these operators have been symbolized in different ways, where the best known are $\Box$ and $\Diamond$ for necessity and possibility respectively. For alternative notations, see appendix 4 in Hugh & Creswell (1968).

4. It is possible in this framework also to evaluate propositions in relation to worlds other than ours. In such a case we would need resemblances among the worlds in question, excluding ours.

5. Prior (1967) argues against the possibility of time branching in both directions: the future and the past. See there for details.

6. As noted by Dowty (1977) it is problematic to talk about relations of times which lie on different branches. For a solution Dowty refers to an unpublished paper of Thomason (1974). Thomason talks of clocks which show the same time along different branches ('scenarios' in Thomason's terms). For our purposes, the effect of Thomason's clock, which runs at the same rate in each possible option, is the R-time to which the speaker refers. (For shortcomings of this solution, see discussion in Dowty.) This may also be captured by the analysis of the habituals in Verkuyl (1993). In general, Verkuyl shows that one refers to real time when the habituals actualize. This real time I understand as the R-time, determined in the actual world, which can be the clock Thomason talks about. See elaboration on this analysis in section 4.1.5 discussing the habituals.

7. There is considerable debate concerning the causal relations in conditionals. The question is if the antecedent of the conditional is necessarily the cause of the consequent, and then the conditional is a special case of strict implication, or the relations between the two parts of the conditional are merely temporal and hence we have here a material implication. This question is beyond the scope of this work and hence will not be dealt with.

8. English does not usually use such sentences for deontic modals, but accepts sentences as (2d) and (3b) repeated here in (i) and (ii) respectively:

   (i) John must go to the beach
   (ii) John may go to the beach.

   In section 4.1.1 I have analyzed the epistemic, non-deontic, reading of these sentences, but they may have a deontic interpretation, too. However, as I noted earlier, I will not deal with the ways English expresses the different kinds of modalities, and will try to find the most obvious ones to demonstrate them.

9. It has been argued sometimes, e.g., Palmer (1986), that negation in general is modalic. I do not agree with this analysis. Consider the following negative assertion:

   (i) John did not go to the beach.

   I claim that (i) does not involve either a possibility or necessity property, and if it is true, it just happened to be true.

10. Traditionally, these are the only forms referred to as modals, since the uses of the *yiqtol* and *wqatal* in generic, habitual and future statements are not recognized as modals.

11. This interpretation, which is the most acceptable one, is found in the Talmud and in Rashi. However, there are other interpretations for the word *na:*, which are discussed in Fassberg (1994).

Chapter 5

The Perfect Aspect: Simultaneity, Anteriority and Backgrounding

One of the most puzzling forms in BH is *qatal*. *Qatal* may appear in clauses reporting situations which precede, are simultaneous with or even follow the situations reported in preceding clauses. Thus some scholars, e.g., Givón (1977, 1982) point only to one of its temporal uses, usually the most frequent one, namely its anteriority use. Other scholars provide lists of uses (Blake 1951, Andersen 1974, Eskhult 1990, Niccacci 1990, among others). In this chapter I will show that all these uses have in common one semantic feature which characterizes the aspect labelled **perfect**. I will show that clauses in the perfect (like progressive clauses) do not introduce their own R-time, but depend on an R-time introduced by the context, e.g., by an adverbial or by another clause. The different uses of the *qatal*, it will be demonstrated, are due to its "parasitic" nature as the perfect aspect in BH. In the first part of this chapter I will discuss the perfect aspect and show the temporal relations that can be denoted by it. In the second part of the chapter I will discuss the perfect form *qatal* in BH.

5.1 Definition of Perfect

The perfect aspect is characterized by its "parasitic" nature with respect to R-time: a clause in perfect cannot introduce a new R-time. Having this feature the perfect results in denoting different kinds of temporal relations.

5.1.1 *Simultaneity*

Simultaneous situations may bear the inclusion relation, i.e., include their R-time, or they may report merely overlapping, where they are included in their

R-time. Here I will use the term "simultaneity" for referring to mere overlapping. In chapter (3) we saw that BH (like English) has a special form for denoting inclusion. For denoting simultaneity, i.e., mere overlapping, BH uses the perfect *qatal*. Note that English does not use the perfect but the simple forms to report simultaneity (as illustrated by the examples under 1 below). This is because the simple forms in English may also be parasitic, as manifested also by its lack of sequential forms (see ch. 2 for discussion). Like inclusive clauses, a clause denoting simultaneity does not introduce its own R-time, but depends on the context for its temporal interpretation. Consider the following sentences:

(1) a) Israel was established in 1948. In that year John's parents left Europe.
b) John opened his mouth and closed his eyes at the same time.

The R-time of both sentences in (1a) is the year 1948, established by the first sentence. The second sentence in (1b) does not establish an R-time either, but uses the one which has already been established by the first sentence, as witnessed by the anaphoric adverbial "at the same time". The R-time in (1b) is not explicit, but is introduced by the event reported in the first clause. We may say, then, that the situations depicted in the second clauses in (1) are "parasitic" on those reported in the first. When discussing example (1a) in chapter (2) I showed that the temporal relations between the events themselves are not determined. In other words, the events' intervals do not necessarily overlap, and the event of leaving Europe in, e.g., (1a) may have happened in May 1948, exactly at the time at which the establishment of the state took place, but also before or after May, of that year. This can be reflected also in the difference between (1) above and (2) below:

(2) In 1948 Israel was established and John's parents left Europe.

The situations reported in the conjoined sentences, like the situations reported in (1), share the R-time denoted by '1948', but unlike the sentences in (1), they are not necessarily interpreted as simultaneous, but (usually) as sequential, where each of the sentences in (2) introduces its own R-time, within the scope of the year 1948. That is, '1948' is used as an explicit 'big' R-time including the 'sub-R-times' of the situations, which bear the sequential relation. This can be illustrated in two ways:

(3) a) $[R=1948[r1]<[r2]]$
b) $[R1 \subseteq 1948]<[R2 \subseteq 1948]$

Note that the simultaneity relation may be assigned to more than two situations, e.g., to the sentences in (1) we can add another sentence denoting a situation which also took place in 1948:

(1') ... and Dan was born.

The simultaneity relation may, naturally, hold not only between past non-modal situations. Situations in any time sphere, modal as well as non-modal, may bear the simultaneity relation, as in the following examples:

(4) a) John is eating and reading the paper. (present time)
b) (John and Mary will perform together); John will dance and Mary will sing. (future)
c) John used to lie on the beach and read the papers. (past habitual)

As noted above, while English uses the simple tense forms for depicting simultaneous situations, BH uses the perfect *qatal*. The use of the *qatal* in BH for denoting simultaneity will be demonstrated and discussed in section 5.2.1.

5.1.2 *Anteriority*

The usual definition of anteriority is that situations are reported in reverse order, as in “When Mary arrived John had already left”. This relationship is usually pointed out as the character of the (past) perfect in English. However, as shown by Comrie (1986) and others the situations may be reported in their chronological order and yet one of them be in perfect, as in “John had already left when Mary arrived.” This suggests that the perfect has a wider scope of functions than what is suggested by the regular definition of anteriority. Hence we need to discern a different feature for the perfect. I argue that it is, indeed, anteriority, but not as defined by traditional analyses. My definition of anteriority is given below under (5a), illustrated by the diagram in (5b):

(5) a) A situation E is anterior iff it precedes its R-time; the R-time is provided by an adverbial or another clause.
b) $E < R$

Situations denoted by sentences in one of the English perfect tenses (as they are traditionally called), the plus-que-parfait in French or the *qatal* form in BH are used to denote situations which precede the R-time, and hence called **anterior**. Since there is more literature on the English tenses, I will discuss the subject using (mainly) English data, and apply it to the Hebrew *qatal*.

Most of the analyses account for the difference between the simple and the perfect tenses in terms of relevance.[1] Compare the following sentences:

(6) a) I ate.
 b) I have eaten.

According to the relevance approach, when speakers utter (6a) they merely report a past-time event, but when uttering (6b) they also indicate that this event has some relevance in S-time (e.g., I am not hungry at the moment). The pragmatic approach does not see a difference in truth conditions between the simple past and the present perfect because it determines the truth conditions of a sentence by S-time and E-time only, as in traditional tense logic analysis. It is correct to claim that the relations of E-time and S-time are identical in (6a) and (6b), since in both sentences E-time precedes S-time. However, Heny (1982) shows that the relations of E-time with R-time also participate in determining the truth conditions of the sentence. He claims that (7a) is true if said on June 12, 1981, but (7b) is not (recall that US president Reagan was shot once, on June 11, 1981):

(7) a) Reagan has only been shot once during 1981.
 b) Reagan was shot only once during 1981.

Similarly, Chomsky (1972, and in other places) shows that the choice of the tense sometimes affects the logical entailments. Consider his example:

(8) Einstein has lived in Princeton.

According to Chomsky, (8) entails that Einstein is still alive, and hence the past simple should be used.[2] Furthermore, the pragmatic approach is forced to treat the present perfect in a different way than the past and the future perfect (Reinhart 1984b, Comrie 1985a and others). While the present perfect is defined only in terms of relevance, past and future perfect clauses are stipulated to denote situations which precede some R-time in the past or in the future respectively. Such an approach cannot account for the similarity of the perfect tenses in English, which seem to differ only in tense (intuitively speaking). Studies such as Salkie (1989) and Hatav (1993) follow Reichenbach, showing that the three forms belong together. This line of analysis accords with Bennett & Partee (1978 [1972]), who claim that the past and the future perfect involve a sentence in the present perfect. According to this analysis, a perfect sentence in the present, the past or the future, expresses anteriority as defined in (5) above. The difference between them is only in the relations of the R-time with R_S, as shown in the sentences under (9), (10) and (11) below.

(9) a) I have eaten. $E<R=R_S$
b) John has finished his article.

(10) a) I had eaten by three. $E<R<R_S$
b) When John came Mary had already left.

(11) a) I will have eaten by three. $E<R>R_S$
b) By the time Mary finishes her thesis, John will have already finished his.
c) John will have eaten the fish by tomorrow. (Bennett & Partee 1972)
d) J. will already have left, by the time M. comes.

Sentence (12) below demonstrates that the perfect aspect may be used in all kinds of modal clauses, not only for futurates:

(12) If you ever cross me again, you will wish you had bought a gun first.

This analysis does not contradict the intuitive feeling that a sentence in perfect (in past and future tenses as well as in present tense) asserts some relevance (or perspective, as seen by Reinhart 1984b) at R-time. The speaker is understood to state that s/he is not hungry at the moment, when uttering (9a), and that s/he was not hungry or will not be hungry at three, when uttering (10a) or (11a) respectively. Moreover, it seems to me that the analysis suggested by Chomsky for example (8) above implies that the relevant characteristic of the perfect may even result in determining truth conditions. The relevance property of the perfect seems to be implicitly incorporated in the works of Moens (1987), Moens & Steedman (1988), Parsons (1990), Kearns (1991), Kamp & Reyle (1993) and others, who argue that the event of a sentence in perfect results in some state obtaining at R-time. McCawley (1971, 1981) and Palmer (1965) disagree with this analysis, claiming that it is invalid to say that a sentence in present perfect necessarily entails a state which is the result of some event, although it is many times the case. Analysing the sentences

(13) a) John has gone to the office.
b) We can't come to your party. The police have arrested my wife.

given by McCawley, Moens (1987: ex. 167-168) admits that it is impossible to predict what results the sentences describe. However, Moens correctly claims that "this does not render false an analysis of the perfect in terms of reference to the consequent (=result) states" (p.72). The result state, according to Moens, is determined by the nature of the event (resulting in a state) and world knowledge. For example, referring to Chomsky's example (given above under 8) Moens argues that it is infelicitous only if we take Einstein's life to be the consequential state we are talking about. However, it can be uttered felicitously to refer to, e.g., the history of Princeton. Parsons (1990) attempts to provide an analysis which will allow predictions. Parsons distinguishes between what he calls "target" state and "resultant (=result, consequence) state" of a sentence in perfect. "If I throw a ball onto the roof", claims Parsons (p. 235), "the target state of this event is the ball's being on the roof, a state that may or may not last for a long time". The result state, on the other hand, is "the state of my having thrown the ball onto the roof, and it is a state that cannot cease holding at some later time." However, it seems to me that Parsons' distinction is valid for simple tensed sentences as well. For example, a sentence such as "I threw the ball onto the roof" would also result in a state of having thrown the ball onto the roof which does not cease holding, and moreover has the target state of the ball being on the roof. Another example would be "Mary killed John" whose result as well as target states will last forever. The target state, as described by Parsons, seems to be the result or the consequence state, which cannot be predicted, as claimed by Moens, but depends on context and world knowledge.

To demand sentences in perfect to always have result states might entail that the situation which results in a state should be an event. This is, indeed, what is argued by Moens (1987, & Steedman 1988). The perfect, according to Moens, is a function which requires its input category to be an event (culmination, in Moens terms). If the input is not an event, he further claims, "the perfect will do its best to coerce it to be one" (Moens & Steedman 1988:18). Depraetere (1995:9) correctly claims that adopting such an approach means that sentences such as "I have lived in London" should be unacceptable. For a situation to result in a state it does not have to be an event. It is possible, for example, to think of a result state for the sentence "I have lived in London", without coercing an eventive meaning on it, e.g., it may be uttered by an Israeli who wants to explain her fluent English. (Though the simple past would be more natural.) More problematic is the fact that a sentence such as "I have lived in London" is true also if I still live in London. This might seem to undermine the definition given in (5) above for the perfect, namely that the situation must precede R-time. In what follows I will show that it does not. As discussed in chapter (2) above, we have the following differences in logical entailments of events vs. states:

(14) a) I ate the apple. → I am not eating the (same) apple now.
b) I was sick. ~ → I am not sick now.

The explanation for the difference between (14a) and (14b) draws attention to the semantic properties of the situations. Recall that both sentences are true iff there is at least one interval at which they are true, and events such as (14a) are true only at one interval due to their non-distributivity character, while states such as (14b) may be true in more than one interval (for being distributive situations). For the same reason we have the following entailments of perfect sentences:

(15) a) I have eaten breakfast. → I am not eating now (breakfast).
b) I have known David since childhood. ~ → I do not know him now.

(16) a) Mary had already eaten at three. → Mary was not eating at three.
b) When Mary met John she had already been in love with David. ~ → Mary was not in love with David when she met John.

We may conclude, then, that in the case of the perfect the sentence denotes a situation which has *at least one* interval preceding the R-time; if that situation is an event, it necessarily precedes the R-time as in (15a) and (16a), but if it is a state it can and usually does overlap it as in (15b) and (16b). However, consider the following sentence from Hornstein (1977):

(17) The secretary had left at 10 o'clock.

As pointed out by Hornstein, (17) is ambiguous between (17'a) and (17'b):

(17') a) The secretary left **before** ten o'clock.
b) The secretary left **at** ten o'clock.

(17'a) is in accord with the analysis I have given so far, but (17'b) is not. As mentioned in chapter (4), Hornstein claims that adverbs may modify either the R-time or the E-time. In this spirit, Comrie (1985a:66) analyses adverbs in cases like (17) as ambiguous between modifying the R-time and the E-time. When the adverb modifies the E-time, claims Comrie, we must look for the R-time somewhere in the context. For example, he argues that in (18a) below the first clause establishes a reference time of midnight, hence the adverbial "at ten o'clock" is forced to take on the interpretation of the time of John's departure (i.e. ten o'clock is E-time). In (18b), on the other hand, "for the text to make sense 'at ten o'clock' must be interpreted as the reference point prior to which John had left":

(18) a) The clock struck twelve; John had already departed at ten o'clock.
b) Mary came to visit John at ten o'clock; but John had already left at ten o'clock.

In Hatav (1993) I show that only according to interpretation (17'a) does the adverb "ten o'clock" modifies the R-time of (17); if the interpretation is (17'b) it is necessarily the E-time which is modified by the speaker. As I mentioned there, Barbara Josman (pc) feels that (17) by itself cannot be interpreted as (17'b) unless it is nested in a discourse such as the following:

(19) When I came to the office at 10:15 nobody was there; the secretary had left at ten.

In (19) it is clear that the R-time is 10:15, not ten; and the only way to interpret "ten" is by attaching it to the E-time. A formal account for the difference is proposed in Nakajima (1991). (A similar account is found in Abusch & Rooth 1990.) Nakajima suggests the following tree for sentences such as (17):

(20)

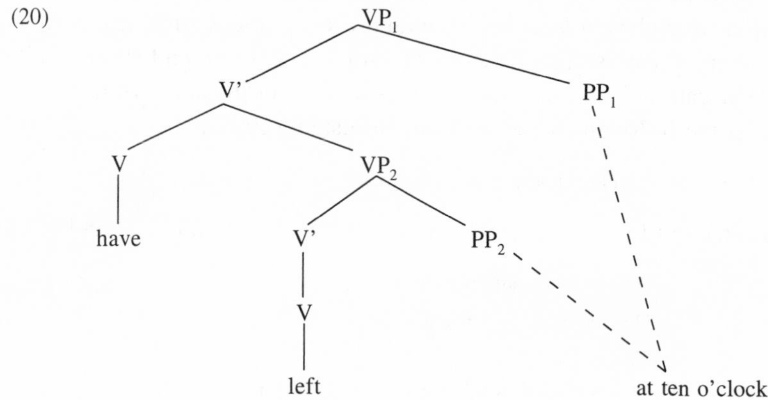

The frame adverb "at ten" can modify either the higher phrase VP_1 or the lower phrase VP_2. Nakajima claims that when the adverb is attached to VP_1 and hence has wide scope over the whole phrase with the auxiliary, it modifies the R-time of the sentence, but when it has narrow scope over the lower phrase VP_2 only, it actually modifies the E-time of the "leaving" event. In my opinion when the adverbial modifies the R-time it adjuncts to a higher phrase IP rather than to VP_1, but this does not affect Nakajima's explanation.

Therefore interpretation (17'a) for (17) corresponds with the modification of VP_1 (or IP), suggesting that the adverb "at ten" is used to modify the R-time, but interpretation (17'b) corresponds with the modification of VP_2, where the adverb modifies the E-time. Nakajima claims that whenever an adverbial has a wider scope than some verbal elements, they may be preposed. Therefore "at ten" may be preposed when it modifies the upper VP_1. In this case, he concludes, the frame adverbial preserves only one interpretation, as being the R-time of the sentence:

(21) At ten o'clock, the secretary had left.

Since situations denoted by perfect clauses may precede the situations of the previous clauses whose R-time they share, the (past) perfect is expected to mark the transition from the main time-line to a subnarrative. This is indeed the case, as illustrated in Reinhart (1984a: ex. 5) and Kamp & Reyle (1993: ex. 5.161). In French it is also the plus-que-parfait and in BH it is the perfect *qatal* which mark the transition to a subnarrative. However, English behaves differently than French and BH with respect to the rest of the clauses in the subnarrative. English uses the past perfect for *all* the clauses, not only for the first one, as illustrated in (22) below:

(22) Last Tuesday Mary got married to Pierre. Three days before she had bought a rotten fish, eaten it and got sick.

The first clause in the second sentence of (22) is in past perfect, since it starts a narrative which took place before the event reported in the previous clause. The other two events reported in the two successive clauses report sequential events with respect to the event of buying a rotten fish, but they are also reported by past perfect clauses rather than simple past. Compare (22) to the French translation (22') below, where 'PS' stands for 'passé simple' and PLP for 'plus-que-parfait' (I thank Bernadette Cailler for the data and the discussion):

(22')	*Marie*	*épousa*	*Pierre*	*Mardi*	*dernier.*	*Trois*	*jours*	*auparavant*	*elle*
	Mary	married:PS	Pierre	Tuesday	last	three	days	before	she
	avait acheté	*du*	*mouvais*	*poisson,*	*le*	*mangea*	*et*	*se sentit*	*malade.*
	bought:PLP	of-the	bad	fish	it	ate:PS	and	felt:PS	sick

The first sentence reports a narrative situation in the past, and hence it is in passé-simple. The second sentence consists of three clauses which report a sequence of events happening before the event of marriage. Hence the first clause is in plus-que-parfait, marking the transition from the main to the sub-narrative. The other two clauses, however, are in passé-simple. In other words, clauses reporting sequences in subnarratives also appear in passé-simple, moving the R-time forward, except for the first one which marks the transition from the main time-line to the sub-sequence. Bernadette Cailler emphasizes that it is also possible for a speaker to refer only to the main R-time of the first sentence, ignoring the sequential relationship between the clauses in the second sentence, and hence the other two clauses may also have the plus-que-parfait. In other words, in French the speaker has the choice between indicating the sequence or ignoring it. In English this choice does not exist, and the speaker has to refer always to the main R-time (but this is not surprising, since English does not mark sequentiality). BH behaves like French in marking the first clause in the sub-narrative by a *qatal* verb where the rest of its clauses are in the sequential form *wayyiqtol*. (See demonstrations in section 5.2.2.) Note, however, that the option of not marking sequentiality in the sub-narrative does not seem to exist in BH. Analysing a similar sequence in English (their example 5.161), Kamp & Reyle would argue that "last Tuesday" in (22) is used as the R-time for all the clauses in the sub-narrative. However, realizing that the clauses form a sequence they claim that also "each clause provides a 'reference time' for the clause following it..." (p. 594). To explain this double referring Kamp & Reyle use their distinction of T_{PT} and R_{PT}, where the former corresponds to the R-time "last Tuesday", and the latter to each of the R-times provided by the clauses. (See section 1.1.1 for an overview of the distinction.) However, since the approach of having two different kinds of R-time was not adopted in this study we have to account for the temporal relations holding between the first clause in the sub-narrative and the clause(s) following it differently. The English case does not pose a problem for our approach, as we stipulate that there is only one R-time, "last Tuesday", for all the situations reported by the clauses of the "flashback" material, and hence the (past) perfect verbs in all of them; the sequence reading seems to be only a pragmatic implicature. However, in the case of French (and BH), we need to account for the sequential forms appearing in the "flashback" clauses. Recall that a sequential form moves its R-time forward, resulting in following the current R-time. Thus we should expect the second clause in the sub-sequence to follow "last Tuesday", counter-intuitively. I want to argue that in flashback narrative, when the narrator introduces a clause which "throws" the text off the main narrative, the current

R-time of the main narrative becomes only one alternative for the next introduced clause; another possibility opens, namely forming a new R-time within the time of the subnarrative. Thus, once we introduce the clause which takes us to the time sphere of the sub-narrative we may choose between two possibilities for locating in time a new sequential clause: the time available in the main time-line, or the time available in the sub-line. To illustrate this let us reconsider ex. (22). The first clause "Mary had bought a rotten fish" takes us to a time preceding the current R-time of her getting married, three days before Tuesday. The narrator may now choose to introduce a new R-time in the new time sphere opened in the discourse, and report a situation with respect to Mary's buying a rotten fish, as done in (22). The other option is to go back right away to the time sphere of the main narrative and introduce a new R-time on the main time-line. In the case of English, the former and the latter choices require different verb forms: a (past) perfect and a simple past respectively. In the case of French and BH both choices require sequential forms. This sometimes results in ambiguity, and only the context could determine whether the sequential clause introduced after the departure from the main time-line is a link on a new (sub) sequence or it is another link following the current one on the main narrative.

5.1.3 *Backgrounding*

Although the R-time of a situation reported by a sentence in perfect is usually mentioned in a phrase following that sentence, there is nothing in definition (5) to block it from preceding it. Example (23a) analyzed in Bennett & Partee (1978) and example (23b) analyzed in Comrie (1986) may illustrate this possibility.

(23) a) John had left when Mary arrived yesterday.
b) Old Sam's boat approached the other side of the pier. He had docked before I began fishing.

Bennett & Partee claim, that (23a) is true at the time of speech if (24) is true when Mary arrived yesterday:

(24) John has left.

In our terms, John's leaving precedes the R-time of Mary's arrival, although it is reported first. This means that when the past perfect sentence is introduced in the discourse it has to wait for another clause for its interpretation. (Recall from our discussion of the progressive in chapter 3, that a prog sentence cannot introduce an R-time and is dependent on the context for its interpretation. When the discourse starts with a progressive sentence, that sentence cannot be interpreted until an adverb or a new clause is introduced, as in "John was eating supper. Suddenly he heard a scream.") The same is to be said about ex. (23b). "He had docked" cannot be interpreted without the second part of the sentence which serves as its R-time. Comrie correctly notes that since the normal way of referring to past events in their chronological sequence is the simple past, "the listener will naturally wonder why a more complex verb form than necessary has been chosen" (p. 20). Comrie claims that in (23b) the past perfect is used to background the event of Sam's docking the boat, to exclude it form the main story-line. This function can also explain the phenomenon of past perfect sentences at the opening of a narrative discourse. Reinhart (1984a) cites the following opening paragraph of Conan Doyle's *The Adventure of the Sussex Vampire*:

(25) **Holmes had read carefully a note** which the last post had brought him. Then, with the dry chuckle which was his nearest approach to a laugh, he tossed it over to me. (*The Complete Sherlock Holmes*, p. 1033)

As the foreground clauses in English are in the simple past, the past perfect in the first clause of (25) marks it as background, although this clause reports an event which is ordered temporally before the next event and could be a candidate for foreground.[3] We can regard the first clause as forming a setting (or as part of it). In terms of R-time, since it is the first clause in the discourse it has to wait for its interpretation until the text provides an R-time, i.e., only when the second sentence is introduced does our clause "have a home". (Note that the second clause is also in past perfect, which suggests that the R-time of the third clause provides the temporal interpretation for two parasitic events in addition to its own event.)

5.1.4 *Counterfactuals*

Counterfactuals, as mentioned in chapter 4, are usually indicated in English by the past perfect:

(26) If you had done this you would have been wrong. (Palmer 1986)

However, as mentioned in chapter (4), the use of the perfect aspect in sentences such as (26) is not limited to English, but is manifested in other languages, too: the plus-que-parfait in French (Barson 1975), the aorist and the pluperfect in Greek and Latin respectively (Palmer 1986), the anterior marker in Creoles (Givón 1982, attributed to Bickerton 1976) and the *qatal* in BH. However, as indicated in chapter (4), the use of the perfect tenses in counterfactuals such as (26) has not to date been given a satisfactory analysis.

5.2 The Perfect Aspect in Biblical Hebrew

In this section I will show that *qatal* is the perfect aspect in BH, used for all the functions described in the first part of the chapter. In section (5.2.1) I will discuss its use in clauses denoting simultaneous situations. Section (5.2.2) discusses the anteriority use of *qatal* which entails its use in marking the transition from the main time-line to subnarrative. In this connection it will be shown that direct-speech is a special kind of subnarrative, whose first clause would have a *qatal* verb (if it is not modal). Section (5.2.3) examines its backgrounding function, and section (5.2.4) shows its behaviour in modal material. Section (5.2.5) summarizes the different uses of the *qatal*.

5.2.1 *Simultaneity in BH*

Being a perfect form in general the *qatal* in BH is used to report simultaneous situations, as in the following example:

(27) 3. *wayhi: miqqe;ṣ ya:mi:m wayyab̲e; qayin mippri:*
wayhi: from-end:of days WAYY:bring:3SG:MASC Cain from-fruit:of
ha:^{ʔa}d̲a:ma: minḥa: layhwh 4. ***wheb̲el he;b̲i: gam***
the-earth present to-the-God and-Abel QAT:bring:3SG:MASC also
hu: mibbk̲o;ro:t̲ ṣo:no: u:me;ḥelb̲e;he:n
he from-firstlings:of sheep-his and-fat-their:FEM
wayyišaˁ yhwh 5. *ˀel heb̲el wˀel minḥa:t̲o:* ***wˀel***
WAYY:accept:3SG:MASC God to Abel and-to present-his and-to
qayin wˀel minḥa:t̲o: lo; ša:ˁa:...
Cain and-to present-his NEG QAT:accept:3SG:MASC
'3. At the end Cain brought some of the produce of the soil as a gift to the Lord 4. **And Abel brought some of the first-born of his flock and their fat portions**. The Lord accepted Abel and his gift 5. **But Cain and his gift he did not accept**...' (Gen. 4:3-5)

The *qatal* verb *he;ḇi:* 'brought' in the boldfaced clause in verse (4) denotes an event which is simultaneous to the event reported in the previous clause.[4] As this clause stands in a parallel structure with the previous clause, Hebraists following Andersen (1974) would claim that the *qatal* verb is used here to build a chiasmus structure. (See section 1.2 for a discussion on Andersen's analysis.) However, although the narrator may have thought of eliciting a poetic effect of chiasmus here, he could not have formed a chiasmus structure by using a *qatal* verb if the situation were in sequence with the previous one. The use of a *qatal* form in negative sentences such as the boldfaced clause in verse (5) is usually explained as a syntactic choice (see, e.g., Bauer 1910). It has been claimed that the *wayyiqtol* is not used here because it is verb initial, and since the Neg particle *lo;* should precede the verb in negative assertions, the *qatal* is used instead. But the syntactic constraint is only part of the picture. Moreover, it is sometimes possible to avoid a negative sentence and then to use the sequential form, e.g., in (27) the speaker could have used a verb such as *mˀn* 'refuse' (to accept the gift). The main reason for using a *qatal* here, as said above, is that its clause denotes a simultaneous situation.

In this sense, the form of *qatal* can be used also to explain, detail and summarize situations reported in previous clauses:

(28)

7. *wayya:ḇo;*	*no;$_{a}$ḥ*	*u:ḇa:na:w*	*wˀišto:*	*u:nše:*
WAYY:come:3SG:MASC	Noah	and-sons-his	and-wife-his	and-wives:of

ḇa:na:w	*ˀitto:*	*ˀel*	*hatte;ḇa:*	*mippne:*	*me:*	*hammabbu:l*
sons-his	with-him	to	the-ark	from-face:of	water:of	the-flood

8. *min*	*habbhe;ma:*	*haṭṭho:ra:*	*u:min*	*habbhe;ma:*	*ˀ^{a}šer*
from	the-beast	the-pure:FEM	and-from	the-beast	that

ˀe:nenna:	*ṭho;ra:*	*u:min*	*ha:ˁo:p̄*	*wḵol*	*ˀ^{a}šer*
NEG-she	pure:FEM	and-from	the-bird	and-all:of	that

ro;me;ś	*ˁal*	*ha:ˀ^{a}ḏa:ma:*	9. ***šnayim***	***šnayim***
QOT:crawl:SG:MASC	on	the-ground	two:MASC	two:MASC

baˀu:	***ˀel***	***no;$_{a}$ḥ***	***ˀel***	***hatte;ḇa:***	***za:ḵa:r***	***u:nqe;ḇa:***...
QAT:come:3PL	to	Noah	to	the-ark	male	and-female

'7. Noah went into the ark with his sons, his wife and his sons' wives because of the waters of the flood. 8. And of all beasts, clean and unclean, of birds and everything that crawls on the ground 9. **two by two came to Noah unto the ark male and female**...' (Gen. 7:7-9)

The *qatal* verb *ba:ˀu:* '(they) came' in the boldfaced clause of verse (9) does not indicate a new event, but explains the event just reported (Noah coming to the ark with his family and the animals). The following example illustrates how a *qatal* verb summarizes a list of situations already reported:

(29) *waydabbe;r mo;še ˀel bne: yiśra:ˀe;l*
WAYY:speak:3SG:MASC Moses to sons:of Israel
wayyo:ṣi:ˀu: ˀet̠ hamqalle;l ˀel miḥu:ṣ
WAYY:take-out:3PL:MASC ACC the-curser:SG:MASC to from-out
lammaḥ^{a}ne wayyirgmu: ˀo;t̠o: ˀa:b̠en ***u:b̠ne:***
the-camp WAYY:stone:3PL:MASC him stone and-sons:of
yiśra:ˀe;l *ˁa:śu: kaˀ^{a}šer ṣiwwa: yhwh ˀet̠*
Israel QAT:do:3PL as-that QAT:command:3SG:MASC God ACC
mo;še
Moses
'Moses spoke to the Israelites, and they took the man who blasphemed out of the camp and stoned him to death. **The Israelites did** as the Lord had commanded Moses.' (Lev. 24:23)

The *qatal* verb *ˁa:śu:* '(they) did' in the boldfaced clause summarizes all the actions of the sons of Israel (taking the man who cursed God and stoning him). (The *qatal* verb in the last clause is an example of the anteriority use of the *qatal*. See discussion on this use in the next section.)

5.2.2 *Anteriority in BH*

Most of the traditional analyses claim that *qatal* clauses indicate not only that an event occurred (in the past), but furthermore that it resulted in a state-of-affairs which holds at the current R-time, like the aorist in Greek. McFall (1982) reports that Turner (1876), for example, argues that *qatal* expresses an "action of state" as the attribute of the person or thing spoken of rather than the verbal action (which can be expressed only by *yiqtol-wayyiqtol* according to Turner). All the historical-comparative theories — Knudtzon (1889), Bauer (1910), G.R.Driver (1936) and Thacker (1954) — trace the *qatal* form back to an original *qatil* which indicated a state. When the Akkadian language was discovered in 1841 it was realized that it lacked an active *qatal* but had a stative (permansive) *qatil*. It has been claimed, that after the split of Akkadian had occurred, the active *qatal* was developed in West-Semitic[5] from this stative meaning as follows: 'he is old' developed to 'he has become old'; 'he is clothed' became 'he has clothed (himself)', etc. Although it does not account for all the uses of the BH *qatal*, this analysis seems to capture one of its major uses, the one parallels to the English perfect, namely anteriority, as it discussed in section 5.1.2.

Since the BH verb system does not express tenses, as demonstrated throughout this work, *qatal* clauses reporting anterior situations (the subject of the present section) may be interpreted in English as a present, a past or a future perfect, depending on the context. First consider present perfect interpretation. The natural environment for such interpretation in a narrative discourse is direct speech:

(30) *wayyakki:ra:h* *wayyo;mer* *kt̲o;net̲* *bni:*
WAYY:recognize:3SG:MASC-her WAYY:say:3SG:MASC robe:of son-my
ḥayya: ***ra:ʕa:*** ***ʔak̲a:la:t̲hu:*** ***ṭa:ro;p̄***
beast evil:SG:FEM QAT:eat:3SG:FEM-him INF:devour
ṭo;rap̄ ***yo:se;p̄***
QAT:be:devoured:3SG:MASC Joseph
'Jacob recognized it, and said, It is my son's robe. **A wild beast has eaten him. Joseph has been devoured**.' (Gen. 37:33)

The cry of Jacob over his son is intuitively understood as being relevant to the time he utters the words, i.e., to R_S. Hence it is likely that Jacob will use a form which corresponds to the present perfect in English. It is not surprising, therefore, that he uses the *qatal* form. As expected from the analysis of the anteriority function of the perfect (in section 5.1.2), the event in the "parasitic" *qatal* clause is understood to precede the time of Jacob's speech. The analysis also predicts that if the "parasitic" situation is a state rather than event it may be interpreted as overlapping the S-time. Consider the following examples:

(31) a) 4. *wayyišlaḥ* *yaʕaqo;b̲* *wayyiqra:* *lra:ḥe;l*
WAYY:send:3SG:MASC Jacob WAYY:call:3SG:MASC to-Rachel
ulle;ʔa: *haśśa:d̲e* *ʔel* *ṣo;no:* 5. *wayyo;mer*
and-to-Leah the-field to flock-his WAYY:say:3SG:MASC
la:hen *ro;ʔe* *ʔa:no;k̲i:* *ʔet̲* *pne:*
to-them:FEM QOT:see:SG:MASC I ACC face:of
ʔab̲i:k̲en *ki:* *ʔe:nennu:* *ʔe;lay* *kit̲mo;l*
father-yours:PL:FEM that NEG-he to-me like-yesterday
šilšo;m ***we;lo;he:*** ***ʔa:b̲i:*** ***ha:ya:***
the-day-before-yesterday and-God:of father-my QAT:be:3SG:MASC
ʕimma:d̲i: **6.** ***wʔatte;na:*** ***yd̲aʕten*** *ki:* *bk̲ol*
with-me and-you:PL:FEM QAT:know:2PL:FEM that in-all:of
ko;ḥi: *ʕab̲a:d̲ti:* *ʔet̲* *ʔab̲i:k̲en*
strength-my QAT:work:1SG ACC father-yours
'4. Jacob sent to fetch Rachel and Leah to his flocks out in the field. 5. and said to them, I see that your father is not as well disposed to me as once he was; **yet the God of my father has been with me.** 6. **You know** how I have served your father to the best of my power.' (Gen. 31:4-6)

b) *wayyo;mer* *qaḥ* *na:* *ˀeṯ*
WAYY:say:3SG:MASC IMP:take:2SG:MASC please ACC
binḵa: *ˀeṯ* *yḥi:ḏka:* *ˀᵃšer* ***ˀa:haḇta:...***
son-yours:SG:MASC ACC only-yours:SG:MASC that QAT:love:2SG:MASC
'He (God) said, Take your son, your only son, **whom you love**...' (Gen. 22:2)

c) 4. ... *wayyiḇku:* *gam* *bne:* *yiśra:ˀe;l*
WAYY:cry:3PL:MASC also sons:of Israel
wayyo;mru: *mi:* *yaˀᵃḵi:le;nu:* *ba:śa:r*
WAYY:say:3PL:MASC who YIQ:feed:3SG:MASC-us meat
5. ***za:ḵarnu:*** ***ˀeṯ hadda:ḡa:*** *ˀᵃšer* *no;ḵal* *bmiṣrayim*
QAT:remember:1PL ACC the-fish that YIQ:eat:1PL in-Egypt
ḥinna:m...
for-free
'4. ...The children of Israel also wept, and said, Who shall give us meat to eat? 5. **We remember the fish** which we used to eat in Egypt freely...' (Num. 11:4-5)

In chapter (3) we mentioned a group of verbs, namely the verb 'be' and what I called "mental state verbs" such as 'love', 'know', 'remember', and the like, which cannot have the inclusive form, e.g., the progressive in English and the form *qotel* in BH. When such verbs are understood as inclusive, I claim, they actually have the form of the perfect. For example, in (31a) the last clause of verse (5) has the verb 'be' in *qatal* which is translated in English by a present perfect verb. This clause is to be interpreted as denoting a situation included in R_S of Jacob's speech event, but since this situation is a state it can include the event of the speech, rather than precede it. The other boldfaced clauses in (31) contain verbs from the group of "mental state verbs": 'know', 'love' and 'remember' in (a), (b) and (c) respectively. Hence they are in *qatal* form and are analyzed the same way as the 'be' clause in (a).[6]

The following discussion demonstrates the different uses of the perfect aspect *qatal* when it is interpreted as denoting anterior situations in the past. Consider the following example:

(32) 17. *wayya:qom* *yaʕᵃqo;ḇ* *wayyiśa:* *ˀeṯ* *ba:na:w*
WAYY:rise:3SG:MASC Jacob WAYY:set:3SG:MASC ACC sons-his
wˀeṯ *na:ša:w* *ʕal* *haggmalli:m* 18. *wayyinhaḡ* *ˀeṯ*
and-ACC wives-his on the-camels WAYY:lead:3SG:MASC ACC
kol *miqne;hu:* *wˀeṯ* *kol* *rḵušo:* ***ˀᵃšer ra:ḵa:š...***
all:of cattle-his and-ACC all:of property-his that QAT:acquire:3SG:MASC
19. ***wla:ḇa:n*** ***ha:laḵ*** *liḡzo;z* *ˀeṯ* *ṣo;no:...*
and-Laban QAT:go:3SG:MASC to-INF:shear ACC flock-his

'17. Jacob set his sons and his wives on camels, 18. and drove off all the herds and livestock **which he had acquired**... 19. **And Laban had gone to shear his sheep**...' (Gen. 31:17-19)

It is well acknowledged that the first clause in verse (19) denotes an event preceding the event reported in the previous clause (see, e.g., Qimron 1980). However, the use of the *qatal* form in the boldfaced clause of verse (18) is commonly explained syntactically, as in the case of verse (5) in example (27) above. E.g., Bauer (1910), followed by modern Hebraists such as Qimron (1980), claimed that the verb in the boldfaced clause of verse (18) is in *qatal* form because it appears in a subordinate clause, and hence has to be preceded by a particle "which", not allowing the verb initial form *wayyiqtol* to appear. But, as claimed also in connection with example (5), this analysis does not contradict ours. The following example demonstrates a "mental state verb" in past perfect *qatal* (but see FN 6 above):

(33) 2... *wayya:b̲e;* *yo:se;p̄* *ˀet̲* *dibba:t̲a:m*
WAYY:bring:3SG:MASC Joseph ACC report-their:MASC
ra:ˤa: *ˀel* *ˀᵃb̲i:hem* 3. ***wyiśra:ˀe;l*** ***ˀa:hab̲***
bad:SG:FEM to father-their:MASC and-Israel QAT:love:3SG:MASC
ˀet̲ ***yo:se;p̄*** ***mikkol*** ***ba:na:w***...
ACC Joseph from-all:of sons-his
'2. ... Joseph brought their father a bad report of them. 3. **Now Israel loved Joseph more than any other of his sons**...' (Gen. 37:2-3)

Since it may be interpreted as a past perfect, *qatal* functions also to mark a transition to a subnarrative. Consider the following example:

(34) 33. *wayya:b̲o;* *la:b̲a:n* *bˀo;hel* *yaˤᵃqo;b̲* *u:b̲ˀo;hel*
WAYY:come:3SG:MASC Laban in-tent:of Jacob and-in-tent:of
le;ˀa: *u:b̲ˀo;hel* *šte:* *ha:ˀᵃma:ho;t̲* *wlo;*
Leah and-in-tent:of two:FEM:of the-maids and-NEG
ma:ṣa: *wayye;ṣe;* *me;ˀo;hel* *le;ˀa:*
QAT:find:3SG:MASC WAYY:go:out:3SG:MASC from-tent:of Leah
wayya:b̲o; *bˀo;hel* *ra:ḥe;l* 34. ***wra:ḥe;l***
WAYY:come:3SG:MASC in-tent:of Rachel and-Rachel
la:qḥa: ***ˀet̲*** ***hattra:p̄i:m*** ***wattśime;m***
QAT:take:3SG:FEM ACC the-idols WAYY:put:3SG:FEM-them:MASC
bk̲ar ***hagga:ma:l*** ***watte;šeb̲*** ***ˤᵃle:hem***
in-pillow:of the-camel WAYY:sit:3SG:FEM on-them:MASC
waymašše;š *la:b̲a:n* *ˀet̲* *kol* *ha:ˀo;hel* *wlo;*
WAYY:touch:3SG:MASC Laban ACC all:of the-tent and-NEG

ma:ṣa:
QAT:find:3SG:MASC
'33. Laban went into Jacob's tent and Leah's tent and that of the two slave girls, but he did not find anything. He came out of Leah's tent and went into Rachel's. 34. **Rachel had taken the household gods and put them in the camel-bag and sat on them**. Laban went through everything in the tent and did not find anything.' (Gen. 31:33-34)

The context makes it clear that the boldfaced clauses in verse (34) denote events all of which precede the event reported in the last clause of verse (33) (and maybe even the situations preceding it too). That is, they all report anterior events. But, since their events follow each other their verbs are in the sequential form *wayyiqtol*, except for the first clause. In the first clause we have a *qatal* verb to indicate anteriority, and hence mark the transition to the subnarrative. Note that, as predicted by the analysis given above, the transition back to the main time-line is not marked, and the clause appearing in it is interpreted as being part of the main rather than the subordinate narrative only due to context.

Niccacci (1990) claims that the language in direct speech ("discourse", in his terms) differs completely from the language in the narrative text. Thus, according to Niccacci, the forms *qatal* and *wayyiqtol* function differently in the narrative and in the direct speech text. One of his arguments is that unlike a regular narrative, the time line within a direct speech starts with a *qatal* rather than with a *wayyiqtol* clause. I disagree with Niccacci. Direct speech, I argue, is a special kind of subnarrative, and therefore their first clause marks a transition from the main to the subordinate discourse, and hence its *qatal* verb. (An indication of that is the fact that a direct speech text may abandon the current R-time and use another R-time, e.g., R_S as in ex. 30.) This finds support in the findings that when the time line does *not* start at the opening of the direct speech text its first clause is in *wayyiqtol*. Consider first an example where the first clause of the narrative direct-speech is also the first clause in the direct speech text. (The boldfaced clauses are part of the main rather than the subsidiary time-line):

(35) 6. ***wayyo;mer*** ***hannaˤar hammaggiḏ*** ***lo:*** *niqro;*
WAYY:say:3SG:MASC the-boy the-tell:QOT:SG:MASC to-him INF:happen
niqre;ṯi: *bhar* *haggilbo;$_{a}^{ʕ}$whinne;* *ša:ˀu:l nišˤa:n*
QAT:happen:1SG in-mount:of the-Gilboa *whinne;* Saul QOT:lean:SG:MASC
ˤal ḥ^{a}ni:ṯo: *whinne;* *ha:reḵeḇ* *u:ḇa^{ʕa}le:* *happa:ra:ši:m*
on spear-his *whinne;* the-chariot and-owners:of the-horses

hidbi:quhu: 7. *wayyip̄en* *ˀaḥ^a^ra:w*
QAT:catch:3PL:MASC-him WAYY:turn:3SG:MASC behind-him
wayyir?e;ni: *wayyiqra:* *ˀe;lay wa:ˀo;mar*
WAYY:see:3SG:MASC-me WAYY:call:3SG:MASC to-me WAYY:say:3SG:MASC
hinne;ni: 8. *wayyo;mer* *li:* *mi:* *ˀa:tta:* *wa:ˀo;mar*
hinne;-me WAYY:say:3SG:MASC to-me who you:SG:MASC WAYY:say:1SG
ˀe;la:w *ˁ^a^ma:le;qi:* *ˀa:no;k̲i:* 9. *wayyo;mer* *ˀe;lay*
to-him Amalekite:MASC I WAYY:say:3SG:MASC to-me
ˁ^a^mod̲ *na:* *ˁa:lay* *u:mo;t̲te;ni:* *ki:*
IMP:stand:2SG:MASC please on-me and-IMP:kill:2SG:MASC-me because
ˀ^a^ḥa:z̧a:ni: *haššа:b̲a:ṣ* *ki:* *k̲ol-ˁo:d̲* *nap̄ši:* *bi:*
QAT:catch:3SG:MASC-me the-convulsion because yet soal-my in-me
10. *wa:ˀe^ˁe^mo;d̲* *ˁa:la:w* *wa^ˀa^mo;t̲te;hu:* *ki:* *ya:d̲aˁti:*
WAYY:stand:1SG on-him WAYY:kill:1SG-him because QAT:know:1SG
ki: *lo;* *yiḥye* *ˀaḥ^a^re:* *nip̄lo:* *wa:ˀeqqaḥ* *hanne;zer*
that NEG YIQ:live:3SG:MASC after INF:fall-his WAYY:take:1SG the-crown
ˀašer *ˁal ro;šo:* *wˀeṣˁa:d̲a:* *ˀ^a^šer* *ˁal* *zro;ˁo:*
that on head-his and-bracelet that on arm-his
wa:ˀ^a^b̲i:ˀe;m *ˀel* *ˀ^a^d̲o;ni:* 11. *he;nna:* ***wayyaḥ^a^ze;q***
WAYY:bring:1SG-them:MASC to lord-my here-to WAYY:hold:3SG:MASC
da:wid̲ ***bib̲ḡd̲a:w*** ***wayyiqra:ˁe;m*** ***wḡam*** ***kol***
David in-clothes-his WAYY:tear:3SG:MASC-them:MASC and-also all:of
ha:ˀ^a^na:ši:m ***ˀ^a^šer*** ***ˀitto:***
the-people that with-him

'6. **The lad who was telling him the story said**, I happened on Mount Gilboa and there was Saul leaning on his spear and the chariots and horsemen closing in on him. 7. He turned, saw me, and called me. I said, Here I am. 8. He asked me, Who are you? I said, An Amalekite. 9. He said to me, Come and stand over me and dispatch me, because the throes of death have seized me. 10. I stood over him and gave him the death blow; for I knew that he would not live after having fallen. I took the crown from his head and the armlet from his arm, and brought them here to you sir. 11. **David caught at his clothes and rent them, and so did all the men with him**.' (SamII. 1:6-11)

The direct speech in (35) is composed of a story which was supposed to take place *before* the events of the main narrative, and hence it should be considered as a subnarrative. Since the first clause in this subnarrative is also the first clause of the direct speech, it functions as a transition marker from the main to the subordinate time-line, and hence its verb is in *qatal* — *niqre;t̲i:* 'I happened'. (The infintival *niqro;* preceding this verb is an example of the use of the absolute infinitive as a tautological infinitive, as labelled by

Goldenberg 1971. See section 1.2 for more details.) Now, after reporting the first event of the subnarrative in the non-sequential form *qatal*, the narrator can carry on the sub-narrative with the sequential form *wayyiqtol*, up to verse 10 where the sub-narrative ends. In verse (11) the text switches back to the main time-line (without marking the transition, as expected). Now consider a narrative within direct speech where the time line does not start at the opening of the direct speech:

(36) 9. *wayysappe;r* *śar* *hammašqi:m* *ʕeṯ* *ḥ^{a}lo;mo:*
WAYY:tell:3SG:MASC minister:of the-beverages ACC dream-his
lyo:se;p̄ *wayyo;mer* *lo:* *baḥ^{a}lo:mi:* *whinne;* *gep̄en*
to-Joseph WAYY:say:3SG:MASC to-him in-the-dream-my *whinne;* vine
lp̄a:na:y 10. *u:ḇggep̄en* *šlo;ša:* *śa:ri:gim* *whi:*
to-front-my and-in-the-vine three:MASC branches and-she
ḵp̄o;raḥaṯ *ʔa:lṯa:* *niṣṣa:h* *hiḇši:lu:*
as-QOT:blossom:SG:FEM QAT:rise:3SG:FEM flower-her QAT:ripen:3PL
ʕašklo;ṯe:ha: *ʔ^{a}na:ḇi:m* 11. *wḵo:s* *parʔo;* *bya:ḏi:*
clusters-her grapes and-glass:of Pharaoh in-hand-my
wa:ʔeqqa:ḥ ***ʔeṯ*** ***ha:ʕ^{a}na:ḇi:m*** *wa:ʔeśḥaṭ* *ʔo;ṯa:m* *ʔel*
WAYY:take:1SG ACC the-grapes WAYY:squeeze:1SG them:MASC to
ko:s *parʕo;* *wa:ʔetten* *ʔeṯ* *hakko:s* *ʕal* *kap̄* *parʕo;*
glass:of Pharaoh WAYY:give:1SG ACC the-glass on palm:of Pharaoh
12. *wayyo;mer* *lo:* *yo:se;p̄...*
WAYY:say:3SG:MASC to-him Joseph....

'9. The chief butler of beverages told Joseph his dream. He said, In my dream, there was a vine in front of me. 10. On the vine there were three branches, and as soon as it budded, it blossomed and its clusters ripened into grapes. 11. Now I had Pharaoh's cup in my hand, **I took the grapes**, crushed them into Pharaoh's cup and put the cup into Pharaoh's hand. 12. Joseph said to him... (Gen. 40:9-12)

The story of the chief butler starts at verse (9) with a description of the vine, which continues in verse 10. The first clause in verse 11 is also a description. The time-line starts at the boldfaced clause in verse 11, and indeed, its verb is in *wayyiqtol*, not *qatal*. The transition from the main narrative to the sub-narrative within the direct speech is naturally marked by the *first* clause in the direct speech. In (35) the first clause happens to be the first link on the time-line of the subnarrative, and therefore the first link has a *qatal* verb; in (36) in contrast, the first link of the time-line is not the first clause of direct speech, i.e., it does not function to mark the shift from the main to the sub narrative and hence it is in *wayyiqtol* as any other narrative clause. This explains also the fact that when a direct speech opens with a clause which is the first link of a modal sequence that clause has the non-sequential form *yiqtol* (which is the usual case as in ex. 81 in ch. 4). But when the sequence does not open the direct speech it starts, as predicted, with a *wqatal* clause, as in example (83) in chapter (4) repeated here under (37) below:

(37) 10. *wayyaˁan* *na:ḇa:l* *ˀeṯ* *ˁaḇḏe:* *da:wiḏ*
WAYY:answer:3SG:MASC Nabal ACC servants:of David
wayyo;mer *mi:* *da:wiḏ* *u:mi:* *ḇen* *yiša:y* *hayyo:m*
WAYY:say:3SG:MASC who David and-who son:of Jesse today
rabbu: *ˁaḇa:ḏi:m* *hammiṯpa:rṣi:m* *ˀi:š*
QAT:increase:3PL slaves that-QOT:burst:PL:MASC man
mippne: *ˀaḏo;na:w* 11. *wla:qaḥti:* *ˀeṯ* *laḥmi:* *wˀeṯ*
from-face:of master-his WQAT:take:1SG ACC bread-my and-ACC
me:may *wˀeṯ* *ṭiḇḥa:ṯi:* *ˀašer* *ṭa:ḇaḥti:*
waters-my and-ACC slaughter-my that QAT:slaughter:1SG
lḡo;zza:y *wna:ṯati:* *laˀana:ši:m* *ˀašer* *lo;* *ya:ḏaˁti:*
to-shearers-my WQAT:give:1SG to-people that NEG QAT:know:1SG
ˀe: *mizze* *he;mma:*
where from-this they:MASC
'10. Nabal answered David's slaves, Who is David and who is this son of Jesse? In these days every slave who breaks away from his master sets himself up as a chief. 11. Am I to take my food and my water and the meat I have provided for my shearers and give it to men who come from I know not where?!' (SamI. 25:10-11)

The first clause of Nabal's speech appears in verse (10), followed by two more clauses, none of which reports sequentiality. Nabal's speech continues at verse (11), but there it opens a series of two modal events chronologically ordered. Therefore the first clause in verse (11), as well as the second sequential clause, is in *wqatal*. However, we do have counter examples. For instance, Gen. 44:18-19 does not open with the sub-time-line of the direct speech, yet the first clause of the time line is in *qatal*.

5.2.3 *Backgrounding*

The above discussion has demonstrated that *qatal* is the perfect aspect, i.e, does not introduce its own R-time, but is always "parasitic" on an R-time introduced by other clauses, and therefore does not form a sequence. However, there is a very small number of cases — 1% of all the occurrences in our sample (see table 2.1 in chapter 2) — where it appears in sequential clauses where the *wayyiqtol* form is expected. Consider the following fragment of discourse — the boldfaced clause is a sequential clause with a *qatal* verb:

(38) 17. *wayyišmaʕ* *ʔelo;hi:m* *ʔel le;ʔa:* *wattahar*
WAYY:hear:3SG:MASC God to Leah WAYY:conceive:3SG:FEM
watte;led *lyaʕaqo;b* *be;n* *ḥami:ši:* 18. *watto;mer*
WAYY:bear:3SG:FEM to-Jacob son fifth:MASC WAYY:say:3SG:FEM
le;ʔa: *na:tan* *ʔelo;hi:m* *śka:ri:* *ʔašer* *na:tatti:*
Leah QAT:give:3SG:MASC God hire-my that QAT:give:1SG
šipḥa:ti: *lʔi:ši:* *wattiqra:* *šmo:* *yiśśa:śka:r*
maid-my to-man-my WAYY:call:3SG:FEM name-his Issachar
19. *wattahar* *ʕo:d* *le;ʔa:* *watte;led* *be;n*
WAYY:conceive:3SG:FEM more Leah WAYY:bear:3SG:FEM son
šišši: *lyaʕaqo;b* 20. *watto;mer* *le;ʔa:*
sixth:MASC to-Jacob WAYY:say:3SG:FEM Leah
zba:dani: *ʔelo;hi:m* *ʔo;ti:* *zebed* *ṭo:b* *happaʕam*
QAT:endow:3SG:MASC-me God me dowry good:SG:MASC the-time
yizble;ni: *ʔi:ši* *ki:* *ya:ladti:* *lo:*
YIQ:dwell:3SG:MASC-me man-my because QAT:bear:1SG to-him
šišša: *ba:ni:m* *wattiqra:* *ʔet* *šmo:* *zbulu:n*
six:MASC sons WAYY:call:3SG:FEM ACC name-his Zebulun
21. ***wʔaḥar*** ***ya:lda:*** ***bat*** *wattiqra:* *ʔet*
and-afterwards QAT:bear:3SG:FEM daughter WAYY:call:3SG:FEM ACC
šma:h *di:na:*
name-her Dinah
'17. God heard Leah's prayer, and she conceived and bore a fifth son to Jacob. 18. Leah said, God has rewarded me, because I had given my slave-girl to my husband. And she named him Issachar. 19. Leah again conceived and bore a sixth son to Jacob. 20. Leah said, God has endowed me with a noble dowry. Now my husband will treat me in princely style, because I have born him six sons. And she named him Zebulun. 21. **Then she bore a daughter** and named her Dinah.' (Gen. 30:17-21)

(39) ***wʔaḥar*** ***ba:ʔu:*** ***mo;še*** ***wʔaharo;n*** *wayyo;mru:* *ʔel*
and-then QAT:come:3PL Moses and-Aaron WAYY:say:3PL:MASC to
parʕo;...
Pharaoh
'**After this, Moses and Aaron came to Pharaoh** and said...' (Ex. 5:1)

The whole paragraph in (38) reports similar events: Leah conceives, gives birth, says something and then names the baby. All these sequential events are reported by *wayyiqtol* verbs, except for the last event of giving birth.[7] This event is reported by a *qatal* verb, although it moves the R-time forward.

However, note that the conjunction *w^{ʔ}aḥar* 'and afterwards' is attached to the verb, which suggests that it is not the verb but the conjunction which moves the R-time forward. Similarly the *qatal* verb of the first clause of the narrative discourse in (39) is also modified by this conjunction. This hypothesis seems reasonable in view of the fact that half the sequential *qatal* clauses have such a conjunction attached to them, which reduces the percentage of the counter-examples to 0.6%. The question which arises is why the conjunction 'afterwards' was chosen for this purpose instead of the sequential form *wayyiqtol*? The answer may be pragmatic, similar to a past perfect sentence in English or a *qatal* clause in BH opening a narrative discourse (see discussion on examples 23 and 35 above). That is, although they are sequential, these clauses are part of the background. The definition of the narrative sequence, as phrased in chapter (2) above, involves the requirement that the R-times be associated. That is, when there is a "jump" in the time the clause in question either starts a new time-line or is part of the background material. The foreground clauses are not modified by conjunctions denoting sequentiality; they are understood as such merely by their linear order.[8]

Since *qatal* cannot introduce an R-time it cannot open a narrative line (unless it is used to mark a transition to a subnarrative, as demonstrated in ex. 35 above). However, there are cases where a qatal verb opens a narrative discourse. But in these cases, as claimed in chapter (2) above, the *qatal* clause is not the first link of the time-line but is part of the setting. That is, these cases are explained in a similar way to the English examples (25 in the previous section) where the first clause is in past perfect. Reinhart (1984a), as mentioned in FN (3), explains that the choice of the past perfect clause instead of a past simple in example (25) above lies in the difference in punctuality between the reported events. However, since the principle of punctuality does not apply to the Biblical narrative, I have looked for another reason to explain the choice of verb. It seems to me that the principle determining the choice of the form in cases such as example (40) below is inferability. Whenever a *qatal* verb appears in what I identified as a setting, it did not represent a new situation, but retold it as an old one (Cf. Niccacci 1990):

(40) ***wyo:se;p̄*** ***hu:raḏ*** ***miṣray:ma:***
and-Joseph QAT:be:brought:down:3SG:MASC Egypt-to
wayyiqne;hu: *po:tip̄ar...* *miyyaḏ* *hayyišmʕe;li:m*
WAYY:buy:3SG:MASC-him Potiphar from-hand:of the-Ishmaelites
^{ʔa}*šer* *ho:ri:ḏuhu:* *ša:mma:*
that QAT:bring:down:3PL-him there-to

'and Joseph had been taken down to Egypt, and Potiphar bought him... from the Ishmealites who had brought him there.' (Gen. 39:1)

The fact reported in the first (boldfaced) clause of chapter (39) was told before in chapter (37):

(41) ... *wayyimkru:* *ˀeṯ* *yo:se;p̄* *layyišmˁe;li:m* *bˁeśri:m*
WAYY:sell:3PL:MASC ACC Joseph to-the-Ishmaelites in-twenty
ka:sep̄ ***wayyaḇi:ˀu:*** ***ˀeṯ*** ***yo:se;p̄*** ***miṣra:yma:***
silver WAYY:bring:3PL:MASC ACC Joseph Egypt-to
'...They sold Joseph for twenty pieces of silver to the Ishmaelites, **and they brought Joseph to Egypt**.' (Gen. 37:28)

Commentators of the Bible, trying to explain the use of the form *qatal* in (40), usually point to the fact that it is a second report of the same story.[9] In other words, when the information is inferable the Biblical narrator tends to put it in the background. However, consider the following case:

(42) ***wha:ˀa:ḏa:m*** ***ya:ḏaˁ*** ***ˀeṯ*** ***ḥawwa:*** ***ˀišto:***
and-the-man QAT:know:3SG:MASC ACC Eve wife-his
wattahar *watte;leḏ* *ˀeṯ* *qayin...*
WAYY:conceive:3SG:FEM WAYY:bear:3SG:FEM ACC Cain
'**The man lay with his wife Eve**, and she conceived and gave birth to Cain.' (Gen. 4:1)

The event of Adam's knowing Eve had not been told before chapter 4, but nevertheless the verb reporting it is in *qatal*. Many commentators such as Rashi, Ibn-Ezra and others claim that the sexual act took place **before** the exile from the Garden of Eden, which is reported in the last clause of the preceding chapter. Rashi even emphasizes that had the action of Adam knowing Eve occurred after the exile a *wayyiqtol* form would have been used — *wayye;ḏaˁ*. (Furthermore, Rashi claims that the conceiving and the bearing of the child also took place before Adam and Eve departed from the Garden of Eden. In other words, according to Rashi, the report of events in our example forms a subnarrative.) This line of commentary is in accord with the explanations given to the phrase *ˁe;ṣ haddaˁaṯ* 'the tree of knowledge' as the tree which acquainted Adam and Eve with the secrets of sex.[10] An apparent counter-example is the first verb in the Bible:

(43) 1. ***bre;ši:ṯ*** ***ba:ra:*** ***ˀelo;hi:m*** ***ˀe;ṯ*** ***hašša:mayim***
in-beginning:of QAT:create:3SG:MASC God ACC the-heavens

> ***wʔe;ṯ ha:ʔa:reṣ*** 2. *wha:ʔa:reṣ ha:yṯa: ṯo;hu:*
> and-ACC the-earth and-the-earth QAT:be:3SG:FEM chaos
> *wa:ḇo;hu: wḥo;šeḵ ʕal pne: ṯho:m wru:$_a$ḥ ʔelo;hi:m*
> and-void and-darkness on face:of abyss and-spirit:of God
> *mraḥep̄eṯ ʕal pne: hamma:yim* 3. *wayyo;mer*
> QOT:hover:SG:FEM on face:of the-water WAYY:say:3SG:MASC
> *ʔelo;hi:m yhi: ʔo:r wayhi: ʔo:r*
> God JUS:be:3SG:MASC light WAYY:be:3SG:MASC light
> '1. **In the beginning of creation, when God made heaven and earth** 2. the earth had been without form and void, with darkness over the face of the abyss, and the spirit of God hovering over the face of the waters. 3. God said, Let there be light, and there was light.' (Gen.1:1-3)

Since this is the first clause of the Bible, the boldfaced clause in (43) cannot be interpreted as reporting a simultaneous event or be considered as a second report of an event, and therefore the use of the *qatal* verb *ba:ra:* is problematic. However, most of the commentators (Rashi, Ibn-Ezra and others) argue that this clause does not report an event but serves as a temporal adverbial which consists of *b* 'in' and a genitive construction (called *smixut* in Hebrew) of the noun *re;ši:ṯ* 'beginning' (the construct = *nismax*) and the verb *ba:ra:* which functions just like the infinitival *bro;* (the *somex*). In other words, the phrase *bre;ši:ṯ ba:ra:* is parallel to *bre;ši:ṯ bro;*. Rashi and Ibn-Ezra base their argument on the pointing ("niqud") of the word *bre;ši:ṯ* 'in the beginning of'. This word has the form of the *nismax*, the first noun phrase of a compound, and therefore it has to be complemented by another noun phrase. Had this adverb been punctuated as an independent noun phrase *ba:re;ši:ṯ* it would have been complemented by a finite verb. (Cf. *batthilla:* 'at the beginning' in Gen. 43:18, Jud. 1:1 and elsewhere vs. *biṯḥillaṯ* 'at the beginning of' in SamII 21:9 and KingsII 17:25.) This use of a verb as part of a compound is not isoteric to BH. Shlomo Izre'el (personal communication) pointed out to me that it is common in Semitic languages, notably Akkadian, to nominalize a sentence for creating a compound which is to be used as an adverb. The following three clauses of (43) form a setting, where the first is a "parasitic" 'be' clause ("The earth had been..."), and the other two are *qotel* clauses, reporting inclusive situations. In other words, the time line starts only in the third verse starting with the *wayyiqtol* verb *wayyo;mer* 'said'. (Cf. Niccacci 1990 for a similar account of these verses.)

5.2.4 *The Perfect Aspect and Modality*

Since this is the only form to report anteriority, the *qatal* is used in modal clauses, too, when the situation reported is anterior. Consider the following examples:

(44) *w^{ʔ}im* *ko; yo;mru:* *^{ʕa}lu:* *^{ʕ}a:le:nu:*
and-if so YIQ:say:3PL:MASC IMP:go-up:2PL:MASC on-us
w^{ʕ}a:li:nu: ***ki:*** ***nṯa:na:m*** ***yhwh***
WQAT:go-up:1PL because QAT:give:3SG:MASC-them:MASC God
bya:ḏe;nu: *wze* *lla:nu:* *ha:^{ʔ}o:ṯ*
in-hands-our and-this:MASC to-us the-sign
'and if they say "Come up to us", we will go up; this will be the sign that **the Lord has put them into our power**.' (Sam.I 14:10)

(45) *bišnaṯ* *hayyo:ḇe:l* *ya:šu:ḇ* *haśśa:ḏe* *la^{ʔa}šer*
in-year:of the-Jubilee YIQ:return:3SG:MASC the-field to-that
qa:na:hu: ***me;^{ʔ}itto:...***
QAT:buy:3SG:MASC-him from-him
'At the year of Jubilee the land shall revert to the man **from whom he had bought it**.... (Lev. 27:24)

The causative clause *ki: nṯana:m...* 'the Lord has put them into our power' in (44) describes a situation that will (possibly) take place **before** the situations described in the conditional sentence preceding the causative clause. Therefore, the verb in this clause is in *qatal*. (45) states a law determining that in the year of the Jubilee, a field given to the temple through a buyer should be given back to that buyer. This particular part of the law is mentioned after the (possible) event of giving back the field, although it would be carried out after it. Hence the verb in the relative clause is in *qatal*.

Just like in the case of English and other languages (see discussion in section 5.1.4 above), the perfect form in BH, i.e., the *qatal* is usually used for counterfactual clauses in BH. Since I already discussed this function of the *qatal* in chapter (4), this comment is sufficient for the present section. (See table 4.3 in chapter 4 for the distribution of *qatal* in modal clauses, followed by discussion.)

For the same reason that *qatal* is used in anterior modal clauses we would expect simultaneity, too, to be denoted by *qatal* in such clauses. However, it seems to be the case that a modal clause indicating simultaneity has a *yiqtol* verb instead. Consider the following examples:

(46) *wṣippi:ṯa:* *ʔo;ṯo:* *za:ha:ḇ* *ṭa:ho:r* ***mibbayiṯ***
WQAT:overlay:2SG:MASC him gold pure:SG:MASC from-house
u:miḥu:ṣ ***tṣappennu:***
and-from-out YIQ:overlay:2SG:MASC-him
'And overlay it with pure gold, within and without overlay it.' (Ex. 25:11)

(47) ...*wha:rḡu:* *ʔo;ṯi:* ***wʔo;ṯa:k̲*** ***yḥayyu:***
WQAT:kill:3PL:MASC me and-you:SG:FEM YIQ:make-live:3PL:MASC
'...And they will kill me but let you live.' (Gen. 12:12)

The verse cited in (46) is an excerpt from a list of directions God gives Moses. In our particular verse God commands Moses to overlay the ark of the temple with gold. This command is given in the first clause, and repeated with more specification in the second, i.e., the second clause does not report a new event which God wants Moses to make happen. The verb in the second clause, therefore, is expected to be in *qatal* form, just like in the (non-modal) example (28) above. Similarly, in (47) Abraham tells Sarah the possible course of events he is afraid of, where the Egyptians will kill him but let her live. The possible situation of letting her live is to take place when the possible killing of Abraham happens. Here, too, we expect a *qatal* rather than a *yiqtol* verb clause reporting the simultaneous possible situation, contrary to what we have in the actual text. This may be explained in the same line as the fact that *qatal* does not function to denote inclusive situations. As there is a special form *qotel* for inclusion, the *qatal* is not used for this function. Similarly we may conclude that *qatal* is not used to denote simultaneous situations of modals, because there is a special form *yiqtol* for that purpose. Another line of explanation may be the different possible options involved in modal assertions. When a (second) clause in *yiqtol* is introduced into the discourse it is not always clear whether it denotes a (possible) simultaneous situation (although it is clear that it does not indicate a sequential or an anterior one). Consider one of many examples:

(48) *wayyo;mer* *ʔelo;hi:m* *yišrṣu:* *hammayim*
WAYY:say:3SG:MASC God YIQ:teem:3PL:MASC the-water
šereṣ *nep̄eš* *ḥayya:* ***wʕo:p̄*** ***yʕo:p̄e;p̄***
creeping-animal soul alive:SG:FEM and-bird YIQ:fly:3SG:MASC
ʕal ha:ʔa:reṣ ʕal pne: rqi:ʕa haššа:ma:yim
on the-earth on face:of heaven:of the-sky
'God said, Let the waters teem with countless living creatures, **and let birds fly above the earth across the vault of heaven**.' (Gen. 1:20)

It seems to me peculiar to interpret verse (20) in Genesis as indicating that God insists that the situations will necessarily be included in exactly the same R-time. Rather, it seems that God wants them to share the same branching options (which, according to his will, have to be the whole set), and possibly the R-times, too. This line of explanation might be adequate for negative modals, too:

(49) 16. *Wayṣaw* *yhwh* *ʔelo;hi:m* *ʕal ha:ʔa:da:m* *le;mo;r*
WAYY:order:3SG:MASC God God on the-man to-INF:say
mikko;l *ʕe;ṣ* *hagga:n* *ʔa:ko;l* *to;ke;l*
from-all tree:of the-garden INF:eat YIQ:eat:2SG:MASC
17. *u:me;ʕe;ṣ* ***haddaʕat*** ***ṭo:b*** ***wa:ra:ʕ***
and-from-tree:of the-knowledge good:SG:MASC and-bad:SG:MASC
lo; ***to;kal*** ***mimmennu:...***
NEG YIQ:eat:2SG:MASC from-him
'16. And the Lord God commanded the man, saying, Of every tree of the garden you may eat. 17. **But of the tree of the knowledge of good and evil, you must not eat of it**;...' (Gen. 2:16-17)

The assumption that a (possible) situation reported in a modal clause such as the negative (boldfaced) clause in verse (17) is not to be interpreted as bearing the simultaneous relation with the previous reported (modal) situation, finds support in the interpretation of the *yiqtol* clauses. The two clauses express different kinds of directives, where the first is permission (requiring existential quantification over branching options), and the second is a command (involving universal quantification).

There is also a small number of *qatal* verbs in clauses where a *yiqtol* form is expected (40.7% in our sample — see table 4.3 in chapter 4). In these cases a *yiqtol* verb could easily replace the actual *qatal* verb. These cases were discussed in chapter (4), illustrated by examples (102a-b).

In ex. (27) above there was one negative clause "and Cain and his gift he did not accept". In discussing this clause I claimed that what determines the choice of the verb form, i.e., the *qatal*, is the fact that the situation reported by this clause bears the simultaneity relation with the situation reported in the previous one. Negative assertions may also negate anterior situations (e.g., Gen. 2:20, 20:4, 38:16). In both cases the clauses do not move the R-time forward, which is compatible with the choice of the *qatal*. However, as mentioned in chapter (4), there are cases when we interpret negative sentences as denoting sequential events, as in (50) below:

(50) a) John fell down the stairs but did not get hurt.
b) Mary greeted John, but he did not reply.

Such examples are found also in the Bible:

(51)

8. *wayšallaḥ*	*ˀet̲*	*hayyo:na:*	*me;ˀitto:*	*lirˀo:t̲*	
WAYY:send:3SG:MASC	ACC	the-dove	from-him	to-INF:see	
h^{a}*qallu:*	*hammayim*	*me;ˁal*	*pne:*	*ha:ˀ*^{a}*d̲a:ma:*	
QUE-QAT:abate:3PL	the-water	from-on	face:of	the-earth	
9. ***wlo;***	***ma:ṣˀa:***	***hayyo:na:***	***ma:no;*$_{a}$*ḥ***	***lk̲ap̄***	***rag̅la:h***
and-NEG	QAT:find:3SG:FEM	the-dove	rest	to-sole:of	foot-her
watta:šob̲	*ˀe;la:w*	*ˀel*	*hatte:b̲a:...*		
WAYY:return:3SG:FEM	to-him	to	the-ark		

'8. He released the dove from the ark to see whether the water on the earth had subsided. 9. **The dove did not find a place where she could settle**, and came back to him to the ark...' (Gen. 8:8-9)

The context makes it clear that the dove did not find a place to settle **after** Noah had released her from the ark, not at the same time or before it. This sequential feeling I have explained as due to other branching options in which the event of finding a place has taken place. (See section 4.1.7 in chapter 4 for a more detailed discussion).

5.2.5 *Conclusion*

It has been demonstrated that the *qatal* is the general perfect form in BH, and therefore it cannot provide its own R-time, but depends on explicit adverbials or neighboring clauses for its temporal interpretation. Being a "parasitic" form *qatal* was shown to be unable to move the R-time forward, and hence not found in sequential clauses of a narrative. Instead *qatal* has several functions in the non-sequential material, all resulting from its "parasitic" characterization: a) It may denote simultaneous clauses which use the R-time of the previous clause to be included in; b) It may denote anterior situations, parallel to the English perfect, where the situation precedes the R-time. For being the form to denote such situations in all time spheres, the *qatal* is used also in clauses marking the transition from the main time-line to some subnarrative, including direct speech texts which were shown to be a special kind of subnarrative; c) It is used also for putting a clause in the background material, e.g., in settings of narrative.

NOTES

1. The following discussion of the perfect tenses in English touches only on the points relevant to its "parasitic" character and its anteriority meaning. It does not intend to provide a full description of the studies dealing with the subject. Good surveys of the different approaches with their shortcomings are provided in McCoard (1978) and Binnick (1991). Other works dealing with the perfect tenses in English are Palmer (1965), Heny (1982), Mittwoch (1988), McCawley (1971, 1981), Comrie (1976, 1985a), Salkie (1989) among others. Some of the points in the following discussion I already discussed in Hatav (1993).

2. However, Chomsky himself points out the fact that it is not always the case, e.g., (i) cannot entail that Einstein is alive:

   (i) Einstein has died.

   Furthermore, McCawley (1971) shows that (8) does not entail that Einstein is alive if the tone shifts to 'Princeton'. It seems to me that what Chomsky refers to here is related to the property of relevance, to which I will return shortly.

3. Reinhart explains this choice in the difference in punctuality between the first and the third reported events. She claims that the event depicted by the first clause of the first sentence is durative compared to the event reported in the second sentence. However, this explanation cannot be adopted in the case of Biblical narrative, since the principle of punctuality does not apply there, as shown in chapter (2) above and in Hatav (1985). For an alternative explanation see the next section.

4. Note the difference between the original Hebrew text and the English translation. The two events of bringing are denoted by different verb forms in the Biblical original text — the first is in *wayyiqtol* for denoting a sequential event and the second in *qatal*. However, since English does not have different forms to distinguish between sequential and simultaneous situations, and since it does not use the perfect for denoting simultaneity, the two occurrences of 'bring' have the same form — 'brought'.

5. Only a few scholars, such as Nöldeke (1880), claimed that active *qatal* existed originally in Proto-Semitic, but was lost at a later stage from the East-Semitic (Akkadian) language, and remained or reappeared in the West Semitic languages such as in Hebrew.

6. It is peculiar that in English these verbs have the form of the present simple instead of the present perfect. It is questionable why they may (or must?) have the form of the present perfect if they are modified by adverbs, as in the following examples:

   (i) I have known David for many years.
   (ii) I have loved him since childhood.

7. Note that this is not the only difference between the reports in this and the preceding clauses: The "formula" used in this paragraph first tells that Leah conceived, and only then that she gave birth. In the case of Dinah the text "skips" the conceiving event. Moreover, in each case Leah explains the names she gives her sons, but in the case of her daughter we are only told that she named her Dinah, without explaining why.

8. Cf. the English translation where in (38) the last sequential clause is modified by the adverbial "then" and the first clause in (39) is modified by "after this". Ruth Berman

(personal communication) has pointed out to me that children violate the narrative discourse rules by, inter alia, adding such modifiers to their clauses.

9. Talmon (1980) addresses the question of why the Bible tells the same story twice. His answer is that the story of Joseph was interrupted by another story, and therefore when the narrator of the Bible comes back to it he reminds the reader of the last occurrences relevant to the current happenings.

10. Could it be that eating the fruit of the tree of knowledge is a figurative illustration to report the sexual act itself?

Chapter 6

Conclusions and Suggestions for Future Research

This book has tackled one of the most puzzling problems in Biblical Hebrew (BH), namely the semantics of its verbal system. The verbal oppositions have traditionally, and recently, been an area of great controversy with different scholars generating different analyses of the semantics involved. In chapter (1) a survey was given of the various theories, mainly to point to their inadequacies, showing the necessity of a new analysis. However, to provide a new account of the BH forms, a general analysis of temporality in language had to be developed first. Thus, the aim of this book has been twofold: To analyze the temporal system in language in a general theoretical fashion; and to deal with the verbal system in Biblical Hebrew in detail. English was usually used to account for the theoretical discussion, resulting in some analysis of the English temporal system, too.

The book starts with the assumption that TAM, i.e., the Tense-Aspect-Modal system in language, should be defined within truth conditional semantics, in terms of temporality, rather than within a pragmatic approach which deals with it in terms of perspective, attitude, and the like. However, since pragmatics is not irrelevant, it has also been taken into account.

In determining tense and aspect I assumed a neo-Reichenbachen distinction of S(peech)-time, E(vent)-time and R(eference)-time. Tense has been defined as a function from the intervals of S-time and R-time to truth values. I have shown that contrary to what is claimed in tense oriented theories (notably the *waw*-conversive theory of the scholars in the Middle Ages and the historical comparative theory of Bauer 1910), BH is a tensless language. The BH verb forms do not encode the three-place distinction of past, present and future, and therefore a sentence may be given tense interpretation only by linguistic means such as adverbs, or by the context. Aspect has also been defined as a function, but rather from the intervals of R-time and E-time to truth values. In language, different kinds of relationships may hold between the R-time and the E-time, in different combinations. This work has shown that BH uses three relations, resulting in three different aspects: sequentiality, inclusion (progressive) and perfect.

Sequentiality has been shown to be a central factor in determining the choice of the verb form in BH. This has been observed already by Driver (1874) and other traditional and more recent analyses (e.g., Joüon 1947, Givón 1982, Longacre 1981). The definition of sequentiality which seems to be assumed implicitly in those studies is that a sequential clause reports an event which follows in time the event reported in the previous clause. However, this line of definition cannot explain the appearance of such clauses at the beginning of a narrative, and their occurrence in isolation. I have shown that replacing the traditional account of sequentiality by the analysis of Discourse-Representation-Structure (DRS) developed by Kamp (1979, & Reyle 1993) captures its nature, while avoiding the shortcomings of the more traditional account. Kamp defines *sequence* in terms of time movement, where a sequential clause is claimed to move the R-time forward. When such clauses appear in discourse with other clauses which also move the R-time forward it will form with them a sequence. The temporal interpretation of the clauses in a given discourse would be elicited by the DRS rules he developed, where the total of the sequential clauses would be recognized as the time-line. Kamp shows that French clauses with verbs in passé simple move the R-time forward, and therefore they would be interpreted as sequential, forming together a time-line. English lacks a special verb form for moving the R-time forward, and therefore the general concept of the sequence aspect has been dealt with in this study mainly through French. In applying Kamp's analysis to BH, I showed that BH is even more strict than French. Not only does BH have a special form, *wayyiqtol*, for the clauses on the time line, but it also has a special form, *wqatal*, for sequential clauses in the modal material.

Adopting Kamp's definition for sequence I have, furthermore, argued that a clause moves the R-time forward iff the situation it reports introduces its own R-time to be included in it. The characteristics of the non-sequential aspects revolve from this characterization. If the situation does not have its own R-time, but rather it is "parasitic" on another R-time provided by the context, it cannot move the R-time forward, and hence cannot be a link in a sequence. This has been shown to be the case with the inclusion (progressive) and the perfect aspects.

As the studies within truth-conditional semantics discussed in chapter (3) show, the *progressive* in English does not introduce its own R-time, but uses an R-time introduced explicitly in the context. In other words, the progressive is, indeed, "parasitic". These studies further show that the function of the progressive is to report situations which include their R-time; hence the label "inclusion" given here to this aspect. When applying the analysis of the English progressive to BH, I have shown that the form *qotel* functions as its inclusion aspect. It was interesting to see that its characteristic parallels that of the English progressive almost detail by detail.

The *perfect*, too, has been shown in this work to be a parasitic aspect, whose clauses are dependent on some R-time provided explicitly by the context for their temporal interpretation. However, unlike the progressive, it has been shown that the perfect in BH and English parallel only partially. While the "parasitic" characteristics of the perfect is common to both languages, only some of its uses are. In English as well as in BH the perfect is used to express the relation of "anteriority", which I defined in terms of precedence, where the situation was claimed to precede the R-time. It is usually the case that the R-time on which the clause depends is provided by the previous clause, resulting in a reverse order of the depicted situations. However, it was shown by Comrie (1986) and Reinhart (1984a) that this is not a requirement, since there are marked cases of the English perfect where those situations are reported in their chronological order. According to Comrie and Reinhart, in such cases the speaker is merely interested in backgrounding those clauses. I have shown that the BH *qatal* behaves like the English perfect in denoting anteriority, and in being used for backgrounding.

However, there is at least one "parasitic" use of the *qatal* which does not coincide with the English perfect, namely the relation of simultaneity, where the situation of a given clause is interpreted to be included in the R-time of the situation depicted in the previous clause. For such situations BH uses the *qatal* (which may cause ambiguity between an anteriority and simultaneity meaning), but English uses the simple tenses rather than the perfect. Thus, BH shows more consistency in using only parasitic forms in reporting parasitic situations. Moreover, for lack of a sequential aspect English uses the simple tenses also in reporting sequential situations, resulting many times in ambiguity between the sequential and the simultaneous interpretation.

To account for the sequential vs. non-sequential interpretation in English, the interesting theory of Hinrichs (1986) has been discussed. Since

Hinrichs' theory relies on the notion of *aktionsarten* (which distinguishes, for example, between events and states), this notion has been given a thorough discussion in this work, adopting, like Hinrichs, interval semantics as the adequate analysis for the various distinctions. Hinrichs has claimed that aktionsarten determine semantically whether a simple past tensed clause in English be interpreted as sequential or non-sequential. Although Dowty (1986) shows that, contrary to what Hinrichs claims, aktionsarten are not a semantic factor in determining the temporal relations in English, he still agrees that they may be responsible for the temporal interpretation in discourse, though through pragmatic inferences. I have shown that aktionsarten have some impact on the temporal interpretation also in languages like French and BH, which mark the sequence aspectually.

While sequentiality was usually recognized in the literature as a crucial factor in the semantics of the verbal forms in BH, *modality* was acknowledged only as bearing pragmatic significance. Most Hebraists, e.g., Joüon (1947), define modality in pragmatic terms as a volitive property, expressing some attitude of the speaker, their wishes, desires, intentions, and the like. Thus, they point to three forms of the directives — the jussive, the cohortative and the imperative — as comprising the suppletive paradigm of the modal system in BH. However, it is well acknowledged that the forms *yiqtol* and *wqatal* are also used to express volition, yet they are not considered modal since they appear in other kinds of sentences, too (conditionals, generics, futurates, etc.). Having modal clauses with forms which are considered non-modal has been one of the most puzzling phenomena in the study of the verbal forms in BH. Another phenomenon which the pragmatic approach cannot explain is the fact that the forms *yiqtol* and *wqatal* are found in future propositions as well as in past habituals. Both problems have been nicely solved in the present study within the framework of modal logic. According to the logical approach, a modal proposition has a necessity or possibility operator, analyzed as involving, respectively, universal and existential quantification over a set of possible worlds. I have applied this analysis to the different uses of *yiqtol* and *wqatal*, showing that they all exhibit modality of some kind. And vice versa, all modal functions recognized by the general account were shown to be expressed by one of these forms (which differ in their sequentiality). Since future and habitual statements were shown to be modal, it was predicted that they both would be expressed by *yiqtol* or *wqatal*. Now since BH does not encode tenses, habituals in all time sphere, including the past, were expected to be expressed by one of the forms, resolving the seeming problem of habituals in the past being expressed by the same forms as future statements.

The possibility of using the forms *yiqtol* and *wqatal* for expressing directives is also explained by the logical theory. It has been shown in the literature (Kratzer 1981a and elsewhere) that directives, too, have a modal operator of necessity or possibility, and therefore involve quantification over possible worlds. It is not surprising, then, that the neutral modals *yiqtol* and *wqatal* are not blocked from expressing directives. Since directives are recognized as one kind of modal, the forms of the imperative, the jussive, and the cohortative comprise a subcategory of modals. Like the neutral forms they meet the general requirement of modality, namely they have a modal operator of necessity or possibility, but in addition they also meet further semantic conditions restricting their functions to expressing only directives (which are characterized by the pragmatic definition in an intuitive way as volitive). Evidence that the directive forms in BH are, indeed, a subcategory of modals is their morphology, which shows that they all derive from *yiqtol*: The jussive is a short *yiqtol*, the cohortative is a long *yiqtol*, and the imperative is a *yiqtol* without the person prefixes.

In my final remarks, I want to point to some directions for future research.

First consider the corpus. For reasons explained in the first chapter, this study has not analyzed the full Bible, but limited itself in genre and chronology.

Regarding genre, the present study has examined only the prose portion of the Bible (including the law part). It would be interesting to examine the functions of the verb forms in the poetic clauses with respect to the findings in the prose. This, naturally, would necessitate an account for the poetry in the Ancient East in general, and the Bible in particular.

Regarding chronology, this work has dealt only with the books attributed to the First Temple, namely Genesis through Kings. There have been a few treatments for the verbal system in the Post Biblical period, but to my knowledge there is no systematic account for the verb forms in the Biblical books attributed to the Second Temple. Most studies of BH do not acknowledge the importance of separating the two periods. The scholars who do acknowledge the difference (e.g., Hurvitz 1972) usually note briefly that the verbal system in the Second Temple had been in transition, not crystallized, a claim which is usually illustrated by examples showing strange morphology, or misuse of the forms. However, it seems to me that a systematic research might reveal some consistency in the use of the different forms in the books attributed to the Second Temple period, and outline the conditions of the changes occurring after the First Temple.

The second topic awaiting future research is the two kinds of infinitives found in BH — the absolute and the inflective infinitive. Within the prose discourse of the First Temple, all verb forms were discussed exhaustively, accounting for counter-examples and providing statistical findings. The only forms I have not discussed were the infintivals. The inflective Infinitive is known from other languages, so a general analysis might reveal its use in BH, too. The absolute infinitive, to my knowledge, has been found so far only in BH, and therefore determining its characteristic seems to be more problematic. It will be interesting if future research will show it not to be, after all, so language specific.

A third issue awaiting an adequate analysis is counterfactuals. Although counterfactuals are analyzed in the literature (e.g., Lewis 1973) as involving quantification over possible worlds, they are not expressed in BH by one of the modal forms, but rather by the perfect. However, it has been shown that this problem is not specific to BH. This suggests that a general account for the use of the perfect in counterfactuals is yet to be developed, in order to account for the phenomenon in BH.

The fourth issue I acknowledge as deserving further research is the pragmatics of the modal forms in BH. As emphasized above, this book was concerned mainly with the semantics of the verbal system in BH, while pragmatic considerations were only occasional. Since the forms *yiqtol* and *wqatal* are used for all modal functions, clauses in these forms may sometimes be ambiguous. Linguistic clues such as adverbials may appear in such clauses, eliciting unambiguous interpretations. When an explicit phrase is absent in a modal clause the context may sometimes point to its specific function. This was shown occasionally in the present work, but no systematic account was developed.

A related topic is the choice of the verb form in directives. Since BH allows the speaker to use either the neutral forms *yiqtol* or *wqatal* to express volition, or the more specific forms of the directives, the question arises when does the Biblical writer use the neutral forms, and when does he use the more specific ones when expressing speech acts like commands and requests? This question, it seems to me, should be answered within a pragmatic rather than semantic theory, and therefore it has been left open for future research.

A completely different area of future investigation is the tense and the modal systems in English.

Although English was the meta language used in this work for the theoretical discussion of modality (as of other issues), its modal system has not been given a systematic analysis. However, the theoretical account developed here may be applied now to English. This is a good place to point to the interaction between the theoretical and the BH analyses. Recall that what motivated the general investigation of modality in language was to explain the use of the same forms *yiqtol* and *wqatal* in BH for expressing future statements as well as habituals in the past. The conclusion reached by the general analysis (that both futurates and habituals are modal) enabled me to solve my original problem of the BH forms. The general account of modality, which was motivated in the first place by BH, may be now applied to English (and other languages), closing the circle.

Similarly, the study of tenses in English may benefit from the study of the BH system. Tense, in English, interwines with aspect, raising some difficulty in distinguishing between them. Since BH lacks tenses, the notion of tense and the semantics of the various tenses were not dealt with in detail. However, the lack of tenses in BH has enabled me to isolate issues of tense and aspect, which now enables us to recognize the tense morphemes in English (or other languages) more easily.

To summarize, on one hand the study of the theoretical notions has given special insight into the verbal system in BH. On the other hand, the systematic treatment of the BH verb system has enabled theoretical generalizations of tense, aspect, and modality to be reached, which may now be applied to other languages.

References

Abusch, Dorit and Mats Rooth. 1990. "Temporal Adverbs and the English Perfect". *NELS* 20. Amherst, MA.

Allen, R.L. 1966. *The Verb System of Present-Day English*. The Hague: Mouton.

Andersen, Francis I. 1974. *The Sentence in Biblical Hebrew*. The Hague and Paris: Mouton.

Bach, Emmon. 1980. "Tense and Aspect as Functions on Verb Phrases". In C. Rohrer (ed.), *Time, Tense and Quantification Proceedings of the Stütgart Conference on the Logic of Tense and Quantification*. Tübingen: Niemeyer.

———. 1981. "On Time, Tense and Aspect: An Essay in English Metaphysics". In P. Cole (ed.), *Radical Pragmatics*. New York: Academic Press.

———. 1982. "The Algebra of Events". Paper read at *Sloan Conference on Tense and Aspect* at the Ohio State University, Columbus. Republished in: *Linguistics and Philosophy* 9:1, 1986, 5-16.

Barson, John. 1975. *La Grammaire à L'ouvre*. Deuxième édition. Corte Madera, California: Holt, Rinehart and Winston.

Barwise, John and Robin Cooper. 1981. "Generalized Quantifiers in Natural Language." *Linguistics and Philosophy* 4:2, 159-219.

Bauer, Hans. 1910. *Die Tempora im Semitischen, Beitrage zur Assyriologie und Semitschen Sprachwissen Schaft* 8:1, 1-53.

Ben-Ḥayyim, Zeev. 1977. "zmane hapo'al bilshon hamikra umasoret hashomronim bahem". In *Sefer Dov Sadan*. Tel-Aviv: Hakibbutz ha-meuchad. [In Hebrew]

Bennett, Michael. 1971. "A Guide to the Logic of Tense and Aspect in English". *Logique et Analyse* 20: 491-517.

———. 1981. "Of Tense and Aspect: One Analysis". In P.J.Tedeschi and A. Zaenen (eds.), *Syntax and Semantics 14: Tense and Aspect*, New York: Academic Press, 13-29.

——— and Barbara Partee. 1978. *Towards the Logic of Tense and Aspect in English*. Bloomington: Indiana University Linguistics Club. Revision of 1972 ms.

Bergsträsser, G. 1918. *Hebräisch Grammatik*. Leipzig. Reissued in Hildsheim, 1962.

———. 1972. *Dikduk ha-lashon ha-ivrit*. Translated from German by M. Ben-Asher. Jerusalem: The Magness Press, The Hebrew University. [In Hebrew]

Berlin, Adele. 1983. *Poetic Interpretation of Biblical Narrative*. England: The Almond Press [*Bible and Literature Series* 9].

Berman, Ruth (Aronson). 1978. *Modern Hebrew Structure.* Tel-Aviv: University Publishing Projects.

Biblia Hebraica. 1937. R. Kittel (ed.) and P. Kahle (Text Masoretic). Stüttgart: Urttembergidche Bibelanstalt.

Bickerton, D. 1976. "Creole Tense-Aspect Systems and Universal Grammar". A paper read at *The Society Linguistics Conference*, Georgetown.

Binnick, Robert I. 1991. *Time and the Verb: A Guide to Tense and Aspect.* New York and Oxford: Oxford University Press.

Blake, F.R. 1951. *A Survey of Hebrew Tenses.* Rome.

Blau, J. 1972. *Torat ha-hege ve-ha-tsurot.* Tel-Aviv: Hakkibutz ha-meuchad. [In Hebrew.]

Bull, W.E. 1963. *Time, Tense and the Verb: A Study in Theoretical and Applied Linguistics, with particular attention to Spanish.* Berkeley: University of California [*Publications in Linguistics* 19].

Carlson, G.N. 1980. *Reference to Kinds in English.* Revised version of author's thesis, U. of Massachusetts, Amherst, 1977. New York and London: Gerland Pub.

Chomsky, Noam. 1972. *Studies on semantics in generative grammar.* The Hague: Mouton.

Chomsky, W. 1952. *David's Kimchi's Hebrew Grammar (Mikhlol) systematically presented and critically annotated.* New York.

Chvany, Catherine. 1980. "The Role of Verbal Tense and Aspect in the Narrative of *The Tale of Igor's Campaign*". In Andrej K., K. Pomorska, and M.J. Conolly (eds.), *The Structure Analysis of Narrative Texts.* Columbus: Slavica, 7-23.

Clifford, John E. 1969. *Tense and Tense Logic.* The Hague and Paris: Mouton.

Comrie, Bernrad. 1976. *Aspect.* Cambridge: Cambridge University Press.

———. 1985a. *Tense.* Cambridge: Cambridge University Press.

———. 1985b. "Causative Verb Formation and other Verb-Deriving Morphology". In Shopen Timothy (ed.), *Language Typology and Syntactic Description*, [Vol. III: *Grammatical Categories and the Lexicon*]. Cambridge: Cambridge University Press,

———. 1986. "Tense and Time Reference: From Meaning to Interpretation in the Chronological Structure of a Text". *Journal of Literary Semantics* 15: 12-22.

Cowley, A.E. 1910. *Gesenius' Hebrew Grammar.* 1909. 2nd English edition. As edited and enlarged by E. Kautzch 28th edition. Translated by A.E. Cowley. Oxford. Reprinted: London 1966.

Dahl, Östen. 1975. "On Generics". In E. Keenan (ed.), *Formal Semantics of Natural Language.* Cambridge: Cambridge University Press, 99-111.

Dalmash, Avram. 1523. *Sefer Mikne Avram. Sha'ar ḥamishi: ḥalukat happe'alim.* [In Hebrew].

Davidson, Donald. 1967. "The Logical Form of Action Sentences". In N. Rescher (ed.), *The Logic of Decision and Action.* Pittsburgh: U. of Pittsburgh Press. Reprinted in Davidson 1980.

———. 1980. *Essays on Actions and Events.* Oxford: Clarendon Press.

——— and Gilbert Harman. 1972. *Semantics of Natural Language.* Dordrecht: Reidel.

De Jong, F.M.G. and H.J. Verkuyl. 1985. "Generalized Quantifiers: the Properness of their Strength". In J. van Benthem and A. ter Meulen (eds.), *Generalized Quantifiers: Theory and Applications.* Dordrecht: Foris, 21-43.

Depraetere, Ilse. 1995. "On the Necessity of distinguishing between (un)boundedness and (a)telicity". *Linguistics & Philosophy* 18: 1-19.

Dowty, David. 1977. "Semantic Analysis of Verb Aspect and the English Imperfective Progressive". *Linguistics & Philosophy* 1: 45-77.

———. 1979. *Word Meaning and Montague Grammar*. Dordrecht: D. Reidel.

———. 1986. "The Effect of Aspectual Classes on the Temporal Structure of Discourse: Semantics or Pragmatics?". *Linguistics & Philosophy*, 9: 37-61.

———, Robert E. Wall & Stanley Peters. 1981. *Introduction to Montague Semantics*. Dordrecht: Reidel.

Driver, G.R. 1936. *Problems of the Hebrew Verbal System*. Edinburgh.

Driver, S.R. 1874. *A Treatise on the Use of the Tense in Hebrew*. Oxford.

Dry, Helen. 1981. "Sentence Aspect and the Movement of Narrative Time." *Text* 1: 233-240.

Eskhult, Mats. 1990. *Studies in Verbal Aspect and Narrative Technique in Biblical Hebrew Prose*. Stockholm: Uppsala, Almqvist & Wiksell International Acta Universitatis Upsaliensis. [*Studia Semitica Upsaliensia*].

Ewald, G.H.A. 1827. *Kritische Grammatik der hebräischen Sprache*. Leipzig.

———. 1870. *Ausführliches lehrbuch der hebräischen sprache des Alten Bundes*. Leipzig. The Syntax of this edition (8th) was translated by J. Kennedy, Edinburgh 1979.

Fassberg, Steven E. 1994. *Sugiyot betaḥbir hamikra*. English title: *Studies in Biblical Syntax*. Jerusalem: The Magness Press, The Hebrew University. [In Hebrew].

Fillmore, Charles. 1971. "Towards a Theory of Deixis." *University of Hawaii Working Papers in Linguistics*, 3: 219-242.

Forsyth, J. 1970. *A Grammar of Aspect: Usage and Meaning in the Russian Verb*. Cambridge: Cambridge University Press.

Gabbay, D. & J. Moravcsik. 1980. "Verbs, Events and the Flow of Time." In C. Rohrer (ed.), *Time, Tense and Quantifiers*. Tübingen: Niemeyer, 59-83.

Garbel, I. 1959. "Ma'amadam hafonemi shel hashwa, shel haḥaṭafim ve-shel begedkefet harefuyot baivrit hamasortit". *Leshonenu*. [In Hebrew]

Garey, H.B. 1957. "Verbal Aspect in French." *Language* 33: 91-110.

Gell, P. 1818. *Observations on the Idiom of the Hebrew Language*. London.

Gesenius, Wilhelm. 1909. See A. E. Cowley above.

Givón, Talmy. 1977. "The Drift from VSO to SVO in Biblical Hebrew: The Pragmatics of Tense-Aspect." In Charles N. Li (ed.), *Mechanisms of Syntactic Change*. Austin: University of Texas Press, 115-63.

———. 1982. "Tense-Aspect-Modality; The Creole Prototype and beyond." In Paul Hopper (ed.), *Tense-Aspect*. Amsterdam and Philadelpha: John Benjamins.

Goldenberg, G. 1971. "Tautological Infinitive." *Israel Oriental Studies* 1: 37-85.

Goldsmith, J. and E. Woisteschlaeger. 1982. "The Logic of English Progressive." *Linguistics Inquiry* 13: 79-89.

Gruber, J.S. 1976. *Lexical Structures in Syntax and Semantics*. Amsterdam: North-Holland.

Gunthner, F., J. Hoepelman and C. Rohrer. 1978. "A Note on the Passé Simple." In C. Rohrer (ed.), *Papers on Tense, Aspect and Verb Classification*. Tübingen: Gunter Nurr Verlag.

Hartmann, R.R.K. and F.C. Stork. 1972. *Dictionary of Language and Linguistics.* London: Applied Science Publishers.

Hatav, Galia. 1977. *Meta'arey hamatsav ba'ivrit haḥadasha.* Unpublished M.A. thesis. The Hebrew University of Jerusalem. [In Hebrew].

———. 1985. "Criteria for Identifying the Foreground." *Theoretical Linguistics* 12: 265-273.

———. 1989. "Aspect, Aktionsarten and the Time Line." *Linguistics* 27: 487-516.

———. 1993. "The Aspect System in English: An Attempt for a Unified Analysis." *Linguistics* 31: 209-237.

Heim, Irene. 1982. *The Semantics of Definite and Indefinite Noun Phrases.* Unpublished diss. Amherst: U. of Mass.

Heny, Frank. 1982. "Tense, Aspect and Time Adverbials, part II." *Linguistics & Philosophy* 5: 109-154.

Hinrichs, E. 1985. *A Compositional Semantics for Aktionsarten and NP Reference in English.* Unpublished diss. Ohio State University.

———. 1986. "Temporal Anaphora in Discourses of English." *Linguistics and Philosophy* 9: 62-82. Revision of 1982 ms.

Hoepelman, J. 1978. "A Note on the Treatment of the Russian Aspect in a Montague Grammar." In C. Rohrer (ed.), *Papers on Tense, Aspect and Verb Classification.* Tübingen: Gunter Nurr Verlag.

——— and C. Rohrer. 1980. "On the Mass-Count Distinction and the French Imparfait and Passé Simple." In C. Rohrer (ed.), *Time, Tense and Quantification. Proceedings of the Stutgart Conference on the Logic of Tense and Quantifiers.* Tübingen: Niemeyer.

Hopper, Paul. 1979. "Some Observation on the Typology of Focus and Aspect in Narrative Language." *Studies in Language* 3: 37-64.

——— and Sandra Thompson. 1980. "Transitivity in Grammar and Discourse." *Language* 56: 251-299.

Hornstein, Norbert. 1977. "Towards a Theory of Tense." *Linguistic Inquiry* 8: 521-557.

Hughes, G. and M.J. Cresswell. 1968. *Introduction to Modal Logic.* London: Methuen.

Hurvitz, Avi. 1972. *Ben lashon le-lashon - letoldot leshon ha-Mikra be-yeme bayit sheni.* English title: *The Transition Period in Biblical Hebrew; A Study in Post-Exilic Hebrew and its implications for the Dating of Psalms.* Jerusalem: Mosad Byalik. [In Hebrew].

Ibn-Janaḥ, Jonah (Abu al-Walid Marwan). ca. 990- ca.1050. *Sefer ha-rikma. sha'ar alef.* Jerusalem. 1964. [In Hebrew].

Jackendoff, R.S. 1976. *Semantic Interpretation in Generative Grammar.* Cambridge, Mass.: MIT Press.

Jespersen, Otto. 1933. *A Modern English Grammar on Historical Principles.* Part VI. London: Allen and Unwin.

Josman, Barbara. 1986. *The Linguistic Encoding of Temporality in Hebrew Narrative.* Unpublished M.A. thesis, Tel-Aviv University.

Joüon, P. 1947. *Grammaire de L'Hébreu Biblique.* Rome. Translated by Muraoka 1993 below.

Kamp, Hans. 1979. "Events, Instants and Temporal Reference." In R. Baurle, U. Egli &

A. von Stechow (eds.), *Semantics from Different Points of View*. Berlin: Springer-Verlag, 376-417.

———. 1981. "Evénements, Représentations discoursive et Référence Temporelle." *Languages* 64: 39-64.

——— and C. Rohrer. 1983. "Tense in Text." In R. Bauerle, C. Schwartze and A. von Stechow (eds.), *Meaning, Use and Interpretation of Language*. Berlin: de Gryter Linguistik, University of Konstanz.

——— and Uwe Reyle. 1993. *From Discourse to Logic; Introduction to Modeltheoretic Semantics of Natural Language, Formal Logic and Discourse Representation Theory*. Dordrecht, Boston and London: Kluwer Academic Publishers.

Kasher, Asa and Ruth Manor. 1980. "Simple Present Tense." In C. Rohrer (ed.), *Time, Tense and Quantification*. Tübingen: Niemeyer.

Kearns, K.S. 1991. *The Semantics of the English Progressive*. Unpublished diss. MIT, Cambridge, Mass.

Kimchi, David. 1545. *Sefer Mikhlol*. Venice: J. Rittenberg's edition (Lyck, 1862) of this grammar was translated by W. Chomsky (1952) above. [In Hebrew].

Knutzon, J.A. 1889. *Om Det Saakaldte Perfectum Og Imperfectum i Hebraisk*. Denmark.

Kogut, Simcha. 1986. "On the Meaning and Syntactical Status of 'hinne' in Biblical Hebrew." In *Scripta Hieroslymitana*. Jerusalem: Publication of the Hebrew University.

König, E. 1980. "On the Context Dependence of the Progressive in English." In C. Rohrer (ed.), *Time, Tense and Quantification*. Tübingen:Niemeyer.

Kratzer, A. 1981a. "The Notional Category of Modality." In H.J. Eikmeyer and H. Reiser (eds.), *Words, Worlds and Contexts. New Approach in Word Semantics*. Berlin and New-York: de Gruyter.

———. 1981b. "Blurred Conditionals." In W. Klein & W. Levelt (eds.). *Crossing Boundaries in Linguistics*, 201-209.

———. 1981c. "Partition and Revision: the Semantics of Counterfactuals." *Journal of Philosophical Logic* 10: 201-216.

Krifka, M. 1992. "Thematic Relations as Links between Nominal Reference and Temporal Constitution." In Ivan A. Sag and Anna Szabolcsi (eds.), *Lexical Matters*, [*CSLI, Lectures Notes* 24]. United States: Leland Stanford Junior University, 29-53.

Kripke, Saul. 1959. "A Completeness Theorem in Modal Logic." *Journal of Symbolic Logic* 24: 1-14.

———. 1972. *Naming and Necessity*. In Davidson and Harman 1972, 253-355.

Labov, W. 1972. "The Transformation of Experience in Narrative Syntax." In *Language in the Inner City*. Philadelphia: University of Pennsylvania Press.

Lappin, Shalom. 1982. "On the Pragmatics of Mood." *Linguistics and Philosophy* 4: 559-578.

Lascarides, A. 1988. *A Formal Semantics of the Progressive*. diss. University of Edinburgh.

Lee, S. 1827. *A Grammar of the Hebrew Language*. London.

Leech, G.N. 1968. *Meaning and the English Verb*. London: Longman.

———. 1969. *Towards a Semantic Description of English*. London: Longman.

Lewis, David. 1973. *Counterfactuals*. Cambridge, Mass.: Harvard University Press.

———. 1975. "Adverbs and Quantification." In E. Keenan (ed.), *Formal Semantics of Natural Language*. Cambridge: Cambridge University Press, 3-15.

Longacre, R. 1981. "A Spectrum Profile to Discourse Analysis." *Text* 1: 337-359.

Lyons, John. 1977. *Semantics*. Cambridge: Cambridge University Press.

McCawley, James, D. 1971. "Tense and Time Reference in English." In C.J. Fillmore and D.T. Langendoen (eds.), *Studies in Linguistic Semantics*. New-York: Holt, Rinehart and Winston, 97-113.

———. 1981. *Everything that linguists have always wanted to know about logic but were ashamed to ask*. Chicago: University of Chicago Press.

McCoard, Robert W. 1978. *The English Perfect: Tense Choice and Pragmatic Inferences*. Amsterdam: North-Holland.

McFall, Leslie. 1982. *The Enigma of the Hebrew Verb System: Solutions from Ewald to the present day*. Historical Texts and Interpreters in Biblical Scholarship 2. Sheffield, England: The Almond Press.

Miller, George A. and P.N. Johnson-Laird. 1976. *Language and Perception*. Cambridge, Mass.: Harvard University Press.

Mittwoch, Anita. 1988. "Aspects of English Aspect: on the Interaction of Perfect, Progressive and Durational Phrases." *Linguistics & Philosophy* 11: 203-254.

Moens, Marc. 1987. *Tense, Aspect and Temporal Reference*. Edinburgh: Center for Cognitive Science; University of Edinburgh.

——— and Mark Steedman. 1988. "Temporal Ontology and Temporal Reference." *Computational Linguistics* 14: 15-28.

Montague, R. 1968. "Pragmatics". In Raymond Klibansky (ed.), *Contemporary Philosophy: A Survey*. Florence: La Nuova Italia Editrice, 102-22. Reprinted in Montague (1974), 95-118.

———. 1970. "Universal Grammar." *Theoria* 36: 373-98. Reprinted in Montague (1974), 222-246.

———. 1973. "The Proper Treatment of Quantification in Ordinary English." In J. Hintikka et al. (eds.), *Approaches to Natural Language: Proceedings of the 1970 Stanford Workshop on Grammar and Semantics*, 221-42. Dordrecht: Reidel. Reprinted in Montague (1974), 247-70. Generally referred to as "PTQ".

———. 1974. *Formal Philosophy*. Ed. Richmond Thomason. New Haven, Conn.: Yale University Press.

Mouralatos, Alexander P.D. 1978. "Events, Processes and States." *Linguistics & Philosophy* 2: 415-432. Reprinted in: P. Tedeschi and A. Zaenen (eds.), *Syntax and Semantics 14: Tense and Aspect*. 1981. New York: Academic Press.

———. 1981. See (1978).

Muraoka, T. 1993. Paul Joüon, S.J.- T. Muraoka. *A Grammar of Biblical Hebrew*. Translated and revised by T. Muraoka. Roma: Editorice Pontificio Instituto Biblico. Subsidia Biblical: 14/11.

Nakajima, Heizo. 1991. "Transportability, scope ambiguity of adverbials and the generalized binding theory". *Journal of Linguistics* 27: 337-374.

Nerbonne, J. 1986. "Reference and Time in Narration". *Linguistics & Philosophy* 9: 83-95.

Niccacci, Alviero. 1990. *The Syntax of the Verb in Hebrew Prose*. Translated from Italian (1986) by W.G.E. Watson. Sheffield, England: Academic Press.

Nöldeke, Th. 1880. *Syrische Grammatik.* Leipzig. Translated by J.A. Crichton (1904). *Compendious Syriac Grammar*. London.

Palmer, F.R. 1965. *A Linguistic Study of the English Verb.* London: Longman's Linguistic Library.

———. 1986. *Mood and Modality*. Cambridge: Cambridge University Press.

Parsons, Terence. 1990. *Events in the Semantics of English; A Study in Subatomic Semantics*. Cambridge, Mass.: The MIT Press.

Partee, Barbara H. 1973. "Some structural analogies between tenses and pronouns". *The Journal of Philosophy* 70: 137-166.

———. 1984. "Nominal and Temporal Anaphora." *Linguistics & Philosophy* 7: 243-286.

Polani, L, and P. Hopper. ms. "A revision of the foreground-background distinction." Paper presented to the Winter Meeting (1981), LSA, New York.

Prior, A.N. 1967. *Past, Present and Future*. Oxford: Oxford University Press.

Qimron, Elisha. 1980. *Le-shimushey ha-zmanim ba-mikra*. Jerusalem: The Hebrew University. [In Hebrew].

———. 1986-1987. "Consecutive and conjunctive imperfect: the form of the imperfect with WAW in Biblical Hebrew." *The Jewish Quarterly Review* LXXVII: 149-161.

Rabin, Chaim. 1965. *Taḥbir leshon ha-mikra*. Jerusalem: Akademon. [In Hebrew]

———. 1971. *Mashma'uyotehen shel ha-tsurot ha-dikdukiyot bi-lshon ha-mikra u-vi-lshon yamenu*. Jerusalme: Akademon. [In Hebrew]

Reichenbach, Hans. 1947. *Elements of Symbolic Logic*. New York: Free Press.

Reinhart, Tanya. 1981. "Pragmatics and Linguistics : An Analysis of Sentence Topics." *Philosophica* 27: 53-94.

———. 1984a. "Principles of Gestalt perception in the temporal organization of narrative texts." *Linguistics* 22: 779-809.

———. 1984b. "Temporal categories and reference time." Paper read at the conference *Language and Cognition*, Tel-Aviv University. [In Hebrew]

———. 1986. "States, Events and Reference time." Handout of a lecture given in MIT.

Ring, I. 1967. *Mavo le-sifrut ha-tanakh.* Tel-Aviv: Yavne. [In Hebrew].

Rubinstein, E. 1980. *Ha-ivrit shelanu ve-ha-ivrit ha-kduma*. Tel-Aviv: Misrad Habitaḥon - ha-hotsa'a la-or. [In Hebrew].

Ryle, Gilbert. 1949. *The Concept of Mind*. London: Barnes and Noble.

Salkie, Raphael. 1989. "Pefect and pluperfect: what is the relationship?" *Journal of Linguistics* 25: 1-34.

Sanford, A.J. and S.C. Garrod. 1981. *Understanding Written Language: Explorations of Comprehension beyond the sentence.* New York: John Willey & Sons.

Scha, Remko. 1983. "The semantics of tense and the syntax of discourse." A talk given in *Amsterdam colloquium on formal semantics* (83/2)/BBN Laboratories.

Schroeder, N.W. 1766. *Institutiones ad fundamenta linguae Hebraicae in usum studiosae juventutis.* Groningae. (3rd. ed. 1810)

Scott, D. 1970. "Advice on Modal Logic." In K. Lambert (ed.), *Philosophical Problems in Logic*. Dordrecht: Reidel.

Searle, J.R. 1983. *Intentionality*. Cambridge: Cambridge University Press.

Silverman, M.H. 1973. "Syntactic notes on the Waw consecutive." In H. Hoffner, Jr. (ed.), *Orient and Occident*. Neukirchen-Vlugn: Neukirchener Verlag.

Smith, Carlota S. 1978. "The syntax and interpretation of temporal expressions in English." *Linguistics & Philosophy* 2: 43-100.

———. 1983. "A theory of aspectual choice." *Language* 59: 479-501.

———. 1991. *The Parameter of Aspect.* Dordrecht: Kluwer. [*Studies in Linguistics and Philosophy* 43].

Sternberg, Meir. 1982. "Lashon, olam uprespektiva bo'omanut ha-mikra: ha-maba' ha-akif ve-ofane ha-ḥadira ha-smuya." *Ha-sifrut* 32: 88-131. Tel Aviv: Tel Aviv University. [In Hebrew].

———. 1985. T*he Poetics of Biblical Narrative.* Bloomington: Indiana University Press.

Strawson, P.F. 1950. "On referring." Mind NS 59: 320-44. Reprinted in Strawson 1971: 1-27.

———. 1971. *Logico-Linguistic Papers.* Oxford: Clarendon.

Talmon, S. 1980. *Darkhe ha-sipur ha-mikra'i.* Jerusalem: Akademon. [In Hebrew].

Taylor, Barry. 1977. "Tense and continuity." *Linguistics & Philosophy* 1: 287-304.

Tedeschi, Philip J. 1981. "Some evidence for a branching futures semantic model." In Tedeschi and Zaenen (1981), 239-69.

——— and Annie Zaenen (eds.). 1981. *Tense nd Aspect.* New York: Academic Press [*Syntax and Semantics* 14].

Tenny, Carol. 1992. "The aspectual interface hypothesis." In I.A. Sag & A. Szabolcsi (eds.), *Lexical Matters,* CSLI Lectures Notes No. 24. United States: Leland Stanford Junior University, 1-27.

ter Meulen, Alice 1984. "Events, quantities and individuals." In F. Landman & F. Veltman (eds.), *Varieties of Formal Semantics.* GRASS 3, Dordrecht: Foris Publications.

Thacker, T.W. 1954. *The Relationship of the Semitic and Egyptian Verbal Systems.* Oxford.

Thomason, Richard H. 1970. "Indeterminist time and truth-value gaps." *Theoria* 18: 265-281.

———. 1974. "Deontic logic as founded on tense logic." Unpublished paper presented at the Temple University Conference on Deviant Semantics, Dec. 1970.

———. 1983. "Conditionals, time and causal independence." (ms.)

Turner, W. 1876. "The tense of the Hebrew verb." *Studies Biblical and Oriental.* Edinburgh, 338-407.

Vendler, Zeno. 1967. Linguistics in Philosophy. Ithaca, New York: Cornell University Press.

Verkuyl, Henk .J. 1972. *On Compositional Nature of the Aspect.* Dordrecht: Reidel.

———. 1993. *A Theory of Aspectuality; The Interaction between Temporal and Atemporal Structure.* Cambridge: Cambridge University Press.

Vlach, Frank. 1981. "The semantics of the progressive." In Tedeschi and Zaenen (1981), 271-92.

Washburn, David L. 1994. "Chomsky's separation of syntax and semantics." *Hebrew Studies*, XXXV: 27-46. Madison, Wisconsin: University of Wisconsin.

Weinrich, H. 1978. *Tempus, le funzione dei tempi nel testo*. Bologna.

Weir, D.H. 1849. "Observations on the tenses of the Hebrew verb." *Journal of Sacred Literature* 4: 308-34.

Zewi, Tamar. 1992. *Ha-hasabot ha-taḥbiriyot ha-kruxot ba-mivne ha- funktsionali shel ha-mishpat ba-ivrit ha-mikra'it*. English title: *Syntactical Modifications Reflecting the Functional Structure of the Sentence in Biblical Hebrew*. Unpublished diss. The Hebrew University of Jerusalem. [In Hebrew].

Name Index

Subject Index

Y

In the STUDIES IN LANGUAGE COMPANION SERIES (SLCS) the following volumes have been published thus far or are scheduled for publication:

1. ABRAHAM, Werner (ed.): *Valence, Semantic Case, and Grammatical Relations. Workshop studies prepared for the 12th Conference of Linguistics, Vienna, August 29th to September 3rd, 1977.* Amsterdam, 1978.
2. ANWAR, Mohamed Sami: *BE and Equational Sentences in Egyptian Colloquial Arabic.* Amsterdam, 1979.
3. MALKIEL, Yakov: *From Particular to General Linguistics. Selected Essays 1965-1978. With an introd. by the author + indices.* Amsterdam, 1983.
4. LLOYD, Albert L.: *Anatomy of the Verb: The Gothic Verb as a Model for a Unified Theory of Aspect, Actional Types, and Verbal Velocity.* Amsterdam, 1979.
5. HAIMAN, John: *Hua: A Papuan Language of the Eastern Highlands of New Guinea.* Amsterdam, 1980.
6. VAGO, Robert (ed.): *Issues in Vowel Harmony. Proceedings of the CUNY Linguistics Conference on Vowel Harmony (May 14, 1977).* Amsterdam, 1980.
7. PARRET, H., J. VERSCHUEREN, M. SBISÀ (eds): *Possibilities and Limitations of Pragmatics. Proceedings of the Conference on Pragmatics, Urbino, July 8-14*, 1979. Amsterdam, 1981.
8. BARTH, E.M. & J.L. MARTENS (eds): *Argumentation: Approaches to Theory Formation. Containing the Contributions to the Groningen Conference on the Theory of Argumentation*, Groningen, October 1978. Amsterdam, 1982.
9. LANG, Ewald: *The Semantics of Coordination.* Amsterdam, 1984.(English transl. by John Pheby from the German orig. edition *"Semantik der koordinativen Verknüpfung"*, Berlin, 1977.)
10. DRESSLER, Wolfgang U., Willi MAYERTHALER, Oswald PANAGL & Wolfgang U. WURZEL: *Leitmotifs in Natural Morphology.* Amsterdam, 1987.
11. PANHUIS, Dirk G.J.: *The Communicative Perspective in the Sentence: A Study of Latin Word Order.* Amsterdam, 1982.
12. PINKSTER, Harm (ed.): *Latin Linguistics and Linguistic Theory. Proceedings of the 1st Intern. Coll. on Latin Linguistics, Amsterdam, April 1981.* Amsterdam, 1983.
13. REESINK, G.: *Structures and their Functions in Usan.* Amsterdam, 1987.
14. BENSON, Morton, Evelyn BENSON & Robert ILSON: *Lexicographic Description of English.* Amsterdam, 1986.
15. JUSTICE, David: *The Semantics of Form in Arabic, in the mirror of European languages.* Amsterdam, 1987.
16. CONTE, M.E., J.S. PETÖFI, and E. SÖZER (eds): *Text and Discourse Connectedness.* Amsterdam/Philadelphia, 1989.
17. CALBOLI, Gualtiero (ed.): *Subordination and other Topics in Latin. Proceedings of the Third Colloquium on Latin Linguistics, Bologna, 1-5 April 1985.* Amsterdam/Philadelphia, 1989.
18. WIERZBICKA, Anna: *The Semantics of Grammar.* Amsterdam/Philadelphia, 1988.
19. BLUST, Robert A.: *Austronesian Root Theory. An Essay on the Limits of Morphology.* Amsterdam/Philadelphia, 1988.
20. VERHAAR, John W.M. (ed.): *Melanesian Pidgin and Tok Pisin. Proceedings of the First International Conference on Pidgins and Creoles on Melanesia.* Amsterdam/Philadelphia, 1990.

21. COLEMAN, Robert (ed.): *New Studies in Latin Linguistics. Proceedings of the 4th International Colloquium on Latin Linguistics*, Cambridge, April 1987. Amsterdam/ Philadelphia, 1991.
22. McGREGOR, William: *A Functional Grammar of Gooniyandi*. Amsterdam/Philadelphia, 1990.
23. COMRIE, Bernard and Maria POLINSKY (eds): *Causatives and Transitivity*. Amsterdam/Philadelphia, 1993.
24. BHAT, D.N.S. *The Adjectival Category. Criteria for differentiation and identification.* Amsterdam/Philadelphia, 1994.
25. GODDARD, Cliff and Anna WIERZBICKA (eds): *Semantics and Lexical Universals. Theory and empirical findings.* Amsterdam/Philadelphia, 1994.
26. LIMA, Susan D., Roberta L. CORRIGAN and Gregory K. IVERSON (eds): *The Reality of Linguistic Rules.* Amsterdam/Philadelphia, 1994.
27. ABRAHAM, Werner, T. GIVÓN and Sandra A. THOMPSON (eds): *Discourse Grammar and Typology.* Amsterdam/Philadelphia, 1995.
28. HERMAN, József: *Linguistic Studies on Latin: Selected papers from the 6th international colloquium on Latin linguistics, Budapest, 2-27 March, 1991.* Amsterdam/ Philadelphia, 1994.
29. ENGBERG-PEDERSEN, Elisabeth et al. (eds): *Content, Expression and Structure. Studies in Danish functional grammar.* Amsterdam/Philadelphia, 1996.
30. HUFFMAN, Alan: *The Categories of Grammar. French lui and le.* Amsterdam/ Philadelphia, 1997.
31. WANNER, Leo (ed.): *Lexical Functions in Lexicography and Natural Language Processing.* Amsterdam/Philadelphia, 1996.
32. FRAJZYNGIER, Zygmunt: *Grammaticalization of the Complex Sentence. A case study in Chadic.* Amsterdam/Philadelphia, 1996.
33. VELAZQUEZ-CASTILLO, Maura: *The Grammar of Possession. Inalienability, incorporation and possessor ascension in Guaraní.* Amsterdam/Philadelphia, 1996.
34. HATAV, Galia: *The Semantics of Aspect and Modality. Evidence from English and Biblical Hebrew.* Amsterdam/Philadelphia, 1997.
35. MATSUMOTO, Yoshiko: *Noun-Modifying Constructions in Japanese. A frame semantic approach.* Amsterdam/Philadelphia, n.y.p.
36. KAMIO, Akio (ed.): *Directions in Functional Linguistics.* Amsterdam/Philadelphia, n.y.p.